BALLPARKS

YESTERDAY AND TODAY

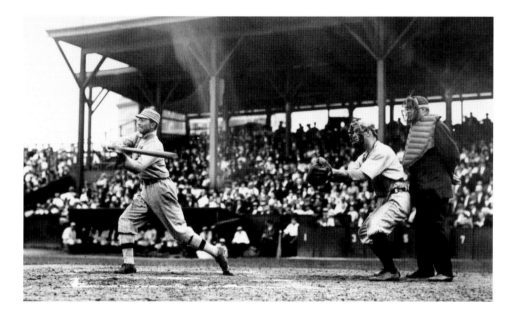

BALLPARKS
YESTERDAY AND TODAY

CHARTWELL
BOOKS, INC.

This edition published in 2007 by

CHARTWELL BOOKS, INC.
A Division of
BOOK SALES, INC.
114 Northfield Avenue
Edison, New Jersey 08837

ISBN-10: 0-7858-2321-2
ISBN-13: 978-0-7858-2321-6

Design: Ian Hughes/Compendium Design.

Acknowledgments
This is a revised and combined version of the books *Ballparks* and *Historic Ballparks*. Thanks to Jim Sutton for reading through the text of the combined volume, and Getty Images (Marc Seigerman), Corbis (Katie Johnston), the Baseball Hall of Fame, the Library of Congress, and the John Pastier collection for the illustrative material. Some of the images—particularly the postcards—are old and do not reproduce perfectly. The Publisher feels that the cons are outweighed by the historic subjects they portray. The text is a combination of various authors: John Pastier wrote the Introduction and many of the captions; Jim Sutton, Marc Sandalow, Michael Heatley, and Ian Westwell's work appears in the gazetteer; Don Gulbrandsen edited. The splendid artwork on pages 14–18 is reproduced courtesy Rick Okkonen. Photographs are from the John Pastier collection unless credited otherwise.

Above: Infield 13, Smyrna Beach, Florida. *Jim Vecchi/Corbis*

Page 1: John Franklin Baker of the Philadelphia Athletics swings as Roger Bresnahan of the St. Louis Cardinals catches during a 1910 game at St. Louis' Robison Field. *MLB Photos via Getty Images*

Page 2: A general view of the stands of Detroit's Tiger Stadium. *Getty Images*

CONTENTS

CONSTRUCTING PARADISE:
THE EVOLUTION OF THE BALLPARK
by John Pastier

Mickey Mantle of the New York Yankees swings at a pitch during a exhibition game. Mickey Mantle played for the New York Yankees from 1951 to 1968. *MLB Photos via Getty Images*

IN THE BEGINNING: PITTSFIELD TO THE ELYSIAN FIELDS

Angelo Bartlett Giamatti, Renaissance scholar, president of Yale University, and seventh commissioner of Major League Baseball, often compared the historic playing fields of his favorite sport to paradise. He liked to point out that the word "paradise" came from Persian, and meant an enclosed green space.

Bart Giamatti's analogy is not mere poetry, but captures the contradictory essence of his favorite sport and the fields on which it is played. Baseball is both "natural"—pastoral and freed from the dictates of the clock—yet is also a product of artifice, largely the creation of an urban society and governed by an intricate web of rules. And so, too, are its theaters. Ballparks are a yin-yang symbiosis of an expansive and constant core of soft grass and earth that's shaped and protected by hard-edged structures that have mutated and grown increasingly complex over time; a lush velvet hand nestled inside an ever more high-tech steel glove. Baseball's earliest roots lie in English stick-and-ball games, but it may be older than rounders and cricket. At first, its American evolution was largely centered in the towns and cities of the northeastern United States.

The sport has two major creation myths. One is that Abner Doubleday invented it in the upstate village of Cooperstown, New York, in 1839, a fabrication that no informed fan of the game takes seriously. The other is that the first organized competitive contest (played under a codified set of rules devised in this case by Alexander Cartwright) took place in a Hoboken, New Jersey, park on June 19, 1846. (A more up-to-date revision of the story now puts the date at October 21, 1845.) [insert Currier & Ives print nearby] This account contains far more truth than the Cooperstown canard, but still oversimplifies a complex history. There were organized, rules-based games played in New York and Brooklyn earlier in 1845, and somewhat differently structured games played even before then. The Gotham Base Ball Club was founded in New York in 1837, and there may well be other precedents waiting to be discovered.

Indeed, in 2004, a discovery by researcher John Thorn revealed that baseball was explicitly mentioned in the legal system as early as George Washington's first presidential term, in the 1791 bylaws of Pittsfield, Massachusetts. There, rules were drawn to protect the town's new meetinghouse from structural and window damage caused by ballgames played on the town square. Specifically, baseball and other ball games were prohibited within 80 yards of the building. Not only were New Englanders playing the sport so early, but they were also doing so in the urban core, not just in fields outside of their towns and villages. And three years before Thorn, a New York University librarian, found newspaper articles from 1823 showing that an organized form of "base ball" was being played in Manhattan at least 23 years before the traditional Hoboken milestone.

Thus, from the beginning baseball was more urban and context-sensitive than is generally realized, and it is the result of a long evolutionary process that shows no sign of abating. The same things can be said of ballparks, and this essay hopes to illuminate the largely urban nature and the ongoing adaptation of this fascinating and increasingly specialized building type over the last 160

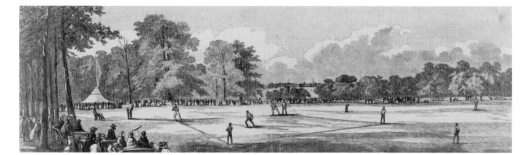

Left: "A base-ball match at the Elysian Fields, Hoboken." Wood engraving in *Harper's Weekly*, October 15, 1859.

Right: Match between the Cincinnati Red Stocking and the Brooklyn Atlantics.

The 1845 and 1846 Hoboken games were played somewhere within the 100-acre expanse of the Elysian Fields (Giamatti relished that paradisiacal place name immensely), a highly popular pleasure-grounds reached by ferry from lower Manhattan. The game took place in a tree-ringed grassy clearing about 600 feet square bordering the Hudson River. The contesting New York clubs had been displaced from their playing grounds near Madison Square by increasing urbanization. (Ironically, Hoboken would eventually develop to a population density even higher than New York's.) Their Jersey playing field was not a ballpark, for such a thing had not yet been imagined, nor was it needed at that point.

The Elysian Fields provided half of the ballpark package—the pastoral playing grounds—but not the constructed frame. There were no fences or other structural boundaries, and no grandstands, shelters from the elements, bleachers, or even seats. Spectators stood nearby in scattered clumps, if a famous Currier & Ives print, showing an 1865 or 1866 contest, is representative. Some depictions of the period show spectators lounging on the grass at other matches. Life was simple and carefree in Elysium.

Games in this era also took place in such ad-hoc settings as college quadrangles, city parks, vacant lots, prep-school lawns, town squares, and even in Confederate prison camps during the Civil War, where Yankee captives taught the game to their Dixie captors.

Below: A Currier & Ives lithograph titled "The American National Game of Baseball" shows an early baseball game watched by a crowd of well-dressed people, 1866. *Getty Images*

ENCLOSING THE GREEN SPACE: THREE BALLPARKS GROW IN BROOKLYN

If there was a big bang in the ballpark cosmology, it occurred seventeen years after Hoboken, fueled by the greatly increased popularity of baseball. William Cammeyer, owner of a six-acre lot near the East River in Brooklyn's Williamsburgh section, had the notion in 1862 to enclose his property with a seven-foot high board fence, and offer baseball in the warmer months and ice-skating in the winter. This simple act helped to fundamentally change baseball by allowing admission to be charged, thus aiding the professionalization of what was up to then an amateur pastime primarily pursued by white-collar gentlemen. It also gave a competitive incentive to improve the spectator experience. (Here too, recent research discoveries enrich the picture. Cooperstown researcher Tom Shieber has found newspaper accounts showing that the New York Excelsior Club enclosed their Brooklyn ball grounds in 1860, not to charge admission, but to exclude ungentlemanly riffraff.) At first, access to Union Grounds ball games was free, but soon Cammeyer began charging fans a dime each to see the contests. (That tariff was not quite a baseball first; in 1858 fans paid fifty cents a game to see a three-game charity series between New York and Brooklyn all-star teams held at a racetrack, the Fashion Race Course in Newtown, Queens.)

The three clubs originally based at the Union Grounds received no share of the gate; Cammeyer kept the proceeds, arguing that he had provided the teams with a superior playing surface and a "commodious" clubhouse (large enough for all three teams) without charging them rent. In addition to the clubhouse and a well-tended lawn, the Union Grounds had a saloon, an odd hexagonal steepled tower in center field, a long shed providing benches and shelter for the ladies, and exposed benches scattered around the grounds. Altogether, the seating capacity was about 1,500, with space for many more spectators standing or sitting on the field. Others could watch the game for free from adjoining embankments and buildings, or by perching on carriages and wagons parked just outside the fences.

Eventually Cammeyer agreed to share gate receipts with the clubs, admission rose to a quarter and then fifty cents, and the Union Grounds became home to several major league teams, since there wasn't a big-league park in New York proper (i.e., Manhattan) until 1883. Brooklyn wasn't part of New York until 1898, but its park was the leading baseball site for the metropolitan region. Although it was home to six major league teams at various times, its greatest historical moment arguably predated the birth of major league baseball. On June 15, 1869, the Cincinnati Red Stockings, the first openly professional club, visited Brooklyn to play the New York Mutuals in the midst of a long undefeated streak that spanned parts of three seasons. In those days most ballgames were sloppy, high-scoring, error-riddled, and one-sided (Cincinnati outscored its opponents by 95 runs or more three times during its streak), but this match was a tightly-played 2-2 tie through eight innings until the visitors rallied to win 4-2. The next day, the Cincinnati Daily Gazette declared that "the game was the toughest, closest, most brilliant, most exciting in baseball annals."

Two years after the Union Grounds' debut, baseball's second commercial enclosed park, the Capitoline Grounds, opened a mile and a half to the south in Brooklyn's Bedford-Stuyvesant district. Built by Reuben Decker, it too combined ice skating with baseball, and saw major league activity. Its greatest moment came on July 2, 1870, when a crowd variously reported between 9,000 and 20,000 watched the Brooklyn Atlantics finally snap Cincinnati's 84-game unbeaten streak by a score of 8-7 in an extra-inning thriller. The Red Stockings' young president called it "the finest game ever played."

Right: Baseball on iceskates at Washington Park, New York.

THE MAJOR LEAGUES AND THE AGE OF WOOD

The year 1871 marked the birth of major-league professional baseball under the auspices of the National Association. The first big league game was played on May 4th in a most unlikely place—Fort Wayne, Indiana, a city of 18,000 that

was the 83rd-largest in the country. Its ballpark, Hamilton Field, was reputedly "a beautiful ornamentedgrandstand christened 'The Grand Dutchess,' so lavish was its construction." Before a modest crowd of fewer than 500 fans, the home-team Kekiongas beat the Cleveland Forest Citys 2-0 (remember that in those days a low score was proof of a skillfully played game), but Fort Wayne quit the league after losing 12 of its next 18 games.

No photographs of the "Grand Dutchess" seem to survive, but we can be sure that it was similar to the other earliest ballparks, which were built of entirely of wood—the supporting structure; the grandstand walls, floors, seats, roofs, and decorative features;

the perimeter fences; the outbuildings; and the bleacher sections. Wood's advantages were many—it was plentiful, inexpensive, of good quality (the virgin timberlands of the time yielded larger and better lumber than today's second-growth forests), easily worked, and permitted rapid construction. For most of the nineteenth century, it was America's default building material, even for many public and commercial buildings. Timber had only one great disadvantage—it burned easily and often, sometimes wiping out entire urban cores, as it did in Chicago in 1871. One victim of that Great Chicago Fire was Lake Park, a downtown ballyard that had logged not quite one full season of National Association service before its demise.

Lake Park was but one of scores of ballparks that burned down over the years. The combustible ballparks of the nineteenth and early twentieth century were short-lived, numerous and usually not well documented. They were often ornate, with turrets, spires, and cupolas embellishing their rooflines. (A surviving building with hints of that style is the old grandstand at Louisville's Churchill Downs racetrack, built in 1895, with its familiar pediments and spires.) Some of the most interesting of the wooden parks were found in Providence, Chicago, St. Louis, and Pittsburgh.

The Providence Grays played at the Messer Street Grounds from 1878 to 1885. In 1884 their ace, "Old Hoss" Radbourn,

Above left: The wooden Union Grounds (1869-70) was home to the nearly invincible Cincinnati Red Stockings, baseball's first openly professional team.ark in Oklahoma City.

Left: An early 20th-century minor league wooden ballpark in Oklahoma City gives a good idea of how major league parks looked a generation earlier.

Below: An 1893 woodcut of the proposed grandstand for Chicago's new West Side Grounds. The three spires were never built, probably for economic reasons.

Right: An advert for Spalding's Official Baseball Guide of 1885. Albert Goodwill Spalding (1850-1915) was a star for the Boston franchise in the National Association, joined the Chicago White Stockings in 1876, later becoming the team president. An entrepreneur, Spalding established a sporting goods company and published an annual guide. *Swim Ink 2, LLC/Corbis*

pitching in this highly lopsided park (281 feet to the left-field fence, 318 feet to center, and 431 feet to right) set a still-standing record by winning 59 games. In contrast to its ornate contemporaries, its straight eight-bay grandstand had a clean-lined functional beauty, with both a wooden roof and a lower projecting canvas awning, and an enclosed press box below the public seating. A horsecar spur track came right up to its front gate. Judged by modernist standards, it may have been the most handsome seating structure of its century.

Chicago's Lakefront Park was a paragon of its decade, deemed by Harper's magazine to be, after its 1883 remodeling, "indisputably the finest in the

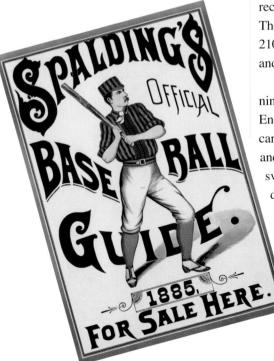

world in respect of seating accommodations and conveniences." These included eighteen private boxes "cozily draped with curtains to keep out the wind and sun, and furnished with comfortable armchairs," a telephone for the owner's box, and forty-one uniformed attendants, including eight musicians. Its major drawback was a tiny playing field, with foul lines of 180 feet and 196 feet. In 1883, balls hit over those short fences were ground rule doubles, but in 1884 they counted as home runs. The home team White Stockings had four players hit between 21 and 27 home runs, all shattering the previous league record of 10, and collectively hit more than 92 percent of its four-baggers at Lakefront. The team's 142 home runs broke the league record of 34 by a factor of more than four. The next year, the National League decreed a 210-foot minimum distance for home runs, and Chicago's total dropped by 62 percent.

The architectural crown jewel of nineteenth-century parks was Boston's South End Grounds, a virtuoso exercise in Victorian carpentry featuring carved columns, a steep and lofty double-decked grandstand built in a sweeping arc, and a sharply pitched dormered roof surmounted by six spires of various sizes and shapes. Its distinction went beyond surface appearance—some of its lower deck structure appears to have been iron or even steel. Nicknamed the Grand Pavilion, it served the Beaneaters (later called the Braves) from 1888 to 1894, when it

succumbed to fire, a fate also met by three other major-league parks that year. Because it was badly underinsured, its replacement lacked both its height and its decorative splendor, and Boston was never again to see a true double-decked ballpark. The Huntington Avenue Grounds was located about 700 feet away, making these the closest active parks in big-league annals. Huntington's center field, estimated as 635 feet by historian Bob Bluthardt, was the longest field dimension ever in the majors.

At various times in its several late-nineteenth century incarnations (the stands burned down with alarming frequency, with five major fires in the 1890s alone), St. Louis' Sportsman's Park offered a plethora of amusements besides baseball. Under the helm of flamboyant saloon-keeper and team owner Chris Von der Ahe, the Browns' home grounds had an on-field roller coaster, a merry-go-round, lawn bowling and handball, a Buffalo Bill and Sitting Bull wild west show, bicycle races, a horse race track, and an in-play picnic grounds and beer garden within fair territory. Not amused, the Sporting News decried such antics as "the prostitution of a ballpark." Yet one wonders whether this unembarrassed promoter of "the Coney Island of the West" might not be hailed as a marketing genius in today's overheated revenue-maximizing climate. Interestingly, this master of hoopla was also capable of structural innovation, installing six bays of cast-iron structural columns and arches in his otherwise wooden

grandstand in 1893.

Pittsburgh's Exposition Park (1890), [Anorax 0872]sited on the flood-prone north bank of the Allegheny River, boasted a twin-spired grandstand, an immense outfield whose shortest point was 400 feet, and the most dramatic downtown view of any pre-1960s ballpark.

Hilltop Park, home of the Highlanders (later the Yankees) from 1903 to 1912, was the last wooden park built in New York, a process that took just six weeks. In those days, neither the park nor the team was particularly distinguished. The Giants played there for ten weeks in 1911 while their burnt-down Polo Grounds was being rebuilt.

Although the American League's last wooden structure, Washington's American League Park, was built in 1904, and the National's last wooden-park game was played at St. Louis' Robison Field in 1920, timber construction long remained suited to the minor leagues, and several carry on even today. Three outstanding ones are found in the lumber-industry region of the Pacific Northwest: Olympic Park in Hoquiam Washington, Civic Field in Eugene Oregon, and the monumental, often-remodeled Civic Stadium (currently PGE Park) in Portland, Oregon, which has a wooden plank-and-beam roof above a concrete substructure. In keeping with a drizzly climate, all have notably deep roofs sheltering their grandstands.

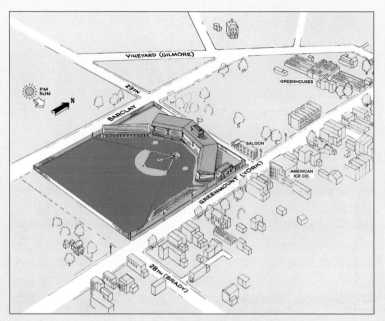

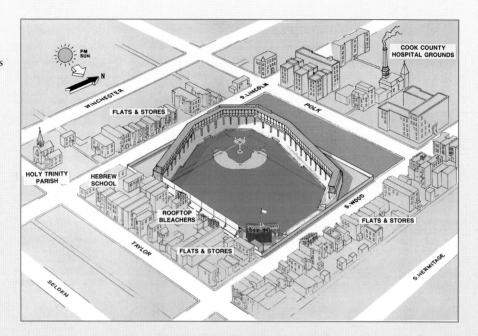

Left: American League Park in north Baltimore saw only two years of big league play (1901 and 1902), but then served the International League Orioles for the next thirteen seasons until they moved a block north to Terrapin Park in 1916. Its outfield was large and oddly shaped.

Right: Chicago's West Side Grounds (1893-1915) shown here circa 1909, was home to the Cubs before they moved to their present North Side home. It was impressively spacious when first built, with about 16,000 seats, a second deck, and a center field approaching 500'.

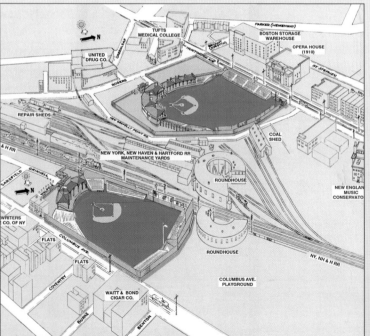

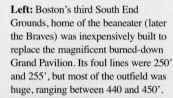

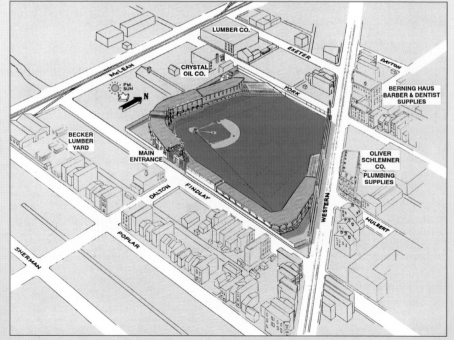

Left: Boston's third South End Grounds, home of the beaneater (later the Braves) was inexpensively built to replace the magnificent burned-down Grand Pavilion. Its foul lines were 250' and 255', but most of the outfield was huge, ranging between 440 and 450'.

The Huntington Avenue Grounds (1901-11) occupied a very eclectic district, with rail yards, a warehouse, a medical college and an opera house as its immediate neighbors. The first World Seroes was played there in 1903, with the home team Pilgrims (later, Red Sox) conquering the Pirates.

Right: Cincinnati's Palace of the Fans (1902-11) had baseball's first reinforced concrete grandstand, a neoclassically syled structure with an elaborate main entrance. Most seats, however, were found in more modest wooden stands down the lines and in rigjht field, where the foul line measured a formidable 450'.

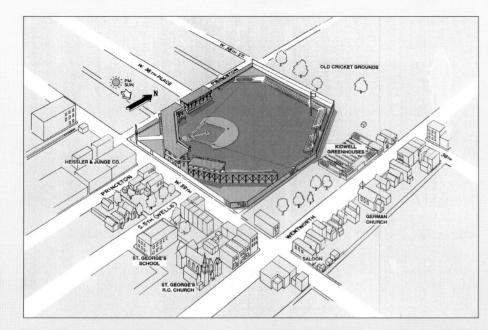

Left: Chicago's South Side Park home of the White Sox from 1901 to 1910, saw 21 seasons of Negro Leagues ball after its original tenants left for Comiskey park a few blocks away. The bleachers in left, right, and center field were a rarity at the time of this 1906 view. This 15,000 seat park burned down in 1940.

Right: An earlier version of Chicago's West Side Grounds than the one shown on p. 14.

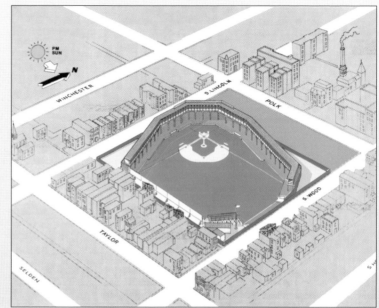

Left: Cleveland's first League Park (1891-1909) had a right field line of about 240' because the Indians neglected to acquire several properties on Lexington Ave. When the team rebuilt in steel in 1910, they bought the rest of the block, but the resulting 290' line was still not a significant challenge to lefty sluggers.

Right: Located in Detroit's Corktown neighborhood, Bennett Park occupied the same location as its successors — Navin Field, Briggs Stadium, and Tiger Stadium — albeit on a smaller piece of property. The later parks shifted home plate to Bennett's LF corner so that the setting sun wouldn't shine in batters' eyes.

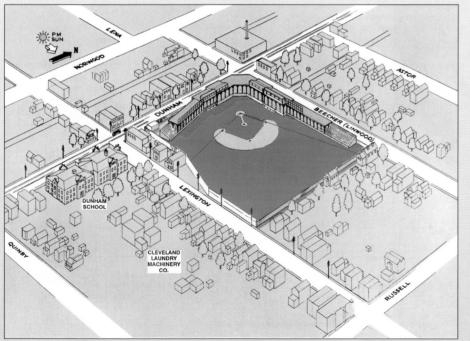

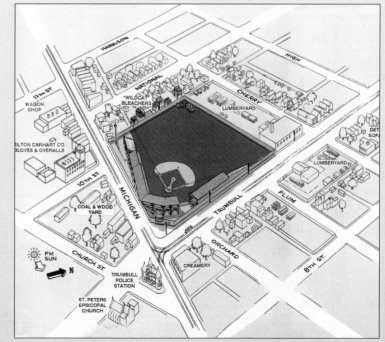

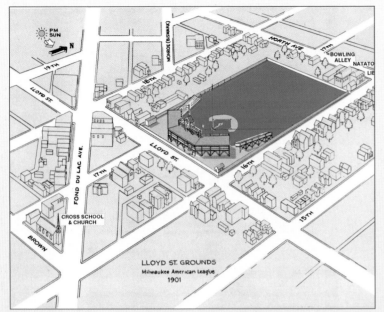

LLOYD ST. GROUNDS
Milwaukee American League
1901

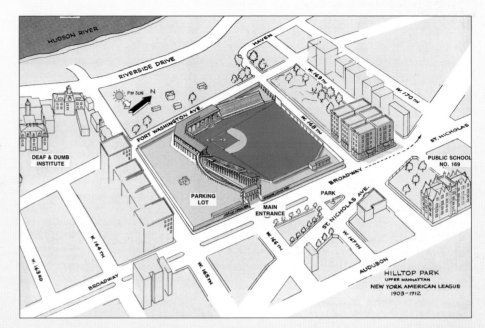

HILLTOP PARK
UPPER MANHATTAN
NEW YORK AMERICAN LEAGUE
1903-1912

Left: Milwaukee's Lloyd Street Grounds saw one season of big-league ball in 1901. Its outfield was shaped like home plate, a common layout in the 19th and early 20th century that was best and most recently exemplified by the Polo Grounds.

Right: Hilltop Park (1902-11) was New York's northernmost major-league park and its last wooden one. Many tenants of the apartments at 168th St. and Broadway had a good view of the game. Its site is now part of the Columbia-Presbyterian Medical Center.

Left and Right: Three different ballparks called the Polo Grounds sat below Coogan's bluff at 8th Ave. and 157th St. in upper Manhattan, but the upper-class equestrian sport was never played on that site. (The name was a holdover from an earlier Giats oark at a different location.) These views show the wooden double-decked second version in 1900 and 1909. The earlier one had a 500' center field where well-to-do fans watched the game from their carriages parked on the field. The later one had more egalitarian outfield bleachers that shortened the CF distance to 433'. The ballpark burned down on April 15, 1911, and by June 28 a partly-completed steel and concrete replacement was pressed into service.

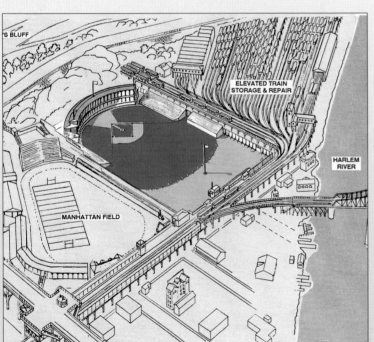

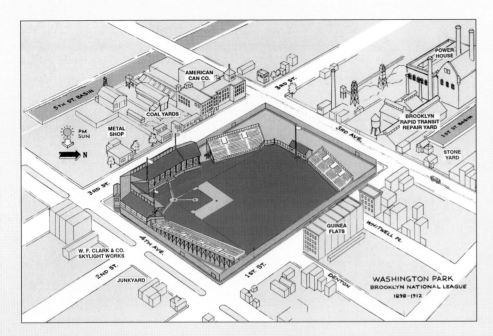

WASHINGTON PARK
BROOKLYN NATIONAL LEAGUE
1898-1912

Left: The second Washington Park served the Brooklyn Dodgers from 1898 to 1912. This view shows the park after a major expansion in 1908. Its name honors George Washington, whose Continental Army unsuccessfully fought British troops in the Battle of Long Island, which took place nearby in 1776.

Right: Philadelphia National League Park (1895-1938), later called Baker Bowl, occupied a North Philadelphia industrial neighborhood. It was the first ballpark to make extensive use of structural steel, and its notoriously short RF allowed Phillies batters to capture 13 HR titles in 21 years.

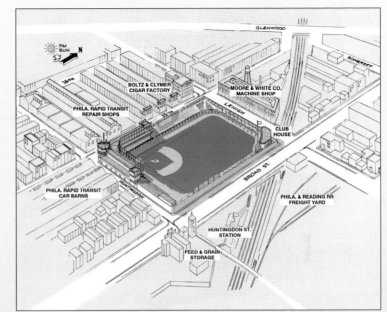

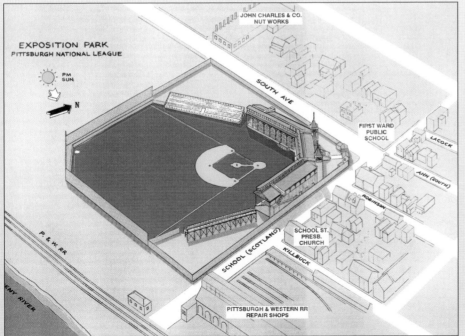

EXPOSITION PARK
PITTSBURGH NATIONAL LEAGUE

Left: Between 1890 and 1915, Pittsburgh's Exposition Park was home to teams in three major circuits — the Players League Burghers, the National League Pirates, and the Federal League Rebels. And later, its site was occupied by Three Rivers Stadium. This twin-spired wooden park was prone to flooding, and had an immense outfield whose shortest distance was 400'.

Right: Columbia Park (1901-08) in Philadelphia's Brewerytown section was well-served by streetcar lines, and hosted a World series, but its small seating capacity and an expiring land lease spurred the A's to build Shibe Park. Occupants of the row houses on 29th and on Columbia had good views of the game.

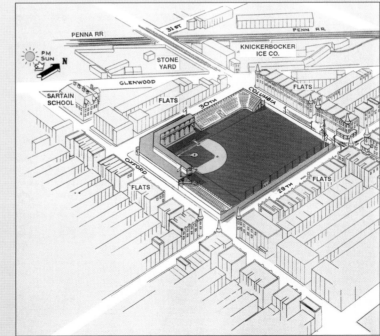

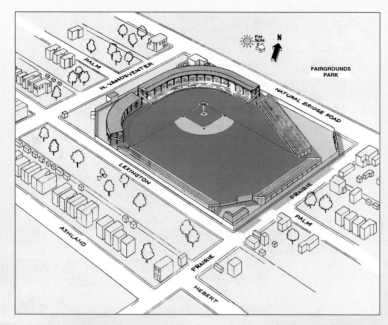

Left: Robison Field, also known as National League Park, was home to the Cardinals from 1893 to 1920 and was the last wooden park to be used in the major leagues. It caught fire more than once. When the Cardinals left it for the safer confines of Sportsman's Park, their journey was just a few blocks long—in mid-season of 1920, the Cards moved three blocks to cohabit with the Browns at Sportsman's Park.

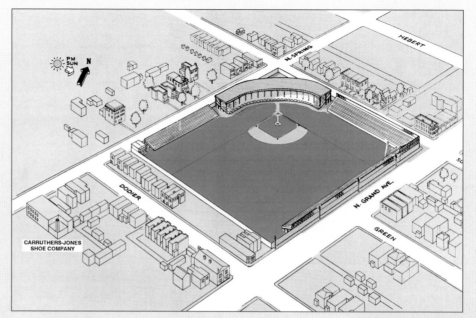

Right: The last wooden version of Sportsman's Park was used by the Browns between 1902 and 1909. The next year, home plate was moved to the right-field corner, and a two-deck steel grandstand rose in that location. Most of the old wooden structure then became outfield seating.

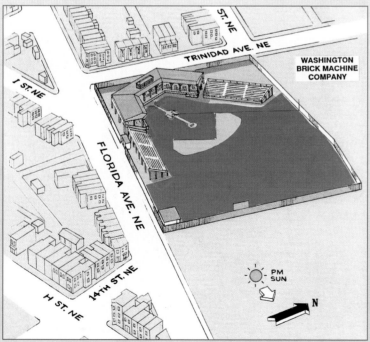

Left: The first American League Park in Washington was a three-year wonder (1901-03) with 10,000 seats and short foul lines. When the Senators moved to larger quarters, down the road, they took much of the wooden seating structure with them. Nevertheless, it had a very deep center field, estimated at well over than 500 feet.

Right: Washington's second American League Park (1904-10), shown here about 1907, occupied the same location as its successor Griffith Stadium, but on a somewhat smaller site. Nevertheless, it had a huge dimensions, with left-center estimated to be about 600'.

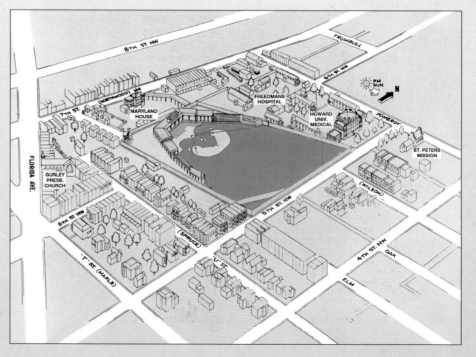

THE FIREPROOF REFORMATION: THE AGE OF STEEL BEGINS

Heavy damage or outright destruction of wooden ballparks by fire was commonplace—major league parks in four cities burned down in 1894 alone. It was a serious enough problem to motivate a structural solution. The process took about fifteen years to become established, but once that point was reached, it spread like wildfire (or anti-wildfire) throughout the major leagues, and to some extent the minor leagues as well.

The solution was to build the grandstands of nonflammable steel, brick, and concrete. This, of course, was far more costly than using lumber, but it provided advantages beyond fireproofing. (And it should be remembered that very few buildings are truly fireproof. Contents can burn, and the early fireproof parks often had substantial wood components—seats and bleacher benches at a minimum, and sometimes wooden structures outside of the main grandstands in the cheaper seating sections.)

Those other advantages dealt with visibility and revenue. Since steel beams and trusses could span greater distances than wood, seating capacities could be larger, and view-obstructing columns could be fewer and farther between. Steel also allowed upper decks and roofs to project farther toward the field in front of the columns. These longer cantilevers meant that there were more clear-view seating rows in front of the column lines, and fewer obstructed ones behind them. Fans today may grouse about having their views blocked by columns at Wrigley Field or Fenway Park, but a far greater proportion of seats had blocked views in the wooden baseball palaces.

In 1894, a sketch of a modestly sized steel-framed grandstand in Cincinnati was published. Little is known about this proposal; it seems structurally naive (the upper columns were more substantial than the lower ones, and the two sets did not align), and it clearly wasn't implemented. But in 1895, the principle of a fireproof structural system became tangible on a grander scale. The previous season, Philadelphia's seven-year-old National League Park had partially burned, and the Phillies' owners decided to rebuild the prime seating areas in steel and concrete. The original park was considered the best in baseball when it opened—it was double decked, had brick exterior walls, seated about 12,500, and sported five picturesque steepled turrets atop its roof. The partial renovation produced a larger steel-framed grandstand with baseball's first cantilevered upper deck.

Left: This sketch of an unbuilt grandstand proposed for Cincinnati, published in 1894, may be the earliest depiction of a steel ballpark structure.

evolution took place in Cincinnati, when the Palace of the Fans, a partial reconstruction of a burned wooden ballpark, opened in 1902. It was the closest thing to a truly fireproof park yet—a distinction gained through then-radical means. Rather than being built of steel columns, beams, girders, and trusses bolted or riveted together, its structure was steel-reinforced concrete, a locally popular new technology that used much less metal and was inherently more fireproof than uninsulated steel framing. Architects Elzner & Anderson and the Ferro-Concrete Construction Company jointly pioneered this structural method in Cincinnati, and they may have worked on the ballpark with Palace architect John G. Thurtle a year before producing the world's tallest reinforced concrete skyscraper in the Queen City's business district. (In another technological feat, The Palace presented an experimental night game between two Elks club teams in 1909.)

Paradoxically, this cutting-edge engineering was used to produce a very traditional-looking result: an impressive pedimented and decoratively columned, classically inspired building that evoked thoughts of a bank, a college, or a museum. This new neoclassical portion of the park featured a slightly projecting roof, nineteen elevated bow-fronted "fashion boxes," and, beneath them, cheap field-level seats and extensive drinking places. Contrary to many published claims, this fireproof park did not

It was the game's state-of-the-art venue; it set a seasonal attendance record in its first year, and cumulatively led the majors in its first seven seasons. Still, the uncovered cheaper seats down the lines were wood, and these were subject to collapse and fire in later years.

The park was later named Baker Bowl to honor a parsimonious team owner, and that's the name that it is remembered by today. Its site was long and narrow, creating a short right field line that varied between 272 feet and 280 feet at different times. The power alley was about 300 feet, and even with a

high wall, home runs were ridiculously easy—doubles were even easier. Phillies sluggers such as Gavvy Cravath and Chuck Klein owed their frequent home-run championships as much to the park as to their skills.

The next step in ballpark structural

burn down, but was razed and rebuilt after ten seasons because it lacked sufficient premium seats.

Three years later and 100 miles to the northeast, another event in the fireproof reformation occurred in Columbus, Ohio. Little is known about Neil Park, but minor league historian Bill O'Neal calls it "baseball's first concrete-and-steel stadium." Actually, like Baker Bowl, it was a hybrid, with extensive wooden bleachers. He also refers to "the concrete grandstand," suggesting that this may have been a reinforced concrete structure rather than a normally steel-framed one. In any case, it could not be the first of either type, due to the precedents of Baker Bowl and The Palace of the Fans. But it seems safe to say that this $23,000, 6,000-seat grandstand, with a small upper deck perched over the main seating tiers, was the most structurally advanced minor league ballpark at the time. Including its wooden bleachers, Neil Park had 11,000 seats, and in its first season it purportedly led all other minor league teams (plus five major league ones) in attendance, thanks in part to the club's 102-win, first-place performance.

Above: Cincinnati's classically styled Palace of the Fans, built in 1902, was the first reinforced concrete grandstand, and the second example of fire-resistant construction in the major leagues. The small top deck, added later, was oddly built of wood.

Right: National League Park in Philadelphia, later known as Baker Bowl, used structural steel in rebuilding its fire-destroyed central grandstand in 1895, thus initiating fire-resistant construction in baseball.

Left: Jay Littleton Ballpark in Ontario Calif. was built by the WPA in 1936. Although many decades newer than the earliest wooden parks, it is representative of the complex carpentry that went into even the most utilitarian of these timber structures.

THE CLASSIC FIREPROOF PARKS

The year 1909 was the most pivotal in the annals of ballpark evolution. It ushered in a new age, new aspirations, and a paradigm shift in both major and minor league facilities. Previously tentative steps toward permanence, fire safety, structural ambition, architectural refinement, and increased revenues suddenly became confident strides. This new momentum would bring about the near-universal replacement of big-league parks within a half-dozen years, and create organizational stability in what had previously been a Brownian motion of emerging, disappearing, and relocating franchises.

The leader of this revolution was Shibe Park, which opened on a 5.75-acre site in north Philadelphia on April 12, 1909. Its enclosed green space was an uncontrived polygon of seven straight sides whose fair territory was a simple 378-foot by 334-foot rectangle with a deepest point about 508 feet from home plate; its total playing surface was about 440 feet by 400 feet. But its constructed frame, designed and built by the firm of William Steele and Sons, was a marvel of complexity. Its exterior was the most elaborate and detailed architectural design ever attempted in a ballpark, a richly eclectic yet tasteful extravaganza in a French Renaissance revival style. Its embellishments included a copper-trimmed green slate mansard roof with thirty-two pedimented dormer windows, a circular corner entrance and four-story office tower topped by an arcaded octagonal cupola and dome plus several flag poles, cornices, belt courses, two monumental arcades each composed of seventeen tall Ionic pilasters flanking sixteen arches, a rusticated stone base, banded red brick walls, and light-colored terra cotta trim. To remind observers bedazzled by all this magnificence that they were actually entering a ballpark and not some major civic institution—although in truth, they were entering a major civic institution—there were bas-relief busts of team owner Ben Shibe and manager Connie Mack.

Inside, patrons saw a less ornate but no less impressive world—a tall, true double-decked grandstand with 5,500 seats below and 4,500 above, and concrete-floored bleachers (with stores and public garages below) that brought the total seating capacity to roughly 23,000—the first time any ballpark had topped 20,000. Standing room in the aisles and on the playing field increased the capacity to more than 30,000. The upper deck and roof cantilevers were unprecedentedly deep, and the roof extended out to the first row of the upper seats. In all likelihood, each of these features was unmatched at the time.

Shibe Park cost $300,000 to construct—about a thousandth of the budget of an economical ballpark today, but far more than anything previously attempted. Ben Shibe's economic gamble proved astute; in 1909 the

Below: Shibe park ca. 1925-30, after most seating expansions, but before the construction of the 34-foot tall right-field wall in 1935 and the addition of lights four years later. *Hall of Fame*

Philadelphia Athletics' attendance was 675,000, about 70 percent higher than the other major league teams, and the highest until then by a non-New York club.

Like nearly all other classic ballparks, Shibe Park was remodeled, reconfigured, and expanded over the years. Seating capacity grew greatly while outfield size shrank somewhat. Eventually, double-decked stands framed three of its sides, while a 34-foot-high wall (the "spite fence") was raised on the fourth to thwart adjacent row-house owners who had built wooden bleachers on their roofs and were charging admission. (Some things never change, as witnessed by the residential buildings across the street from Wrigley Field's outfield.) Lights were added for night games, and the scoreboard got bigger and more informative. Like almost all ballparks of any longevity, Shibe Park was a flexible entity and a work in progress. Most of its changes were for the better, but an insensitive vertical main grandstand expansion marred the superb architectural composition of its exterior.

Pennsylvania's other major-league city opened its own impressive baseball palace hard on the heels of Shibe Park. The Pittsburgh Pirates' Forbes Field was built on a topographically difficult, ravine-cleft, seven-acre site in an astonishing four months, opening in mid-season. Unlike most pre-1966 parks, it wasn't built in a marginal or underdeveloped part of town, but was located in Oakland, the city's cultural centerpiece. Its neighbors included Pittsburgh's two principal colleges, the main library, the leading museum, the symphony, a splendid 300-acre park and conservatory, and upscale hotels and apartments. In terms of prestige and amenity, this was the most favored location for a ballpark in a century-long span, and perhaps ever.

Forbes Field's external architecture was understated but refined, with a lightness and subtle Mediterranean flavor. The street sides had simple ground-floor arches, a curtain wall of large windows and metal spandrels, glazed terra-cotta piers embedded with latticed steel columns, and a copper-sheathed roof. If Shibe Park and the Palace of the Fans achieved their architectural distinction through revival styles and ornate detailing, Forbes did so through a restraint and

Below: Forbes Field before its 1925 right-field expansion.

functionality that could be considered an early form of modern architecture. Its author, Charles Leavitt, was not a traditionally educated architect, but rather a civil engineer with an interest in planning and landscape design. He designed the grandstands for five racetracks, a useful ability in an age when actual ballpark experience was rare among trained professionals.

Forbes had three decks and an initial seating capacity of about 25,000, both records at the time. Among its other functional innovations were interior pedestrian ramps to reach its upper levels, an elevator, and a wide internal promenade to expedite circulation and shelter fans during rain delays. Perhaps its greatest amenity was the scenic panorama of Schenley Park and the Pittsburgh hills visible from most of its seats.

The playing field was asymmetrical and immense, which suppressed over-the-fence home runs and produced an astounding number of triples. In 1912, Pirate outfielder

Chief Wilson set the still-standing single-season triple record with 36 in 1912, 24 of them hit at home. Pittsburgh once smashed eight in a single game, and led the league 30 times in its 62 seasons at Forbes.

Sportsman's Park—at least the fourth ballpark bearing that name on its northside St. Louis site—had its debut as a fireproof park just two days after Shibe. Compared to the Pennsylvania palaces, it was architecturally modest, but satisfying nonetheless, particularly after its 1925 and 1926 expansions. Clean-lined and utilitarian, its expression lay in its structure, and it was beautiful in its understated angular simplicity. For much of its life it was home to both the Browns and the Cardinals, and as a result, more major league games were played on its

and its predecessors' field than anywhere else.

A fourth steel-framed ballpark opened that year, far less well known than the other members of the class of 1909—Swayne Field in Toledo. Its significance was twofold: with a fully double-decked grandstand it was the first fireproof minor league park to match contemporary major league plants

Right: Schenley Park's formal landscaping, with Forbes Field in the background, some time between 1909 and 1925. *Hall of Fame*

qualitatively (albeit at a smaller scale), and it was the first ballpark designed by the Osborn Engineering Company. This Cleveland firm quickly became the reigning designer during the classic ballpark era, and its momentum carried it well into the 1990s, when it was responsible for the structural engineering of Jacobs Field

Osborn's next effort, and its first major league venue, opened the next year. League Park was a fireproof reconstruction of an identically named wooden facility on Cleveland's East Side. Like Baker Bowl, it had a small seating capacity, a short right field with a tall fence, and seating on the other three sides of the field. At 375 feet, its left field was formidable. Its pleasant arched, brick exterior had a picturesque two story semi-detached office building at one corner, an arrangement that was repeated in three other classic ballparks. For several years it was also known as Dunn Field, and its grounds are still used for community sports,

flanked by crumbling fragments of the original grandstands and office.

Chicago's Comiskey Park also opened in 1910 on the city's South Side. It was brick-clad, well proportioned, and subtly decorated, but not as grand as Shibe or Forbes. It strove for perfect symmetry, and its spacious field may have been the first in the majors to strictly achieve that condition. Because the site wasn't symmetrical, the outfield stands were of unequal depth to allow the field to turn out correctly. It was intentionally designed as a pitcher's park with the assistance of White Sox hurler Ed Walsh, and in its first season it yielded just three home runs. But over the years its dimensions were subject to much tinkering: its foul lines were as long as 365 feet and as short as 332 feet, while center field varied between 455 feet and 401 feet. It was large in capacity as well outfield size, with stands completely ringing the field. It sat 28,800 upon opening (a record at the time) and that figure grew to 52,000 seventeen years later.

Even though designed by Osborn, 1911's ballpark crop was architecturally nondescript, but interesting in other respects.

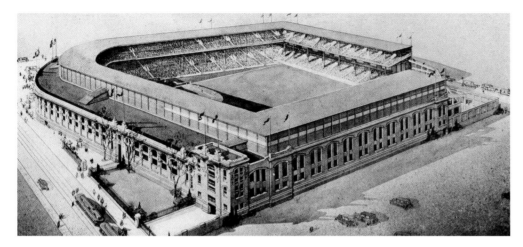

Above: Another Osborn Co. architect's perspective, this time depicting the expanded 52,000-seat Comiskey Park, ca. 1927.

Below: A collector's model of old Comiskey Park capturing its later years after its red brick walls had been painted white to match the color of the home team's socks. Collectible ballpark models, such as the models illustrated here and elsewhere in the introduction, have been part of the scene for the last decade or two. The rarest and most expensive are made of cast metal, but good replicas can also be found in plastic and in painted resin. Sometimes called cold-cast ceramic, the latter material seems to the most popular. Quality varies quite a bit among manufacturers, but the Danbury Mint has consistently managed to produce detailed and credible replicas of both classic and newer ballparks. Among the classics are Detroit's Tiger Stadium, the original Comiskey Park in Chicago (above), Cincinnati's Crosley Field, Forbes Field in Pittsburgh, Washington's Griffith Stadium, and Sportsman's Park in St. Louis, all of which were products of the first great wave of fireproof ballpark construction beween 1909 and 1915. The newer parks include the Houston Astrodome, shown with and without its first-of-its-kind roof, and the initiator of the currently dominant retro-design movement, Oriole Park at Camden Yards in Baltimore.

Griffith Stadium in Washington was very utilitarian, and fronted more on alleys than true streets. Its seating capacity never reached 30,000, but its outfield was immense, (for most of its life, the shortest point between the left field foul line and right-center was 391 feet), handicapping sluggers such as Goose Goslin. Its center field wall bent and jogged to accommodate a tree and the back yards of several row houses. Oddly, its outer foul-

Below: Washington's Griffith Stadium, some time after the double-decking of 1919.

Inset: A post-1980 model of Baltimore's Terrapin Park later renamed Oriole Park.

territory stands were taller than those around the infield. In 1952, Mickey Mantle hit a legendary 565-foot home run that actually carried about 500 feet on the fly, aided by a strong wind.

The Polo Grounds (the fourth park bearing that name) opened in mid-season after a disastrous fire that forced the Giants to share space with the Yankees at Hilltop Park. It too had a spartan exterior, but its field shape was eccentric, with foul lines of 280 feet and 259 feet, and a center field fluctuating in the 480-foot range. Giants outfielder Mel Ott took great advantage of the short dimensions—he hit 135 more home runs there than on the road, enabling him to

first 500-home run player. This also enabled some interesting game action, such as Bobby Thomson's dramatic 1951 pennant-winning homer, which probably would not have cleared the fence in any other park of the period, and Willie Mays' electrifying 1954 World Series catch of Vic Wertz's 415-foot shot, which would have been uncatchable in most other ballyards. Over the years, the Polo Grounds was the full-time home to a record three teams—the Giants, Yankees, and Mets—and was expanded to 55,000 seats, the most in the National League for many decades.

Three ballparks opened in 1912. Fenway Park, the most famous of them, was somewhat nondescript until a comprehensive 1933 rebuilding by new owner Tom Yawkey to Osborn plans, when it began to resemble the magical place of the Ted Williams, Carl Yastrzemski, and Wade Boggs periods. It was the longest-lived single-deck major league park ever, and even with its present partial upper deck it's still the smallest-capacity field in the majors. Its asymmetrical field greatly favors right-handed batters, with a straight left distance of about 320 feet, compared to about 380 feet to straight right. ("Straight" refers not to the foul line, but to the lateral position that the corner outfielders typically take.) In compensation, the 37-foot-high Green Monster left-field wall cuts down on some home runs, but it unfairly stops well-hit line drives while allowing shortish high flies to go for four bases. In its early days, Fenway

Above left: Seating and field diagram of the fully-expanded Polo Grounds.

Above right: Postcard view of the partially expanded Polo Grounds, some time before 1926.

Left: Fenway Park during the 1914 World Series, prior to the 1934 remodeling that produced today's familiar appearance.

Fenway was an unremarkable part of a very diverse ballpark universe, but today it is one of only two survivors of that golden age. With its accumulated patina of history and positive changes, and with most of its peers vanished, it is rightly seen as a unique and irreplaceable national treasure.

Cincinnati's Redland Field, (later Crosley Field), occupied a Mill Creek valley site that housed three parks and 87 seasons of big-league ball. It replaced the architecturally stunning but economically inadequate Palace of the Fans with a more lucrative but less handsome structure. (But its brick office wing did offer a bit of distinction.) Its straightforward character was perfect for its dense urban setting, where brick manufacturing buildings were visible on

Western Avenue just beyond the outfield fences. These factories and laundries provided fine vantage points for watching games, and high-visibility locations for advertising signs.

It started life with an outfield claimed to be baseball's largest (360 feet to left, 420 feet to center, 385 feet to right) and a moderate capacity of 25,000, but seating expansions raised that to a peak of 33,000 while shrinking the field to 328 feet/387 feet/342 feet. On May 24, 1935, it presented the first major league night game. (The minors and the Negro Leagues had initiated night baseball before this.)

Detroit's Navin Field (later Briggs Stadium and then Tiger Stadium) may have been the most underrated of the classic parks.

Its site saw more years of professional baseball than any other, and the ballpark was the first to record 10,000 home runs. It set attendance records in its day, and was the first to be completely double-decked and to have two levels of bleachers.

The park was remarkably intimate, with upper-deck seats very close to the field. This Osborn-designed plant expanded in stages from 23,000 seats to 58,000, providing plenty of cheap tickets for its loyal working-class fans. Those expansions produced many interesting anomalies such as an overhanging right-field upper deck, subtle structural shifts and jogs, and upper deck walkways that projected out over the sidewalk. It was a textbook example of adaptive and pragmatic design, and its accretions gave it convincing

Above: Architect's perspective of the 1934 Fenway Park reconstruction which formed the basis for the venerable ballpark of today.

Right: Cincinnati's Redland Field, later and better known as Crosley Field, was one of several parks to occupy the corner of Findlay Street and Western Avenue. It was home to the Reds and several Negro League teams, and was the site of the first big-league night game in 1935.

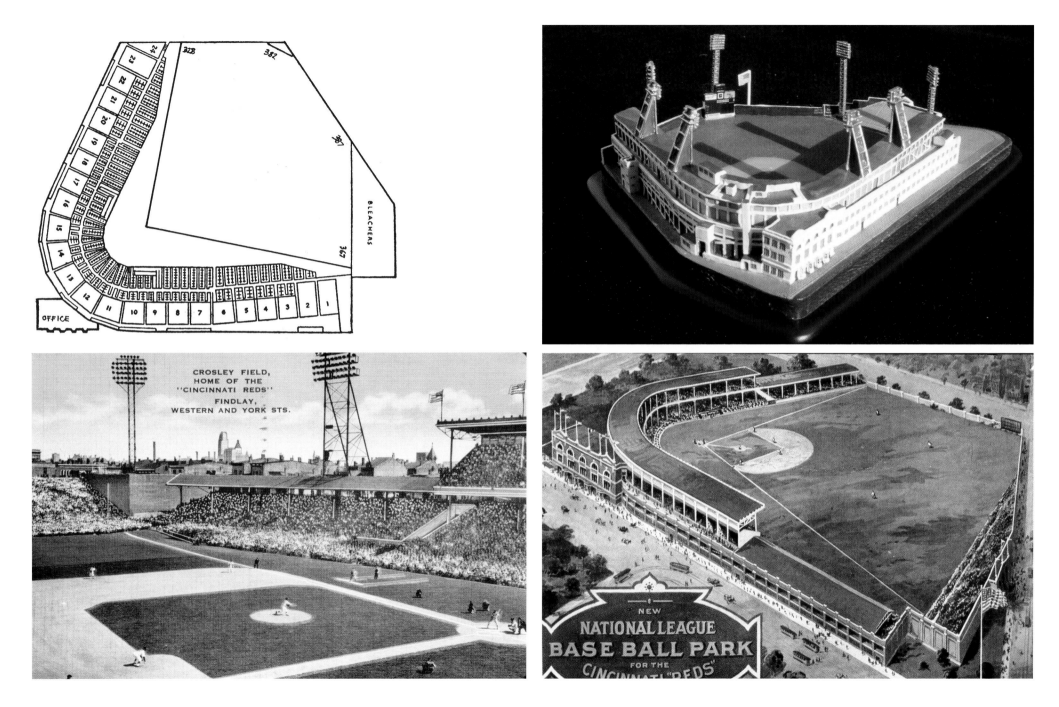

CROSLEY FIELD,
HOME OF THE
"CINCINNATI REDS"
FINDLAY,
WESTERN AND YORK STS.

NEW
NATIONAL LEAGUE
BASE BALL PARK
FOR THE
CINCINNATI "REDS"

character. Designers John and Judy Davids of the Tiger Stadium Fan Club produced a remodeling plan that would have allowed it to continue well into the 21st century as an economically viable structure, but it was rejected by two ownership regimes seeking a nine-figure public subsidy for a new park. Still standing, Tiger Stadium saw its last season of play in 1999.

Ebbets Field, opened in 1913, is probably the all-time sentimental favorite among ballparks—and rightfully so, for we have seen that Brooklyn was the great incubator of ballparks, and this is the masterpiece among them. Designed by Clarence Randall Van

Buskirk and costing $750,000, its architectural quality was second only to Shibe's, and matched or bested that of Forbes. (These are undoubtedly the three great pinnacles of classic ballpark architecture.) The initial grandstand structure had open exterior colonnades on two sides totaling nearly fifty bays, flanking a fourteen-bay arcade along the curve of the home-plate end. Within that arc, past a sweeping metal awning, was an 80-foot diameter entrance and ticket-booth rotunda whose marble floor was patterned in the

image of a baseball, above which hung a chandelier whose dozen arms were shaped like baseball bats. The

basic exterior material was brown brick, but there was plentiful stone or terra cotta ornament in the form of keystones and Corinthian pilaster capitals.

Behind its dignified facade and beyond the impressive entrance, Ebbets Field harbored some of the most colorful players and eccentric fans in baseball. The latter were able to observe the former at close hand, for foul territory was small and its upper deck even closer to the field than Briggs Stadium's. Originally this was a pitcher's park, with a whopping 419-foot left field and a 466-foot center. Seating expansions from 18,000 to 35,000 reduced those to 348 feet and 389 feet, making it a hitter's park in its later years. Right field was always close at 297 feet to 301

This page: Detroit's Tiger Stadium shown in its urban setting (far left) and in model form (center). Above: Early single-decked version with corner office building. Left: The famous right-field home run porch, where the upper deck overhung the lower by ten feet.

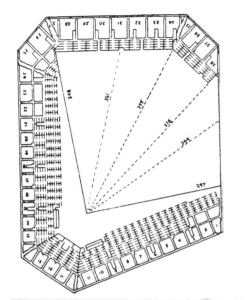

feet, and its original 19-foot concrete wall was heightened to 38 feet by a wire fence as home runs increased during the live-ball era. That wall had about ten different angles or surfaces (a number that's usually greatly exaggerated), which made fielding difficult and gave the Dodgers a home-field advantage. It was dominated by a large scoreboard, and bore

Left: Seating and field diagram of Ebbets Field in its post-WWII configuration.

Below: Brooklyn Dodgers' baseball star Jackie Robinson walks on the sidewalk across the street from Ebbets Field, April 16, 1947. Robinson broke the color barrier in the 1947 season by becoming the first African American to play in the Major Leagues. *Bettmann/Corbis*

prominent advertising signs, including a local haberdasher's famous offer of "Hit Sign, Win Suit."

Ebbets was the site of two events that reshaped 20th-century baseball dramatically, at least as much as the fireproof ballpark revolution itself. One was the first televised major-league game in 1939, which eventually opened the door to greater revenues and popularity for the sport. The second was breaking baseball's color barrier by adding Jackie Robinson to the Brooklyn roster in 1947. Not only did this permit a great increase in the talent level of the sport, but it was a seminal event in the struggle to integrate American society. Not coincidentally, the Dodgers of the Robinson era, bolstered by other African-American stars such as Roy Campanella and Don Newcombe, were the best team in a century of Brooklyn-Los Angeles baseball, and one of the National League's greatest dynasties, winning six pennants in ten years.

The Dodgers' attendance topped one million in each of their last 13 years in Brooklyn, a remarkable feat at the time, especially given their ballpark's modest capacity. In Robinson's first year, they broke the league attendance record with more than 1.8 million. Despite such economic success, Dodger ownership wanted the city to provide land for a new ballpark, and, not getting it, moved the team to Los Angeles after the 1957 season. It was the only time an economically successful team ever relocated,

and was a cruel blow to the borough that invented and perfected ballparks. Yet Ebbets Field lives on in American culture, for Brooklyn is a city of writers, and they have memorialized it and its team eloquently and often.

In 1914, the upstart Federal League declared itself a major circuit and opened shop in eight cities. Although somewhat underfunded and lasting just two seasons, it produced four parks of interest. Baltimore's Terrapin Park, a 12,500-seater, was the youngest wooden structure to claim any major-league status, and it managed to avoid burning down until its luck ran out on the eve of July 4, 1944. Its small skewed outfield (left field 300 feet, straight right about 320 feet) reflected a tiny site, and its right field bleachers were shoehorned between two ranks of row houses.

The other Federal parks were fireproof. Two were designed by C. B. Comstock, a well-connected architect who was one of the league's part owners: Washington Park in Brooklyn (the fourth of that name in the borough), and Harrison Field, just beyond the Newark, New Jersey, city limits. The former was small (18,000 seats and foul lines of 300 feet and 275 feet) and costly (perhaps as much as $500,000), while the latter was spacious (21,000 seats and dimensions of 375 feet/450 feet/375 feet) and economical (somewhat more than $100,000). In 1918, it was the site of Sunday games for all three New York teams.

The Federal League's lasting legacy was Weeghman Park on Chicago's North Side, later known as Cubs Park and ultimately as Wrigley Field. Designed by Comiskey's architect Zachary Taylor Davis, it was originally a simple 14,000-seat, single-deck affair that expanded upward and outward in stages to about 40,000 in 1928 through

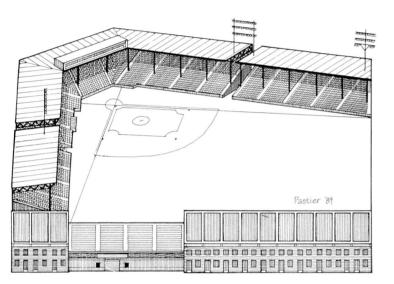

additions undertaken first by Davis and then by Graham Anderson Probst & White, a prestigious Chicago firm. The main grandstand was actually sliced apart and moved 60 feet outward on rollers in 1922-23, and then the structure was double-decked in 1926. Thanks to those added seats and pennant-winning teams, the Cubs became, in 1927, the first club ever to draw a million fans in a season, and then broke that record with

nearly 1.5 million in 1929.

Next, following plans of noted local architects Holabird and Root, the park was completely reconfigured in the foul corners and outfield in 1937-1938 in a somewhat streamlined modern style. It was this remodeling that gave Wrigley its present signature look—the gracefully flowing concave and convex curves of the ivy-clad outfield wall, the distinctive pyramidal bleachers edged by stepped planters, and the large curved-back, hand-operated scoreboard hovering above them. These changes were undertaken by chewing-gum magnate P.K. Wrigley, described by author Mark Jacob as "a remarkably high minded and eccentric owner" who "spent millions on the upkeep of the park when critics were urging him to spend the money on ballplayers instead. He is the primary reason why the Cubs haven't won a World Series since 1908—and also the primary reason why Wrigley Field has survived to this day."

The Cubs' home is both a product and a shaper of its context. When the famous Chicago wind blows in off Lake Michigan, it is a pitcher's park, but more often, when it blows out it is a slugger's paradise, as shown by the unbalanced home and away home run totals of Cubs such as Sammy Sosa, Ernie Banks, and Billy Williams. It exists in symbiosis with its tight urban framework, its home runs often landing in the streets or even bouncing off nearby houses, and allowing neighbors to see into the field and even rent out their vantage points to strangers. It is served by an "L" train stop half a block away, and sustains forty bars and restaurants within a block. It is America's great surviving neighborhood ballpark, and has even given its name to the surrounding district: Wrigleyville.

With the opening of Braves Field, 1915 concluded the tidal wave of ballpark building. By then every one of the traditionally defined major league teams but the St. Louis Cardinals was playing its home games in a fireproof park. (The Yankees were sharing the Polo Grounds with the Giants.) All but Baker Bowl was six years old or less. On paper, Braves Field was a dramatic climax to the wild ride, since it was the first ballpark with 40,000 seats. But in reality, it was a bland, sprawling single-deck affair lacking architectural substance and baseball character. Its outfield was huge—purportedly starting at 402 feet to left, 440 feet to center and 402 feet to right. Over the years

management tinkered with those dimensions with confusing frequency in a futile attempt to get it right. According to ballpark historian Philip Lowry, right field alone changed nineteen times in 32 years, and ranged from 402 feet to less than 298 feet. While Braves Field was its designers' biggest ballpark commission of the period, it was not Osborn Engineering's finest hour.

After this frenzied pace of building nineteen parks in seven years, (including six in the Federal League), baseball built nothing new for the next eight years. The boa constrictor had swallowed a sow, and needed some time to digest it.

Left: Baltimore's wooden Terrapin Park began life as a Federal League venue in 1914, then served the International League Orioles, one of the great minor league dynasties, from 1916 until it burned down 1944. This drawing shows how the right-field bleachers filled the gap between two runs of row houses.

Right: Braves Field's arcaded, dormered, and double-gabled office building was the architectural highlight of an otherwise utilitarian exterior.

Entrance to Braves Field, Boston, Mass.

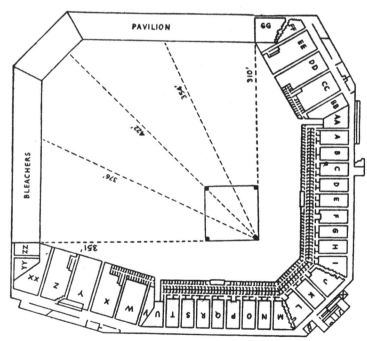

Above and Left: Model and seating diagram of Sportsman's Park in St. Louis. The right field pavilion was the last segregated seating area in major league baseball.

Above right: Ebbets Field was the site of the first major league telecast. *MLB Photos via Getty Images*

Right: The legendary Ebbets Field right-field wall and scoreboard. The bottom half of the wall tilted backwards, while the top half was plumb. Batters hitting the sign at the bottom would win a suit from clothier Abe Stark. *MLB Photos via Getty Images*

SIZE IS EVERYTHING

Opposite: Triple-decked Yankee Stadium as seen from the mezzanine level of its right-field stands.

Below: Field and seating diagram of Yankee Stadium during the 1946-74 period.

Bottom: The Osborn Company's presentation drawing of a fully enclosed 100,000-seat Yankee Stadium. (Never implemented.)

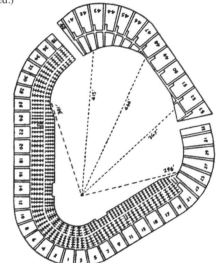

As the final chord of the first fireproof-era symphony, Braves Field's size provided a hint of things to come. Although remaining dormant for nearly a decade, the desire for big ballparks would reassert itself spectacularly in 1923.

It all grew from the greatest player that the sport has yet produced, pitcher-outfielder Babe Ruth. After being sold by the Red Sox to the Yankees, and moving to the Polo Grounds, he raised his season total from 29 at Fenway Park to 54 and then 59 in the home run-friendly New York park, smashing records in the process. His performance electrified the sport, and allowed the Yankees to dethrone the Giants as New York's most-watched team. With the American league tenants outdrawing their National League landlords by nearly 30 percent between 1920 and 1922, combative Giants manager John McGraw convinced team owner Charles Stoneham to serve eviction papers on their guests. "They will have to build a park in Queens or some other out of the way place. Let them go away and wither on the vine," snorted Little Napoleon.

Like the sale of Ruth, it was not a smart move. Rather than relocate in the boondocks, the Yankees found a South Bronx property adjoining a subway stop and less than half a mile from the Giants' home, and proceeded to build the grandest baseball palace to date. Yankee Stadium was planned to be completely triple decked, even in the outfield, and hold 100,000 fans. As first built, it was much less capacious, with 58,000 seats, and single-deck grandstands and bleachers occupied most of the stadium's perimeter. Still, 74,200 fans squeezed inside to watch the first game on April 18, 1923, and 20,000 more were turned away.

Nothing like this $2.5 million monument had ever been built before, and, reflecting its magnitude and grandeur, it was the first ballpark with the word stadium as part of its title. Its exterior architecture was unprecedented as well—the walls were concrete rather than brick or stone, and the style was a minimalist classicism that verged on cautious modernism. Inside, there were decorative touches rendered in copper sheet metal, the most prominent and famous being the scalloped roof frieze 108 feet above the field.

The triple-decked portions of Yankee Stadium (or, as New Yorkers have long called it, The Stadium) were extended in stages until they thrust well into fair territory. This gave the stands a peak capacity of more than 70,000, as well as an impressive and graceful curving sweep that contrasted with the straight-line angularity typical of most contemporary parks. Because the stadium filled its large and oddly shaped site, its outfield dimensions were terribly lopsided. By 1939, right field was short—296 feet down the line, about 344 feet to straight right, and 367 feet to right center. But left field zoomed out from 301 feet at the line to 402 feet straightaway, 457 feet in left center, and

Left: View beneath the upper deck of Cleveland Stadium showing the three-dimensional intricacy of its steel framing system and access catwalks.

Right: Cleveland's two great downtown landmarks: The Terminal tower at upper left was the tallest building outside of New York City for 37 years, and Municipal Stadium at lower right was baseball's largest-capacity stadium for more than 60.

461 feet in dead center. It was a graveyard for righty power-hitters (Joe DiMaggio hit a record 65 more home runs away than at home), and a soft touch for lefties.

No one has ever hit a ball out of Yankee Stadium during a major league game, although Mickey Mantle came very close in 1963. In the mid-1970s it was radically remodeled, diminishing its seating capacity, it oddities, its architectural character, and its grace.

During the 1920s there were many ballpark expansions and alterations, but no new parks other than the monument in the Bronx. Once again there was an eight-year hiatus, followed by another jaw-dropping wonder, this time on the shores of Lake Erie.

During the roaring Twenties, Cleveland was a very ambitious city. It had built a grand master-planned civic center and the tallest skyscraper outside New York, and was planning an immense multi-purpose stadium that would surpass the Yankees' home. It would be a 78,000-seater meant to serve 60 types of events, including track and field, baseball, football, prize fights, grand opera, auto racing, religious convocations, and other mass gatherings. There's a widespread belief that it was being built to allow Cleveland to host the 1932 Olympics, but that was never one of its envisioned purposes, according to Cleveland historian James Toman.

Planning of this superstadium naturally fell to the hometown firm that had become America's preeminent stadium architects and engineers. Kenneth Osborn, the partner who directed the stadium's design, said that its form "evolved from the study of an ideal baseball grandstand." Well, not exactly. Cleveland Municipal Stadium's site was waterfront landfill, extensive and free of any streets. It was thus the first major league ballpark whose shape was not determined or even influenced by its property dimensions, street pattern, or urban context, for there were none of those. Its designers had the freedom to create a unconstrained layout, not exclusively for baseball, but for the combination of various sports and other events. The form it took was a 57-sided egg-shaped polygon, blunted in center field and tightly curved near home plate. It was the first time a ballpark had achieved strict structural and field symmetry.

Baseball needs may have carried the most weight, but this shape was still a compromise between conflicting requirements. One of these was the need for a regulation 440-yard running track, which led to a field size that was far too large for baseball or football, one so vast that Babe Ruth purportedly declared, "A guy ought to have a horse to play the outfield." The central half of the outfield averaged 450 feet, and even with 320-foot foul lines, the overall home run distance averaged about 413 feet.

Osborn may not have known it at the time, but there was no way to meet all those competing requirements successfully. Nevertheless, this was the most functionally ambitious stadium attempted until then, as rationally laid out as possible given the limitations of the running track mandate.

Municipal Stadium was a cornucopia of firsts and superlatives. It had the most seats of any stadium (as opposed to bleacher benches) for baseball or otherwise, the most architectural aluminum ever used on any building of the time (its stepped-back upper exterior walls were completely louvered in this metal), the most ramps (16), the largest scoreboard, and the greatest height (115 feet). It was the first major league ballpark built with public funds, and the most expensive one for more than 20 years (more than $3 million, despite cost-cutting measures and low Depression-era construction wages.). Its inaugural ballgame on July 31, 1932, set an attendance record (80,184), which was broken on September 12, 1954, by 84,587 fans. The season attendance record of 2,620,628 was set in 1948. The stadium could theoretically hold 110,000 for boxing, and was said to have accommodated 125,000 at a religious congress.

Municipal Stadium's immense outfield led to the first significant inner fence in the sport (in 1947), cutting distances by 50 to 75 feet. It had the only long-lived bleachers that were never reached by a home run. It was the first major league park to have permanent field lighting, although not the first to put on a night game. Its architecture was the most modern of its time, with extensive metal cladding and large window walls set between tan brick piers. It was also the least-used new park for several years: its immense capacity and high rent was more than the Indians needed or could afford during the Depression and World War II, and thus it was used only part-time for all but one of its first seventeen seasons.

While only two new parks were constructed in the 1920s and 1930s, it was still an active ballpark-building era as the first generation of fireproof parks expanded through double-decking and second-deck extensions. Several of these, mostly in the American League, topped 50,000 seats in this way: the Polo Grounds reached 55,000 in 1926, Comiskey Park attained 52,000 in 1927, Yankee Stadium exceeded 71,000 in 1937, and Briggs Stadium reached 58,000 in 1938, more than doubling its original 1912 capacity. Also, many minor league parks of

including a pair in Canada, Toronto's Maple Leaf Stadium and Montreal's Delorimier Downs, and two In California, San Francisco's Seals Stadium and Los Angeles' Wrigley Field. Some approached or attained what could have been major-league capacities a generation earlier, including the latter two, and even more notably Jersey City's Roosevelt Stadium, which had somewhere between 26,000 and 30,000 seats in the late 1930s, and was later home to fifteen Brooklyn Dodger games in 1956-1957.

Left: Upon moving from New York to San Francisco in 1958, the Giants played two seasons at the Art Deco-styled Seals Stadium, one of the finest Pacific Coast League parks, before moving to cold and windswept Candlestick Park.

Top and Far right: Jersey City's Roosevelt Stadium, a 1937 WPA project, was a one of the most substantial minor-league parks ever. In 1956 and 1957, it served as the Brooklyn Dodgers' home park for 15 games.

Right: Prototype plan, promoted by the American Institute of Steel Construction in 1930, for a 20,000-seat professional baseball stadium.

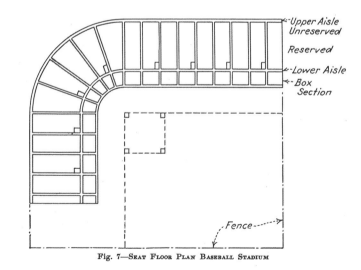

Upper Aisle
Unreserved

Reserved

Lower Aisle

Box Section

Fence

Fig. 7—Seat Floor Plan Baseball Stadium

Right: Durham Athletic Park, built in 1938 and celebrated in the movie Bull Durham, is a classic in-town park. Its signature bull crests the right field wall, ads for local businesses jostle for space below, and an old industrial building provides an easy home run target.

Minor league and amateur ballparks of the 1920s and 1930s, while not as grand as their big-league counterparts, often provided an intimacy, charm and quirkiness that easily made up for their modest size and lack of monumentality.

Above: Built by the Depression-era Works Progress Agency in 1937 to a design of A.H. Morrell, Riverview Park in Clinton Iowa lies near the west bank of the Mississippi. Its Art Deco entry elements and detailing make it a rarity among standing ballparks.

Right: This remarkably elaborate wooden American Legion ballpark, estimated to date from the 1920s, once stood in Houma, a town in southern Louisiana's Cajun country. It showed that even amateur venues in small cities could achieve genuine design distinction.

THE SUBURBANIZATION OF BASEBALL: SHIFTING AND EXPANDED FRANCHISES IN THE EARLY POST-WWII ERA

The years between 1901 and 1952 were a time of absolute major league franchise stability: all of the sixteen teams were faithful to their home city for more than half a century. But then, failing or opportunistic franchises began moving to greener economic pastures: Boston Braves to Milwaukee, St. Louis Browns to Baltimore (becoming the Orioles), Philadelphia Athletics to Kansas City, New York Giants to San Francisco, and, unforgivably, Brooklyn Dodgers to Los Angeles—all in six years. Naturally, these moves stirred up the ballpark mix, bringing seven new temporary and permanent parks into the fold.

Milwaukee County Stadium (1953-2000), the first of this group, was like the Roman god Janus, looking both into the past and the future. Though situated just west of downtown on the site of an abandoned quarry, it is popularly perceived as the first of the modern suburban stadiums, high on efficiency and short on charm and character. Sitting in a sea of 14,000 parking spaces on 110 acres, the structure had Osborn bloodlines (it was their last great design), and the structural form and ambiance of its steel grandstand was largely that of a classic park. But it also reflected Osborn's ongoing search for an ideal baseball layout free of urban constraints, this time unencumbered by a running track, and weighted far more toward baseball's demands than football's. Its pear shape and curved outfield fence became the model for other unconstrained suburban ballyards such as Candlestick Park, and Metropolitan, Dodger, Anaheim, and Royals stadiums, as well as some modern Latin-American ones. County Stadium was the second park built with public money, and grew over the years from 34,000 to 54,000 seats. It set a National League attendance record in its first year, and broke that the next, altogether drawing a then-astounding 10.5 million fans in its first five seasons.

The next year, the Browns migrated from St Louis to become the Baltimore Orioles—the first of only two times that a post-1900 team moved significantly eastward, the other being Seattle to Milwaukee. It, too, occupied a publicly funded symmetrical park surrounded by parking. Memorial Stadium (1954-1991) was the first reinforced concrete ballpark since the Palace of the Fans, and was the first unroofed major league park. Other than having no bleachers in center field, the shape of this oval two-sport facility was very similar to a Cleveland Municipal Stadium.

In 1955, the Philadelphia Athletics decamped for Kansas City, where they occupied a newly double-decked Municipal Stadium, which had been structurally designed by Osborn for just such an expansion when it was built 32 years earlier under the name of Muehlebach Field. Until

Left: Meuhlebach Field, an important minor league park, was double-decked in 1955 to accommodate the Kansas City Athletics. It was also home to the Kansas City Monarchs, a top Negro League team, from 1923 to 1950.

Right: Baltimore's reinforced-concrete Memorial Stadium was a rebuilt football venue, and the first unroofed major league park. It eventually grew to 54,000 seats.

the retro ballpark revival of the last fifteen years, this steel-framed structure was the last major-league park that could be considered a prewar fireproof classic.

The migration of New York's two National League teams to the West coast after the 1957 season, made feasible by improved and cheaper air travel, doubled the east-west span of the major leagues. The Giants were struggling economically, while the Dodgers were doing well but wanted to do even better. When the city couldn't assemble a Brooklyn

ballpark site for them (it offered one in Queens instead), they scheduled several home games in Jersey City in 1956-1957 to dramatize the issue, and then packed up their tent, taking the Giants with them. Upon arrival, the San Francisco Giants played for two years at Seals Stadium, an unroofed single-deck park seating about 23,000. It was a Depression-era concrete structure in a modified Art Deco style, and its playing field was a spacious 365 feet/410 feet/355 feet.

The Los Angeles Dodgers also played in a

single-deck, unroofed concrete venue completed in the early 1930s, but there the resemblances end. The Memorial Coliseum was an immense 94,600-seat track and football stadium unsuited for baseball with field dimensions of 250 feet/425 feet/301 feet, and some seats were more than 700 feet from home plate. Management was willing to overlook the flaws and savor the economics— the Dodgers set an NL seasonal attendance record of nearly 2.3 million in 1960, and several 1959 games drew more than 90,000,

(each of those games exceeding the St. Louis Browns' total attendance in 1933 or 1935) a level never reached before or since.

In 1960, the Giants moved to Candlestick Park at an empty, windswept, bayfront location. The stadium was concrete, and the upper reaches of its exterior had a bit of a Latin-American modernist flair. But it wasn't a good place for a game. It was the last ballpark built with columns in the seating areas, and the outfield seating areas looked unfinished. It was cold, foggy, and windy, and

during the 1961 All-Star game, a sharp gust actually blew hometown hurler Stu Miller off the pitcher's mound. A 1971 expansion for football was meant to block the wind, but it only changed its pattern. During the 1989 World Series, Candlestick was moderately damaged by the Loma Prieta earthquake. For more than a decade, the Giants tried to find a better home, but it wasn't until forty years of purgatory that they were able to find heaven in Pac Bell (now SBC) Park downtown.

The Giants moved from a nice temporary ballpark to a terrible permanent one; their archrivals in Los Angeles reversed the sequence. Dodger Stadium is regarded with near-universal reverence as one of the best ballparks ever, largely for reasons lying outside the park itself. Its weather is good, the views of the San Gabriel Mountains are seductive, the teams have performed well, and the place has always been kept scrupulously clean and well-maintained. It was also the only park constructed with private funds between 1923 and 2000.

But there's another side of the coin. Dodger Stadium received a huge public subsidy in the form of a 300-acre land donation and extensive infrastructure improvements. Its concrete structure eliminates seating-zone columns, but lacks intimacy since its various upper decks are unusually distant from the game action. The stadium is divorced from any neighborhood and inaccessible to pedestrians, has almost no exterior architecture (it's embedded in the

sloping ground), is bland, and produces low-scoring games. Even though it's only 1.3 miles from City Hall, it's the ultimate suburban environment, taking up half a square mile; lacking quirkiness, human scale and a connection to its city; and trapped amid 16,000 parking spaces. Leaving after a game is a stressful experience, as people dodge fast-moving cars on their way to their own vehicles, and then navigate complex internal traffic patterns to find their particular freeway. There have been many worse ballparks in history, but also many better ones.

The expansion Los Angeles Angels also occupied Dodger Stadium for four years, after an initial 1961 season at Wrigley Field. That was one of the finest minor league parks, designed by Zachary Taylor Davis of Comiskey Park and Chicago Wrigley Field fame. This jewel box was double-decked (unusual in the minors) and featured a slender 12-story office tower at its home-plate end. In its single year it set a record with 248 home runs, thanks to cozy 345-foot power alleys, and earlier it was appropriately the setting for the Home Run Derby

Left: Dodger Stadium, isolated and suburban in character despite its proximity to downtown Los Angeles, is much admired for its cleanliness and views of nearby hills and mountains. *Corbis*

Right: A diagram of San Francisco's Candlestick Park. A 360-degree enclosure for football was meant to block its notorious winds, but instead it only made them swirl more unpredictably.

television series. Exploited by its Dodger Stadium landlords, the expansion team renamed itself the California Angels and drove 27 miles down the Santa Ana freeway to settle in Orange County. Steel-framed Anaheim Stadium was designed in the Milwaukee/Dodger Stadium mode by an Osborn alumnus, but with greater intimacy than the latter. It was expanded in 1979 from 43,250 seats to 67,335 to accommodate football, sustained structural damage in a major 1994 earthquake, and then was downsized to 45,000 seats and dramatically overhauled in 1997-1998 under Disney ownership by postmodern architect Robert AM Stern, injecting theme-park elements such as a fake-rock landscape and a 90-foot geyser in the center field stands.

The next franchise shift after the Pacific

coast diaspora was the Washington Senators' metamorphosis into the Minnesota Twins in 1961. Their home, an upgraded five-year-old minor league venue called Metropolitan Stadium, was in the Minneapolis bedroom community of Bloomington, the first time a big-league ballpark had been built in a suburban jurisdiction rather than in a central city. (That process would later be repeated by the Texas Rangers, Kansas City Royals, and Florida Marlins.) The "Met" was a triple-decked steel structure that had the self-revealing nature of a huge Erector set. It was inexpensive, modular, and minimalist modern architecture, meant for football as well as the summer game—none of which would endear itself to baseball traditionalists. Reputedly, it was very poorly maintained, and was abandoned after 21 seasons, replaced by the nation's largest shopping mall.

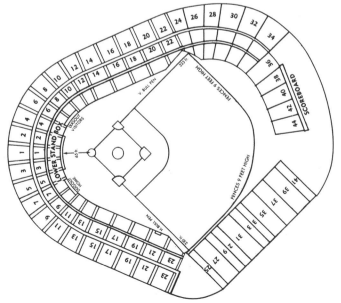

CIRCULAR LOGIC

In 1962, a new form of baseball stadium made its debut, and it swept through the sport like a hurricane through Florida. Depending on how one counts, there were between ten and thirteen of these popular inventions built in a sixteen-year period.

This new gadget was the circular multipurpose facility, and no other type of baseball venue has been so strongly reviled. These round parks have been called cookie cutters and sterile concrete ashtrays, and derided for lacking character and all looking alike. And while it's true that a circle may be nature's perfect form, it's not that for baseball. By their very shape, circular stadiums put too many foul-territory seats too far from the action, and, because they are invariably built to also house football, their size—anywhere up to 73,000 seats—is not conducive to an intimate baseball experience. And a round form leads to a certain sameness of appearance both among individual parks, and between different portions of an individual park; one slice of layer cake is pretty much like another.

But having said all that, there were compelling reasons why circular stadia came into being and became so ubiquitous. It was largely a matter of economy, efficiency, and fiscal responsibility on the part of the local governments that were now expected to pay for big-sport play. With baseball and football teams clamoring for new facilities and threatening, implicitly or explicitly, to move to other cities if denied, combination stadiums were a way to meet those demands and conserve land and taxpayer dollars by avoiding redundancy.

Previously, two-sport stadia either favored one over the other (usually baseball over football), or were neutral, like Cleveland's and Baltimore's oval layouts. But in the 1960s, movable seating allowed straight sections to run parallel to the

Left: When Shea Stadium opened in conjunction with New York's 1964 World's Fair, it had a fussier exterior than the present one shown here. It was baseball's second circular stadium, and the only one that was open in the outfield.

sidelines for football, and converge on the foul lines for baseball. The curved, fixed seating sections were less ideally placed, but the people in the movable lower rows were well treated.

The first application of this principle took place in 1962 at D.C. Stadium (later Robert F. Kennedy Stadium) in the nation's capital. This was probably the most awkward of the circular parks, with an odd undulating roofline, an upper deck in the outfield but none below, and a banal exterior. It hosted the Washington Senators for ten years, saw no big-league baseball from 1972 until 2004, and is now the temporary home of the Washington Nationals, relocated from Montreal, Quebec, and San Juan, Puerto Rico. That 33-season service gap is a major league record.

Shea Stadium, opening in 1964 alongside the New York World's Fair in Queens, was baseball's second round park. The stands don't extend far into fair territory, and thus don't form a complete circle, even though they were designed for such an expansion

option. With four decks, Shea is quite tall, and its seats can be far from the field. Yet seeing a game there is still a good experience, aside from a bland exterior and the noise of planes taking off from nearby LaGuardia Airport. Its ability to frame internal space and yet allow distant vistas is unique among its cohorts.

It's certainly a subjective perception, but some open-air circular parks seem better than others. Shea is above average. Busch Memorial Stadium in St. Louis (1966-2005) was the best, thanks in part to some nice design touches by consulting architect Edward Durrell Stone—its outer roof edge was a graceful series of open scallops that echoed the form of the famous Gateway Arch nearby. Busch was baseball's first downtown park, later joined by others in Cincinnati, Seattle, Minneapolis, Toronto, Baltimore, Cleveland, Denver, Houston, San Francisco, Pittsburgh, and San Diego.

The Oakland Coliseum (1968), sometimes called the Mausoleum, and Arlington Stadium near Fort Worth (1966-1993) are the worst circular parks. Both are sterile, roofless, and occupy auto-dominated suburban settings. Oakland at least has rapid transit access, but it also has some poor sight lines, and in recent years has been disfigured by Mount Davis, a gargantuan football luxury suite structure looming above center field. Arlington was a single-deck minor league park expanded horizontally to not-quite-major-league standards, and was probably

Left: Derided by baseball purists, the better round stadiums such as Shea could attain a certain grandeur through their impressive height and elemental geometry.

the worst big league venue to log 20 years or more of service.

Even nearly identical circular parks can create disparate experiences. Atlanta's Fulton County Stadium (1966-1996) and Cincinnati's Riverfront Stadium (1970-2002) were designed by the same consortium and had identical steel structural systems, but the latter offered a superior ambiance. Cincinnati's foul territory was better shaped, and its river and downtown setting was far more pleasant and convenient than Atlanta's wasteland of parking lots and freeways. Pittsburgh's Three Rivers Stadium (1970-2000) also had a waterside setting near downtown, but fell short of Cincinnati. Its original design would have had a distinctively sloped top profile and allowed spectacular downtown views, but was rejected as too expensive.

Two other open-air parks are usually part of the circular stadium class, but really aren't. San Diego's Jack Murphy Stadium (1969-2003) and Philadelphia's Veterans Stadium (1971-2003) are "superellipses"—multi-radius forms that are bulging squares with rounded corners. This shape is better than a circle for both baseball and football viewing. Philadelphia's is overbearing and externally unimaginative, but San Diego's is an architectural masterpiece. Designed by Gary Allen, it was the first stadium ever to win a national design award from the American Institute of Architects. It boldly expressed its poured-in-place concrete structure, and

articulated each circulation element clearly on the exterior-corkscrew ramps, slantingly ascending escalators, and cylindrical elevator shafts were each put on display like pieces of sculpture. These innovations have been copied in other stadia since. Unfortunately, expansions for football weren't fully sympathetic to the original vision.

Above: St. Louis' Busch Stadium's roofline incorporated scores of scalloped openings whose shape echoed the parabolic form of the city's monumental Gateway Arch nearby.

Below right: A plastic replica of Atlanta's Fulton County Stadium.

Below: Seating and field diagram of Riverfront Stadium, Cincinnati.

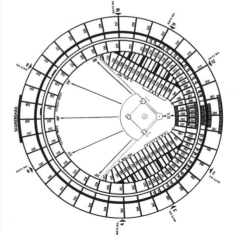

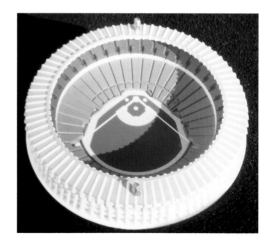

DOMES AND MOVING ROOFS

If open-air round parks were unloved by baseball purists, domed ones were even more disliked. An indoor setting is certainly not Giamatti's paradise; at best it's Dante's Purgatorio, holding out the prospect of relief once the game is over. Like so much of ballpark history, it all began in Brooklyn. The Dodgers' quest for a new ballpark in the 1950s inspired two rough-draft designs for roofed stadiums, from Buckminster Fuller's Princeton architecture students, and from industrial and theater designer Norman Bel Geddes.

Neither came close to being built, but what grew as an idea for Brooklyn would come to actual fruition in Texas. Before moving indoors, the expansion Houston ballclub played three seasons in the temporary Colt Stadium, a spacious (360 feet/420 feet/360 feet) single-decked facility famed for low scoring, poor lighting, high temperatures and humidity, and killer mosquitoes. In 1965, the low scoring persisted but the other problems were eliminated when the team changed its name from the Colt .45s to the Astros and took up quarters in the Astrodome, modestly dubbed "The Eighth Wonder of the World." Despite this hyperbole, the 'Dome truly was a wonder—the first full-sized

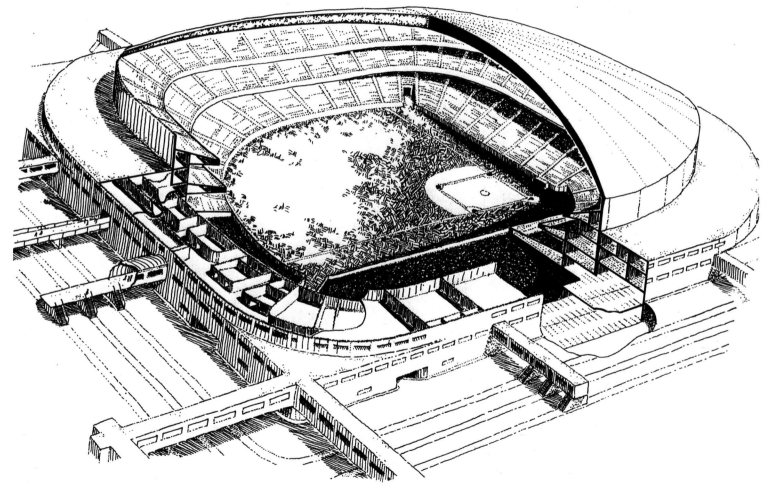

Above: In 1952, at Dodger president Walter O'Malley's behest, industrial and theatrical designer Norman Bel Geddes unveiled this preliminary sketch for a large indoor stadium near downtown Brooklyn.

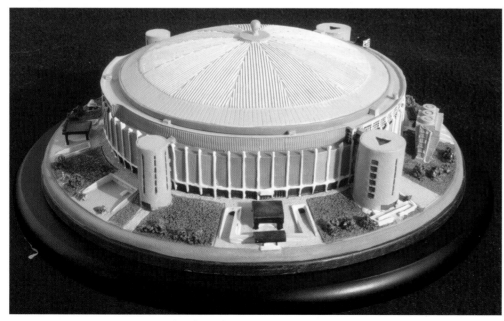

Above and Below: Model of the Houston Astrodome with roof removed and in place, reflecting additions to the original structure.

Right: Seattle's Kingdome was completed in 1976 on reclaimed tideflat land; it was destroyed by implosion in March 2000.

indoor venue for any major field sport (in this case, the customary baseball and football), fully air-conditioned, and supplied with cloth-covered padded seats. It was packed with a variety of restaurants and bars, and it had the world's largest scoreboard, a presidential suite, and a private apartment, chapel, barber shop, and bowling alley for owner Roy Hofheinz. The private amenities reflected a Texas-sized ego, but the public ones later became common in the sport.

The Astrodome's greatest influence on baseball grew out of the law of unintended consequences. In order to admit enough light to allow grass to grow, its plastic-paneled roof also created so much glare that fielders could not see many fly balls. The solution was to paint part of the roof to reduce the light level, but then the grass began dying. In 1966 Hofheinz agreed to the experimental installation of a nylon synthetic grass carpet, and Astroturf was born. It eventually spread to ten ballparks, both indoor and open-air, (as well as countless football fields) until its drawbacks became obvious and its popularity faded. The Astros left the 'Dome after the 1999 season, and now play on real grass.

A decade later, the world's largest domed stadium was built in New Orleans, directly inspired by Houston's, and using the same steel lamella structural system and the same engineers. The Louisiana Superdome's seats are arranged in a superellipse pattern (locally termed a "squircle," or squared circle), making it better suited for baseball than its

progenitor. Fifteen major league teams have played exhibition games there, but the market is too small to attract a big league team. In 2005, the two southern arenas were linked by disaster, when they became emergency shelters for refugees from hurricane Katrina.

Seattle's Kingdome, opened for baseball in 1977, was the world's largest thin-shell concrete dome. (Eight years earlier, Seattle had one tanatlizing season of open-air baseball when the ill-fated Pilots played at Sick's Stadium, a picturesque but inadequate and hastily expanded minor league park.) The Kingdome's seating pattern was a rectangle with rounded corners, even though its outer walls were circular. This layout worked well for baseball, producing a good field shape and a generous crop of home runs. Many observers likened its hulking unadorned exterior, a product of cost cutting, to a gray concrete toadstool. After less than a quarter century of football, baseball, basketball, trade shows, and other uses, the Kingdome fell victim to poor maintenance and stadium politics, and thus was the shortest lived of America's major stadiums. Four separate sports and exhibition buildings costing well over a billion dollars were erected to replace it, but together they didn't have all of the functional capability of the drab workhorse they supplanted.

Montreal also opened a stadium for baseball in 1977, after eight seasons of playing in a temporary ballpark. The contrast was astounding. Parc Jarry was a small,

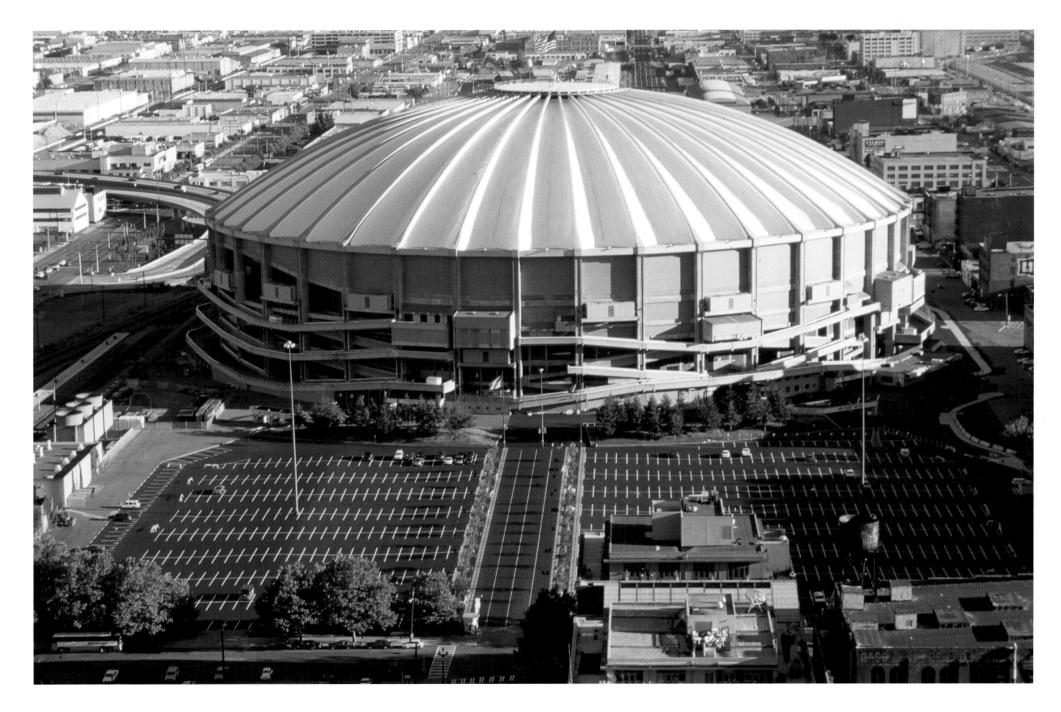

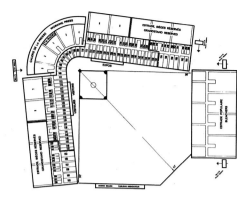

Above: Field and seating diagram of Jarry Park, the Montreal Expos' intimate single-decked temporary home from 1969 to 1976.

Below and Below right: Roof plan and plastic model of Montreal's monumental Olympic Stadium, the billion-dollar home to the Expos from 1977 to 2004.

hastily expanded, single-deck unroofed affair, beloved in retrospect, while Stade Olympique was the most costly and monumental sports structure ever built. Jarry Park was intimate and shaped for baseball, while the Olympic Stadium was a gargantuan concrete sculpture sized for track and field and Canadian football, which has a playing area 63 percent larger than the U.S. variety. Olympique cost about a billion dollars a generation ago—perhaps two billion in today's dollars. Nicknamed "The Big Owe" because of its huge public debt burden, it was the work of Roger Taillibert, a French architect not versed in baseball. It was

designed to have a retractable fabric roof suspended by cables from a tilted 575-foot-tall tower, and after more than a decade of technical and funding problems, the membrane was finally installed only to periodically tear in windy weather. After much unsuccessful tinkering, the fabric roof was redesigned as a fixed element. This fanciful stadium resembles an exotic species of tropical marine life, and its tower can easily be seen from twenty miles away.

Montreal's rival, Toronto, won an expansion franchise that year, and its Blue Jays played in an oddly reworked single-decked stadium that was suited for neither

baseball nor football. Its only covered seats were in the outfield, in an elegantly engineered grandstand that won an architectural medal in 1948. The newer portions, however, looked makeshift and many seats had terrible sight lines, some so bad that they were not offered for sale. This temporary arrangement lasted for a dozen years until Canada's metropolis unveiled a remarkable replacement that will be discussed shortly.

In 1982, yet another multipurpose domed stadium made its debut in downtown Minneapolis. The Hubert H. Humphrey Metrodome introduced air-supported roof

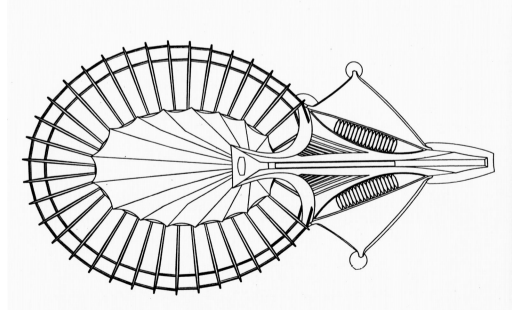

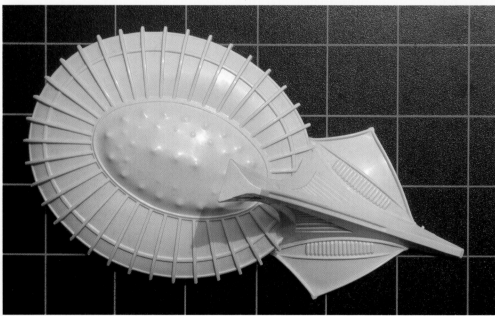

technology to baseball. The fabric ceiling brought some degree of natural light in during day games, but also created visibility problems for fielders, albeit not of the Astrodome's severity. This was the first indoor ballpark to free itself from the straitjacket of circular geometry and, as a rectangle with rounded corners, took on a baseball-friendly shape. In 1990, legendary baseball broadcaster Ernie Harwell said that it his estimation it was the best indoor ballpark then in existence. Alas, since the Metrodome was built to a very tight budget, it doesn't present a very gracious face to its urban environs. Vancouver's 60,000-seat BC Place opened a year later as the world's largest inflatable-roof stadium. Shaped similarly to the Metrodome, it had comparable advantages, but its baseball activity has been limited to a few exhibition games. In 1988, inflatable-roof technology was used to build the Tokyo Dome, a.k.a. "The Big Egg." Asia's premier baseball venue was the site of two official regular-season Cubs-Mets games in 2000.

In their lightness of structure, these air domes were advances over the first generation of heavy conventionally framed roofs, but there was still another significant frontier to be conquered in the world of indoor ballparks. That took place in mid-1989, when Exhibition Place's successor opened in downtown Toronto. The SkyDome was the Astrodome of its day, a technological marvel devoted to creature comforts and a multiplicity of purposes. It married baseball and football with an in-house hotel, bars, restaurants, a nightclub, and many private luxury suites, all of which had views of the field. It also had an immense matrix TV screen, a health club, and a television studio. All this was centrally located, near the subway, the main train station, and the CN Tower, the world's tallest freestanding structure.

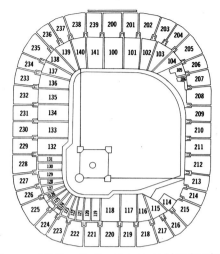

Above and Below: Seating diagram and interior view of the Hubert H. Humphrey Metrodome in Minneapolis, featuring the major leagues' first air-supported roof.

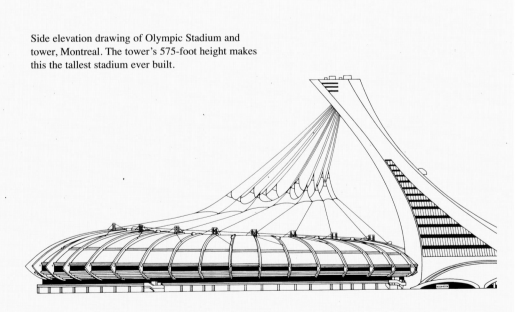

Side elevation drawing of Olympic Stadium and tower, Montreal. The tower's 575-foot height makes this the tallest stadium ever built.

But none of that was SkyDome's main virtue—its centerpiece was the first large, workable moving roof in the field sports world, a 310-foot-tall steel invention of architect Rod Robbie. Three sliding and rotating panels were tucked under a fourth when the weather was good, or deployed to seal off the field when it wasn't—and, best of all, the complicated machinery worked reliably. Now, with a convertible roof, the Blue Jays could have most of the advantages of both open-air and climate-controlled stadia, and fans flocked to see them, with SkyDome attendance topping an astonishing 4 million for three straight years (1991-1993). This convertible roof stadium was like a rag-top sports car, and in both cases, such flexibility commanded a premium price. But since they were paying little of the cost, several teams would later avail themselves of this intriguing new feature.

Interestingly, the idea of an operating ballpark roof did not begin in Canada with either the SkyDome or Stade Olympique, but rather in a suburb of Kansas City at the Harry S Truman Sports complex. At a time when multipurpose stadia were dominant—only two out of twenty-two permanent parks built between 1960 and 1989 were devoted only to baseball—a visionary Denver architect decided to buck the trend. Firmly believing that the conflicting requirements of baseball and football couldn't be properly served in the same structure, Charles Deaton speculatively drew up preliminary plans for separate stadia served by a single moving roof and showed them to the sports authorities who became convinced by the power of the idea. The roof would be taller and wider than either stadium, and roll on rails from one to the other as the schedule and weather demanded. Eventually it became clear that the migrating roof would be too costly, but the idea of separate stadia sharing the same infrastructure survived. The Kansas City ballpark opened in 1973, one year after the adjacent football-oriented Arrowhead Stadium debuted. The baseball facility was in the Milwaukee/Dodger Stadium mold, but with some unusual twists. The ends of the upper decks tapered down to points, looking like no others in baseball. Seating capacity was less than 41,000, well below the norm of the time, and there were very few fair-territory seats. Instead, there were grassy berms, fountains, and a kitschy crown-topped vertical scoreboard underscoring the point that the home team is named the Royals. All the ballparks built in the next seventeen years were multipurpose, but the latent principle of exclusive baseball use embodied in Royals Stadium (since renamed Kauffman Stadium) would finally emerge to reverse that trend, with all but one of the next nineteen parks being custom-designed for baseball alone.

Left: Night game at Kansas City's Kauffman Stadium, with its over-the-top 120-foot-tall crown-capped center field scoreboard.

RECENT TRENDS

Here we come to the chronological boundary of the topic of historic ballparks, defined in this book as those built prior to 1990. But we cannot just halt the chronicle, for there are three open narrative threads that deserve closure: operable roofs, baseball-only use, and retro styling.

SkyDome was first successful operable-roof, and next-to-the-last multi-purpose big-league stadium. Its technology was used in Japan in 1993 for the titanium-roofed Fukuoka Dome (where the number of roof leaves was reduced from four to three, at some expense, because four is an inauspicious number in the national culture). North America's second reliably operable baseball roof was in Phoenix's arena-like Bank One Ballpark (1998), where the six panels move sideways from the foul corners to meet at the home-plate center field axis. St. Petersburg's Tropicana Field opened for baseball that year as well, but had been completed in 1990 and used for ice hockey in the interim. Its roof isn't operable, but rather is a fixed tensegrity-cable fabric structure. (Since 1990, the only fixed baseball domes have been in Japan: the geodesic Nagoya Dome and the inflatable Osaka Dome—both opened in 1997—and the 1999 Seibu Dome.)

Minor league recent trends

Left: The ingratiating exterior of Lee County Stadium in Fort Myers Florida, designed by Ellerbe-Becket, could easily be mistaken for a resort hotel. It opened in 1991 as the spring training site for the Minnesota Twins.

Below left: Bucking the current near-universal mode of nostalgic ballpark design, the Lancaster Jethawks' stadium, located in a distant exurb of Los Angeles, presents a crisp, clean-lined face to the world. Designed by HOK Sport and opened in 1996, its simplicity resonates with its wide-open high desert environs.

Right: The Diamond in Richmond Virginia reveals its split-level exposed concrete structure boldly and expressively. Built in 1985 shortly before retro design took the stage, it may itself someday become an object of nostalgia.

Overleaf left: Cohen Stadium, designed by Ellerbe-Becket and opened in 1990, occupies a desert landscape on the outskirts of El Paso, and nicely reflects that setting with its warm colors and elemental architectural forms.

Overleaf right: Homestead Stadium's pink stucco exterior conjures up visions of a tropical country club, perhaps in Bermuda. Located south of Miami, this former spring training facility was designed by HOK Sport.

Seattle's Safeco Field (1999) has a heavy steel roof that looms above right field and moves past the left field line to close. Because the area experiences little rain during the baseball season, this roof was an unnecessary owners' indulgence.

Houston's Minute-Maid Park opened a year later. It also had a steel roof that moved similarly to Seattle's, but which was definitely needed for rain protection and climate control in the warm and wet Gulf Coast climate.

The next year, Milwaukee's Miller Park pioneered a radially moving roof system, where five arched leaves rotated from above the foul areas toward the center of the field. This is also the major leagues' only heated park, but only the seating areas are warmed, while the playing field is not. Tragically, the park gained nationwide notoriety before it even opened when a crane collapsed while installing one of the roof panels. Three construction workers were killed and the stadium opening was delayed for a year.

Given the complexity and expense of the technology, the six operating roof parks were a good-sized group, but only a fraction of the twenty-two ballparks (excluding Japan) that opened beginning with Toronto. Introduced

over a span of less than seventeen years, these nearly two-dozen facilities constitute the largest, most diverse, most luxurious, and most expensive crop of stadiums in baseball history.

Most have been open-air, beginning with Chicago's New Comiskey Park (1991)—the first baseball-only venue since Kansas City's—whose seating geometry, symmetrical field shape, and concrete structural system had a kinship with it. Like virtually all other new ballparks in history, it was praised upon opening, especially since it was made for baseball only, and for no other purposes. But savvy White Sox fans soon realized that the new park, for all its comfort, convenience, and dedication to baseball, had little of the charm and intimacy of its predecessor. The large, steep, and distant upper deck, pushed upwards by intervening luxury suite and club levels, drew particular criticism. (It was later reduced and remodeled at some expense.)

Orioles Park at Camden Yards, opened in 1992 in Baltimore, was Comiskey's polar opposite, even though both were designed almost concurrently by the same architects, HOK Sport of Kansas City. It was clearly the most influential ballpark design since the Astrodome's (arguably the most influential since Shibe Park's), for it redefined how a new ballpark should look, feel, and be shaped for game action. When shown the developing design in 1989, baseball Commissioner Bart Giamatti was ecstatic and predicted that

when it opened, everyone would want one like it. For better and for worse, it created a new paradigm, that of the retro ballpark. After eighty years, ballpark design was coming full circle, sometimes honoring the principles that shaped the classic parks, and sometimes simply aping their materials, details, and quirks.

Camden Yards revived many classic ballpark principles and traits. It showed attention to urban context, inflecting to the adjacent brick B&O warehouse and deriving much of its form from the shape of its site.

It reintroduced the steel structural system whose articulation and natural detail gave the old parks much of their character. It rejected curved field symmetry in favor of a natural angular asymmetry growing out of site conditions, and while its dimensions weren't extreme, neither were they fully predictable or conventional. It had an open side that allowed views of the immediate historic environs and the middle-distance downtown skyline. Compared to its contemporaries, it increased viewing intimacy through a compact vertical and horizontal seating layout. And to blend with its historic urban setting, it was the first new major league park in 38 years to be clad in brick, and the first one in 89 years to have exterior arches.

As Giamatti predicted, everyone wanted a park like Camden Yards after it opened, and many teams and cities attempted to follow in its footsteps with varying degrees of success.

The new parks in Cleveland, Denver, San

Francisco, and Pittsburgh carry on the Baltimore tradition best, albeit in different ways. San Francisco, with its bayfront setting, open right field, adaptation to a restrictive site, and understated exterior, is probably the worthiest. But Denver has a problem that cannot be solved through design—its high altitude (5,200 feet) allows fly balls to travel about 10 farther than at sea level. Thus its spacious outfield—347 feet/415 feet/350 feet—is too large for fielders to defend effectively, but its sea-level equivalent is only about 315 feet/377 feet/318 feet, woefully inadequate given today's muscled-up sluggers.

Like its predecessor, Atlanta's Turner Field has unpleasant automobile-dominated environs, but otherwise is a better place to see a game than Fulton County Stadium. Cincinnati's Great American Ballpark duplicates the fine downtown setting of its predecessor, Riverfront Stadium, while providing an improved baseball experience. Comerica Park's location in Detroit is somewhat better than Tiger Stadium's, but this in-town mallpark sorely lacks the older park's intimacy, soul, authenticity, and history, distracting itself with a carousel, ferris wheel, and oversized fiberglass tiger sculptures, perhaps in homage to the spirit of Chris Von der Ahe.

The two Florida parks, St. Petersburg's Tropicana Field and Miami's Dolphins Stadium, and Denver's temporary venue, Mile High Stadium, were multipurpose stadia that opened for baseball after Camden Yards but were built earlier, and thus couldn't benefit from its example. Mile High nevertheless managed to set a seasonal attendance record of nearly 4.5 million that may be unbreakable.

Rolling roofs presented a formidable esthetic challenge to recent stadia, and most were unable to respond convincingly. Those designed in a modern mode, SkyDome and Phoenix's arena-like Chase Field, minimized the disparity between the appearance of the main structure and the roof, but neither were architecturally distinguished totalities. Two of the retro-styled ones, Seattle's Safeco Field and Houston's Minute Maid Park, illustrated the inherent conflict between a nostalgic base and a dominating massively engineered top. Only Milwaukee's Miller Park was able to blend its nostalgic brick-arched base and its vaulting steel roof into a unified, visually pleasing entity, and as a bonus it used generous glass areas to bring natural light inside.

One potentially promising recent development has been to team up design architects and sports specialists on projects involving large-scale development. Two ballparks have tried this so far, with dramatically different results.

In the Dallas suburb of Arlington, the Texas Rangers booted the ball, promising an ambitious ballpark village but delivering only an isolated stadium, and a disappointing one at that. Responding to client directives, designer David Schwartz and technical partners HKS produced a notably unintimate seating bowl whose upper deck is more distant from the field than any other in history, even among parks with far more seats. The architects and clients instead focused on superficial details such as longhorn steer's-head bas reliefs, Texas lone stars, oversized baseball replicas, Yankee Stadium frieze imitations, a "home run porch" having no effect on home runs, and symbolic but ineffectual use of a few columns in seating areas, all of which were vainly meant to recall old urban ballparks.

At San Diego's Petco Park, things went much better. Design architect Antoine Predock and stadium specialists HOK Sport produced an innovative design in the heart of a 33-block mixed-use urban redevelopment area that has successfully extended the boundaries of the city's downtown. The park itself incorporates a historic industrial building, a public "park within the park" just beyond the outfield fences, extensive landscaping, and light stone-clad perimeter buildings recalling indigenous southwestern forms. Deep structural cantilevers put the upper deck close to the field, and a footbridge links the stands to a sleek high-rise hotel. New and adaptively reused residential buildings have also emerged nearby. Despite an arbitrary field-shape quirk or two, this undertaking is a convincing argument for rationality, urban design, historic preservation, honest modernism, integrated landscaping, and comprehensive planning. With its pair of adjoining enclosed green spaces, it's a double helping of paradise that Bart Giamatti certainly would have relished.

John Pastier

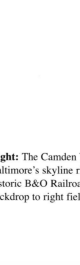
Right: The Camden Yards ballpark nears completion. Baltimore's skyline rises in the distance, and the historic B&O Railroad warehouse forms a close backdrop to right field.

ARCHITECTS AND ENGINEERS

Well over half of the big-league ballparks of the past generation have been designed by one architectural firm, HOK Sport of Kansas City. Historic ballparks (defined here as those older than 20 years) showed greater diversity in their authorship, but there was nevertheless a clear industry leader during the first seven decades of the fireproof ballpark era—the Osborn Company of Cleveland, sometimes known as Osborn Engineering. Its original expertise was steel bridges, and that knowledge lent itself nicely to the design of cantilvered steel grandstands. Between 1909 and 1977 the firm worked on the following fifteen parks:

- League Park, Cleveland
- Polo Grounds, New York (with Henry B. Herts)
- Navin Field (later Briggs Stadium and Tiger Stadium), Detroit
- Griffith Stadium, Washington
- Sportsman's Park, St. Louis
- Braves Field, Boston
- Comiskey Park expansion, Chicago
- Muehlebach Field (later Municipal Stadium), Kansas City
- Yankee Stadium, New York
- Municipal Stadium, Cleveland
- Fenway Park rebuilding and expansion, Boston
- County Stadium, Milwaukee
- Robert F. Kennedy Stadium, District of Columbia (with George Dahl)
- Three Rivers Stadium, Pittsburgh (with Deeter Richey Sippel)
- The Kingdome, Seattle (with others).

Additionally, Osborn designed several minor league parks, including Swayne Field, Toledo, Ohio; Offermann Stadium, Buffalo, New York; Perry Stadium (later Victory field and Owen Bush Stadium), Indianapolis, Indiana; Hartwell Field, Mobile, Alabama; and Firestone Park, Akron, Ohio. It also planned the combined baseball-football stadium for the U.S. Military Academy at West Point, New York.

But many other designers had ballpark opportunities as well. Here is a list of the known designers of pre-SkyDome twentieth century major league ballparks, beginning with those responsible for more than one project:

- Praeger Kavanaugh Waterbury, New York: Dodger Stadium, Los Angeles; Shea Stadium, New York; Yankee Stadium reconstruction, New York; Kingdome, Seattle (with others); also the minor league Metropolitan Park in Norfolk, Virginia.
- Zachary Taylor Davis, Chicago: Weeghman Park, (later Cubs Park and Wrigley Field), Chicago; Comiskey Park, Chicago; Wrigley Field, Los Angeles.
- Skidmore Owings & Merrill, San Francisco and Chicago: Oakland Coliseum; expansion of Anaheim Stadium; Hubert Humphrey Metrodome, Minneapolis.
- C.B. Comstock, New York: Washington Park, Brooklyn; Harrison Park, Newark, New Jersey. (Both were Federal League. Harrison Park also hosted some Sunday games of the Dodgers, Giants, and Yankees.)
- Heery & Heery and Finch, Alexander, Barnes, Rothschild & Paschal, Atlanta: Fulton County Stadium, Atlanta; Riverfront Stadium, Cincinnati.
- Gary Allen, San Diego & Del Mar: San Diego/Jack Murphy Stadium (as designer with Frank Hope & Assoc.); Cashman Field, Las Vegas, Nevada (site of six major league games)

The following firms were involved with single parks:
- John G. Thurtle: Palace of the Fans, Cincinnati (deduced).
- William Steele & Sons, Philadelphia: Shibe Park, Philadelphia.
- Charles Leavitt Jr., New York: Forbes Field, Pittsburgh.
- Harry Hake, Cincinnati: Redland Field, later Crosley Field, Cincinnati.
- Clarence Van Buskirk: Ebbets Field, Brooklyn.
- Otto G. Simonson: Terrapin Park, Baltimore (Federal League)
- John & Donald Parkinson, Los Angeles: Memorial Coliseum, Los Angeles.
- George W. Kelham, San Francisco: Seals Stadium, San Francisco
- Christian H. Ziegler, Jersey City: Roosevelt Stadium, Jersey City, New Jersey.
- L. P. Kooken Co.: Memorial Stadium,

Baltimore.
- Thorshov & Cerny, Minneapolis: Metropolitan Stadium, Bloomington, Minnesota.
- John Bolles, San Francisco: Candlestick Park, San Francisco.
- Sverdrup & Parcel, St. Louis; Edward

Durrell Stone, New York: Busch Memorial Stadium, St. Louis.
- Lloyd & Morgan and Wilson, Morris, Crain & Anderson, Houston: Astrodome, Houston.
- Nobel Herzberg: Anaheim Stadium, Orange County, California
- Deeter Richey Sippel, Pittsburgh (with

The Osborn Co.): Three Rivers Stadium, Pittsburgh.
- Hugh Stubbins, New York; George Ewing, Philadelphia; Stonorov & Haws, Philadelphia: Veterans Stadium.
- Charles Deaton, Denver: Royals Stadium (later Kaufman Stadium), Kansas City
- Marani & Morris, Toronto: Exhibition

Stadium original grandstand, Toronto.
- Roger Taillibert, Paris: Stade Olympique, Montreal.
- Naramore Bain Brady & Johanson, Seattle; Skilling Engineers, Seattle; The Osborn Co., Cleveland: Kingdome, Seattle

Swayne Field, Toledo, designed by The Osborn Co. and opened in 1909, was the most advanced minor league park of its day.

SOUVENIRS

Ballparks have a tendency to take whimsical forms or show up in unusual guises. Ashtrays are a favorite, as witnessed by the ceramic Dodger Stadium and Tokyo Dome, and the metal Fukuoka Dome. Seating diagrams of several pre-WWII classic parks form the pattern for a silk necktie. St. Louis' Busch Memorial Stadium provides the subject matter for an embossed sheet-copper postcard, and the background image for a fan's bank check. And, like a modern-day Colossus of Rhodes, a collectible figurine of home run king Hank Aaron stands astride a plastic model of Atlanta-Fulton County Stadium, where he hit 190 of his round-trippers.

BALLPARKS YESTERDAY AND TODAY

compiled by Michael Heatley, Marc Sandalow, Jim Sutton, and Ian Westwell

ALBUQUERQUE, NEW MEXICO

While never possessing a team in the major leagues, Albuquerque is still a baseball town. It's history littered with such minor league teams as the Cardinals and the Dukes. Baseball shrines in the form of ballparks ranged from the New Mexico State Fairgrounds to Tingley Field, but it was only in 1969 that a lasting home was found at the Albuquerque Sports Stadium.

The Dukes began the tenure there as Albuquerque's team, but the first game to be played was a showcase between the San Francisco Giants and the Cleveland Indians, with legend Willie Mays the first batter at the plate.

The Dukes entered the Pacific Coast League in 1972 and entertained the locals at the Sports Stadium for almost 30 years, amassing eight PCL championships along the way. But it was heartache in 2000 when business tycoons moved the Dukes to Portland, Oregon, and Albuquerque was left without a team to cheer.

With the prospect of baseball returning in time for the 2003 season and the Calgary Cannons moving in, major renovation of the Sports Stadium got underway. Built in a retro style popular among ballparks, Isotopes Park (the team being renamed the Isotopes after a famous Simpsons cartoon episode) now looks totally different from its predecessor, with everything except the playing surface totally rebuilt. This modern ballpark with a historic look, one of the best outside the Major Leagues, will ensure the people of Albuquerque can enjoy baseball for years to come.

Previous pages: Yankee Stadium during the Mets v Yankees World Series, 2000. *MLB Photos via Getty Images*

Far right: Anaheim Stadium in 1966. *Bettmann/Corbis*

Right: Colorful neon and glass welcomes baseball fans to the All-American Baseball Game at Isotope Park on June 13, 2005. *Getty Images*

ANAHEIM, CALIFORNIA

Angel Stadium of Anaheim

Previous names: Anaheim Stadium; Edison International Field

Status: Home of Los Angeles Angels of Anaheim

Address: 2000 Gene Autry Way Anaheim, CA 92806

Capacity: 45,037

Opening day: April 19, 1966

Cost to construct: $24 million, $118 million (renovations)

Architect: N. Herzberg, R. Stern

Dimensions (ft):

Left Field: 330

Left Center: 387

Center Field: 400

Right Center: 370

Right Field: 330

Defining feature: A giant A-frame scoreboard

Most expensive seat: $75

Cheapest seat: $5

World Series: 2002

All-Star Game: 1967, 1989

First constructed in 1964 and currently in its third incarnation, the home of baseball in Anaheim has always been what's affectionately known as the "Big A." When the ballpark first opened as Anaheim Stadium in 1966, it became home to the American League's California—formerly Los Angeles—Angels. After the team's inception in 1961, they spent their first year playing at Wrigley Field in Los Angeles before moving to then-new Dodger Stadium for four seasons. Upon the Angels' arrival in Anaheim they took on the San Francisco Giants in an exhibition game, bringing in a crowd of 31,000.

The original ballpark contained just over 43,000 seats situated primarily on three tiers that stretched down the length of both foul lines. The standout point of the park was found beyond the outfield wall—a giant A-frame scoreboard that attracted the affectionate yet obvious nickname "the Big A."

As originally set up, Anaheim measured 333 feet down both foul lines and 404 fee to straightaway center. Over the years, the team tinkered with the playing field's dimensions as a result of studies conducted to find the fairest balance for both pitchers and hitters, ultimately ending up slightly smaller than the original dimensions.

Regardless of measurements, the stadium played host to many memorable moments in its early years, including the 1967 All-Star Game—the first in which home runs accounted for all the scoring.

Other highlights included two of baseball legend Nolan Ryan's seven career no-hitters and Alex Johnson becoming the first Angel to win a batting title in 1970, on the season's final day against the Chicago White Sox.

Major changes beckoned in the late 1970s when a deal was struck to bring the National Football League Los Angeles Rams to Anaheim. The stadium needed to become enclosed, which caused numerous problems for baseball fans for a number of reasons. In particular, Angels fans lamented the loss of great views—spectators could previously see the local mountains and state highway—and that the famous scoreboard was moved to the parking lot. The changes were complete in time for the 1980 NFL season, and the capacity was duly increased to 65,000.

Regardless of having to share their home with football partners, the Angels recorded many memorable moments at the stadium in the 1980s: In 1982 and 1986 the team won Western Division titles; in 1984 a crowd of nearly 29,000 witnessed home favorite Reggie Jackson hit his 500th career home run; and in 1986, more than 37,000 fans cheered Angels pitcher Don

Sutton to his 300th career victory. The Big A hosted its second All-Star Game in 1989, where it became the Bo Jackson show, the hitter helping to secure the second of back to back All-Star games for the American League.

The Rams moved to St. Louis in 1994 and once again the Angels were the sole inhabitants. The ballpark also incurred damage in the 1994 Northridge earthquake; changes were needed. A deal was struck with the city of Anaheim, ensuring the Angels could stay at their home until 2031; however, they have an option to leave 13 years early. Part of the deal included a new stadium, back in its original baseball-only format. Now reduced to a capacity of 45,000 spectators, the Angels played the 1997 season in the stadium when it wasn't even finished.

Edison International purchased the rights to name the new stadium; it became Edison International Field, and was briefly known to fans as "Big Ed." At the same time the Angels were renamed the Anaheim Angels, but neither of the monikers would last; Edison pulled out of the deal in 2003—a year after the Angels captured their first World Series (against San Francisco) and the stadium was renamed the Angel Stadium. The team reverted to the Los Angeles Angels of Anaheim in time for the 2005 season.

With the Walt Disney Company owning the Angels, and plowing almost $1 million into the park's rebuilding costs, there are a few telltale signs of their input—for example, the sign at the front facade of the stadium is held up by six giant baseball bats, and there are erupting geysers with lights and explosions known as the "California Experience." Disney also considered moving the scoreboard back to its original position, but cost prevented this.

Left: A general view of Edison Field taken in 1998 during an Anaheim Angels game. *MLB Photos via Getty Images*

Right: Entrance to Edison International Field. *Richard Cummins/Corbis*

Overleaf, left: General view of Edison Field. *Allsport via Getty Images*

Overleaf, right: The Indians defeated the Angels 6–4 on April 5, 1998, in this game at the then Edison Field. Anaheim Stadium had become Edison International Field in 1996 under a $50 million, 20-year sponsorship deal. After five years, on December 30, 2003, the Anaheim Angels announced that they were going to rename their ballpark Angel Stadium of Anaheim for the 2004 season because Edison had decided to opt out of its naming rights agreement. *Allsport via Getty Images*

Page 80–81: Anaheim Stadium in May 1981. *Vince Streano/Corbis*

ARLINGTON, TEXAS

Arlington Stadium

Previous Name: Turnpike Stadium

Status: Demolished in 1994

Location: Just west of Six Flags Over Texas amusement park (now a parking lot)

Capacity: 43,521

Opening day: April 23, 1965

First major league game: April 21, 1972

Last game: October 3, 1993

Cost to construct: $1.9 Million, $19 Million (expansions)

Architect: Unknown

Dimensions (ft):

Left Field: 330 Left Center: 380

Center Field: 400 Right Center: 380

Right Field: 330

Defining features: Field was built in a natural bowl 40 feet below ground level. Largest bleachers in the major leagues, running from foul pole to foul pole across the outfield.

World Series: None

All-Star Game: None

Ballpark at Arlington

Address: 1000 Ballpark Way Arlington, TX 76011

Capacity: 49,292

Opening day: April 11, 1994—Milwaukee Brewers 4, Texas Rangers 3

Cost to construct: $191 million

Architect: HKS, Inc. and David M. Schwarz Architectural Services

Dimensions (ft):

Left Field: 332 Left Center: 390

Center Field: 400 Right Center: 381

Right Field: 325

Defining feature: Center field office building Little-known ground rule: Ball lodging in outfield fence padding or in the manually operated scoreboard in left field fence is a ground rule double

Most expensive seat: $75

Cheapest seat: $5

World Series: None

All-Star Game: 1995

Memorable moments:

1994 June 13—Jose Canseco hits three home runs and drives in eight runs in a 17–9 victory over Seattle.

1994 July 28—Kenny Rogers throws a perfect game against the Angels, the first Ranger to do so.

1996 April 19—Juan Gonzelez, Dean Palmer and Kevin Elster combine for 16 RBI as the Rangers beat O's 26–7

1996 September 15—Rangers retire Nolan Ryan's uniform, No. 34.

1997 June 12—In baseball's first regular-season interleague game, San Francisco beats the Rangers 4–3.

Right: The Texas Rangers play the Baltimore Orioles at the Ballpark in Arlington. April 18, 1998. *Joseph Sohm/Visions of America/Corbis*

With the reputation of being the hottest place to play baseball (thanks to temperatures often reaching the 100s), Arlington Stadium was practically still under construction right up to the first pitch! But while the base lines were still being chalked just hours before the first game began in 1965, the plan for a stadium to serve the Dallas-Fort Worth "metroplex" had first been devised in 1959.

Things were changing for the neighboring north Texas cities, recently linked by a freeway. With other plans in the works for shared new facilities like an international airport, the idea of a united baseball team became an increasingly realistic proposal. The proposed location of the new park was a natural hollow in the centrally located suburb of Arlington, adjacent to the freeway and next door to an amusement park—ideal for visitors who wanted extra entertainment on their Texas visits.

Upon completion, the new ballpark—built some 40 feet below ground level—was handed the title of Turnpike Stadium. The Dallas-Fort-Worth Spurs were in the Double A league and eased Turnpike in with minor league baseball. While their seven-year tenure saw only mixed success, they had a tremendous fan following and it was soon clear the original capacity of 10,500 was too small. The stadium's below-ground design meant increasing its capacity was a viable option, and the City of Arlington (which owned the facility) did just that, doubling the capacity to 20,000 in 1970.

The park's increased size and close proximity to a tourist attraction were to prove useful selling points two years later when it was revealed that Major League Baseball's Washington Senators were relocating to Arlington. They were renamed the Texas Rangers and the ballpark was renamed the Arlington Stadium.

The capacity was increased further in the wake of MLB arriving in Arlington, pushing the seating to almost 36,000. A new scoreboard was also added, but the look of the stadium became somewhat distorted due to the continued additions of tiers—some fans started calling it a "mistake." The steel seats, combined with the severely hot Texan weather, also gained it the unenviable nickname of "the World's largest open-air roaster." Indeed, it was so hot in Arlington Stadium that most of the Rangers' games—even those on Sundays—were scheduled for night.

The Rangers beat the California Angels in their first game in Arlington and went on to provide the crowds with many highlights. In 1981, Rick Honeycutt set a club record with his fourth consecutive shutout, a 7-0 five-hitter over the Royals, while in 1989 local boy and legend Nolan Ryan recorded his 5,000th strikeout against Rickey Henderson. The seemingly ageless strikeout king followed that feat with his seventh and final career no-hitter against the Blue Jays in 1991 at the grand old age of 44—the oldest man in MLB history to do so.

On the whole, the Rangers never delivered any real team success, but as one fan put it, "It's hard to be a Rangers fan, but it's not hard to love Arlington Stadium." However much it was liked, the combination of the heat playing a major part in games and the fact the stadium was starting to show its age meant that plans for a new stadium a few hundred yards away were passed. The last game at Arlington was played on October 3, 1993 against the Royals, ending in a 4-1 defeat for the Rangers, and the park was demolished the following year. The site is now a parking lot for the Rangers' newstadium.

Take a bit of Ebbets Field, some Tiger Stadium, a little Yankee Stadium, some Wrigley Field, and a touch of Camden Yards. Mix in a lot of Texas, put it in a suburban parking lot, and you approach the Ballpark at Arlington.

The asymmetrical outfield is like Ebbets Field, with eight facets sending hard-hit balls in different directions The double-decked, right-field porch is like Tiger Stadium, though it is too deep to catch as many home runs. The bleachers recall Wrigley. The canopy lining the upper deck is reminiscent of Yankee Stadium. The brick arches on the exterior feel like Camden Yards.

Yet this is Texas. Cast iron Lone Stars adorn aisles seats, replicating those on the building's facade. Large steer skulls and murals depicting the state's history decorate the walls, and a brick "Walk of Fame," celebrating Ranger's history surrounds the park. The grass in the batter's line of vision in dead center is named Greene's Hill after former Arlington Mayor Richard Greene. There is a Texas-sized dimension to the entire stadium complex, which includes a 12-acre, man-made lake (named for late Rangers broadcaster Mark Holtz), a 17,000 square-foot baseball museum said to be the largest outside Cooperstown, a 225-seat auditorium, a children's learning center, a four-story office building, and a kid-sized park with seats for 650 just outside.

To battle the Texas elements, the stadium is sunken, out of the wind, and enclosed by the office building, home to the Ranger's front office, just beyond center field. A giant windscreen, 42 feet high and 430 feet long, was installed on the roof to further reduce wind. Overhead fans in the upper and lower deck porches help keep patrons cool.

The $191 million park was paid for largely through a sales tax increase, pushed through by the team's managing partner in the early 1990s, George W. Bush.

Right: December 14, 1971—Texas Rangers' Manager Ted Williams walks through a gusty wind as he surveys Turnpike Stadium, the new home of the old American League Washington Senators. *Bettmann/Corbis*

Left: To provide the players some protection from the harsh Texas winds, the playing field is sunken and surrounded by tall, wind blocking structures and screens. *National Baseball Hall of Fame*

Far left: A general view of the exterior of the Ballpark in Arlington before a game between the Seattle Mariners and the Texas Rangers on July 6, 2003. The Rangers defeated the Mariners 5–1. *Ronald Martinez/Getty Images*

Overleaf, left: Another view of the Ballpark in Arlington on July 6, 2003. *Ronald Martinez/Getty Images*

Overleaf, right: Heavy clouds loom over the ballpark during play between the Seattle Mariners and the Texas Rangers at the Ballpark in Arlington on July 6, 2003. *Ronald Martinez/Getty Images*

Pages 90–91: 1998 view of the Ballpark in Arlington. *Joseph Sohm; Visions of America/Corbis*

ATLANTA, GEORGIA

Atlanta-Fulton County Stadium

Previous name: Atlanta Stadium

Status: Demolished in 1997

Location: Adjacent to Turner Field;
now a parking lot

Capacity: 52,013

Opening day: April 12, 1966

Last major league game: October 24, 1996

Cost to construct: $18 million

Architect: Heery, Heery & Finch

Dimensions (ft) Original		Final
Left Field:	325	330
Left Center:	385	385
Center Field:	402	402
Right Center:	385	385
Right Field:	325	330

Defining features: Nondescript, circular, multipurpose stadium. Nicknamed "The Launching Pad" because relatively high elevation helped home runs.

World Series: 1991, 1992, 1995, 1996

All-Star Game: 1972

Turner Field

Location: 755 Hank Aaron Drive Atlanta, GA 30315

Capacity: 49,304

Opening day: April 4, 1997—Atlanta Braves 5, Chicago Cubs 4

Cost to construct: $242.5 million

Architect: Atlanta Stadium Design Team

Dimensions (ft):

Left Field: 335   Left Center: 380

Center Field: 401   Right Center: 90   Right Field: 330

Defining feature: 100 foot-high replica of Hank Aaron's 715 HR ball

Most expensive seat: $45   Cheapest seat: $1

World Series: 1999   All Star Game: 2000

Memorable moments:

1996 July 19—Muhammad Ali lights the Olympic flame a top the stadium that would become Turner Field.

1997 May 16—Michael Tucker breaks up a no-hitter by the Cardinals Alan Benes with two outs in bottom of ninth. Braves go on to win 1–0 in 13 innings.

1999 September 23—Chipper Jones hits his fourth home run in three games to complete a three-game sweep over division rival Mets.

1999 October 19—Andruw Jones draws an 11th-inning, bases-loaded walk to give the Braves a 10–9 victory over the Mets and their fifth National League pennant of the decade.

One of the so-called "cookie cutter" stadiums that became popular in the 1960s and 1970s, the quality of the Atlanta-Fulton has never been in question. Discussions to bring a baseball team in Atlanta had been batted around as early as the 1930s, but it was only until 1956 that things started moving in the right direction. But it would still be a decade before the gates opened.

Left: The world champion Atlanta Braves playing a night game at Turner Field, April 1997. *Joseph Sohm/Visions of America/Corbis*

Below: Postcard showing the interior of Atlanta's Ponce de Leon stadium. *via John Pastier*

Right: 1995 aerial view of the building of Olympic Stadium in Atlanta for the 1996 Summer Olympics. Fulton County Stadium (foreground) was demolished after the Olympics and Olympic Stadium was renamed Turner Field to become the new home of Braves baseball. *Kevin Fleming/Corbis*

When the National League Milwaukee Braves were bought out in 1964, they decided relocation to Atlanta would be the way forward—provided they had a stadium ready by 1966. Work commenced and, with a rapid construction time of just 51 weeks, it was ready in time for the 1965 season, a year earlier than planned.

It was a multipurpose stadium, prepared for both football and baseball, fully enclosed with three tiers of blue wooden seats. Atlanta was awarded an NFL team, the Falcons, that year, but they wouldn't begin their tenure until the 1966 season. The Atlanta Crackers, an International League baseball team, played for a season to fill the time before making way for the Braves and the Falcons.

On April 12, 1966, 51,500 fans watched the Braves' first game as they took on the Pittsburgh Pirates in what was then simply

known as the Atlanta Stadium. They went on to attract 1.5 million spectators over the course of their first season. Attendance would soon drop, however, and the stadium became known for its "ghost town" atmosphere. North American Soccer League team the Atlanta Chiefs would complete a hat trick of different sports, but this took its toll on the playing surface. On top of that, there wasn't even a groundskeeper on the payroll.

The early 1970s would prove to be a decisive period for the Braves and the stadium. In 1972 the Atlanta-Fulton hosted the All-Star game, which was won by the National League. Joe Morgan was named MVP and the Braves' Hank Aaron hit a homer. Two years later in April, Aaron hit the 715th home run of his fabled career against the Dodgers, lifting him above legend Babe Ruth. Despite witnessing moments like that, attendances continued to free-fall, hitting a low ebb when fewer than 1,000 people showed up for a doubleheader between the Braves and the Houston Astros in 1976.

Left: Panorama of Turner Field as the Atlanta Braves play a night game in April 1997.
Joseph Sohm; ChromoSohm Inc./Corbis

Overleaf, left: 1999 view of Turner Field. *National Baseball Hall of Fame*

Overleaf, right: A general view of Turner Field taken during the 2000 All-Star Game on July 10, 2000. *MLB Photos via Getty Images*

140—Ponce De Leon Park, Atlanta.

Left. Postcard showing the interior of Atlanta's Ponce de Leon stadium. *via John Pastier*

That same year the Braves were bought by Atlanta businessman and wrestling enthusiast Ted Turner, who ran several entertaining promotions with the intention of attracting more fans to the stadium. The most famous was the "Wedlock and Headlock" day in which a Braves game was sandwiched between marriages on the field before the game and a wrestling match afterwards. Despite Turner's resourcefulness, the Braves would attract fewer than a million fans per season for almost the next decade.

The departure of the Falcons and the hiring of a groundskeeper in the early 1990s not only coincided with a vastly improved playing surface, but also the Braves' improved performance on the field. It was to prove a glory decade, with six consecutive divisional titles, peppered with trips to the World Series and their first championship in

38 years. For the first time, fans filled Atlanta-Fulton with regularity.

But with Turner at the helm and such unprecedented success, the Braves moved out of the Atlanta-Fulton following Atlanta's 1996 Olympic Games. They carried on their success at Turner Field, just yards away, but their old stadium was demolished in 1997 after its reputation had come full circle.

Turner Field was born an 85,000-seat, Olympic-sized track and field coliseum.

The Olympics came to Atlanta in 1996, just as the Braves were itching for a new home after playing for three decades in oversized Atlanta-Fulton County Stadium. In a confluence of creativity and good timing, the Braves and the city struck a deal.

The city built a $207 million Olympic stadium in the parking lot of the Braves' old home. Athletes from around the world

paraded through the facility. Muhammad Ali lit the opening flame. When the Olympians went home, the Braves spent another $35 million to turn the mega-sports complex into a baseball-only facility.

The grandstands were ripped down and 35,000 seats were removed. Dugouts emerged from underneath Olympic bleachers. The Braves locker room was built in what was originally a basement TV studio.

The final product was a state-of-the-art, designer ballpark. It is more symmetric than the retro-parks now in fashion. But it offers intimate confines, seats angled toward home plate, and a brick and limestone facade reminiscent of Camden Yards.

Turner Field is not as old-fashioned looking as the other instant classics in Baltimore, Cleveland, or Pittsburgh, though it makes frequent gestures to Braves' history. Seats are decorated with a silhouette of Hank Aaron, whom many locals said the stadium should have been named after, rather than team owner Ted Turner.

It takes a close look to detect the stadium's Olympic lineage. One clue is the unusual outfield, where center and left field are curved, like stadiums built in the 1960s, a holdover from the oval-shaped Olympic Stadium, while the right field fence is a straight line consistent with today's old-style parks.

Outside the stadium, the tall posts that surround Monument Grove—a collection of

statues which includes Hank Aaron, Warren Spahn, Eddie Matthews, Phil Niekro, Dale Murphy, and Georgia native Ty Cobb—are the very columns that supported the Olympic Stadium bleachers.

Off the field, the Brave's home resembles a theme park as much as a ballpark. Games, concessions (including food to reflect the visiting team, such as cheesesteaks when the Phillies are in town), and television monitors are ubiquitous. Near a Hall of Fame museum there is a video wall with televisions showing every major-league game in progress. The first fan who catches a home run in a far-away section in the third tier of left field has been promised $1 million, something that baseball experts and those who understand physics agree is unlikely to ever happen.

The Grand Entry Plaza features food and games, and is anchored by a 100-foot-in-diameter photograph of Hank Aaron's actual 715th home run ball. In 1997, the old stadium was imploded, and is now a parking lot for the new.

Right and Overleaf: Cookie-cutter Atlanta-Fulton County Stadium. *National Baseball Hall of Fame; Getty Images*

Far left: Fulton County Stadium in Atlanta was the site for 1996 Olympic baseball. *Alan Klein Photography/Corbis*

This picture: Inside Atlanta's Fulton County Stadium. *Nik Wheeler/Corbis*

BALTIMORE, MARYLAND

Memorial Stadium

Status: Demolished 2000-2002

Location: Home plate was near
1000 E. 33rd Street

Capacity: 31,000 (opening day); 54,000 (final)

Opening day: 1950

First MLB game: April 15, 1954

Last MLB game: October 6, 1991

Cost to construct: $6.5 million

Architect: L.P. Kooken Company

Dimensions (ft): Initial   Final

Left Field: 309   309

Left Center: 446   378

Center Field: 445   405

Right Center: 446   378

Right Field: 309   309

Defining features: Tall concrete wall
memorial at stadium entrance
commemorating those who fought in two
world wars. Football-friendly layout created
very spacious outfield and foul territories.

World Series: 1966, 1969, 1970, 1971, 1979,
1983

All-Star Game: 1958

Oriole Park at Camden Yards

Status: home of the Baltimore Orioles

Location: 333 West Camden Street
Baltimore, MD 21201

Capacity: 48,876

Opening day: 1992

First MLB game: April 6, 1992

Cost to construct: $110 million

Architect: HOK Sports

Dimensions (ft):

Left Field: 333

Left Center: 364

Center Field: 410

Right Center: 373

Right Field: 318

Defining features: B&O Warehouse in
 right field

World Series: None

All-Star Game: 1993

As soon as you saw the facade of the Memorial Stadium in Baltimore, with the plaque commemorating the city's war dead, you knew it is going to be a stadium full of passion and pride. In its existence it played home to many teams spanning many different sports and leagues and indeed became the pillar of the Baltimore community—but the manner of its destruction left a lot to be desired.

When Oriole Park burned to the ground in 1944, the International League Baltimore Orioles found themselves without a home. They were confined to playing their games in a high school sports facility, the Municipal Stadium. While there, a football team emerged and started to play there also. The Baltimore Colts, as they were known, were brought into the NFL in 1950, and when they moved to a new multipurpose facility— Memorial Stadium—the Orioles followed suit.

With such an impressive stadium, locals began to make it known they wanted Major League Baseball in their town, and in 1954 the St. Louis Browns announced they were relocating to Baltimore and adopting the Orioles name. A second tier was quickly added to the stadium, increasing its original capacity from 31,000 to nearly 48,000. Due to the speed in which the second tier was constructed, thick concrete poles were employed to hold it up, creating many obstructed-view seats on the lower deck. Even though speed was the priority, renovations were not even complete for the Orioles' first game in 1954—there weren't even any floodlights, and had the game not finished before nightfall it would have been cancelled.

Despite these teething problems, the stadium that had become known as "the Grand Old Lady of 33rd Street" after its location on the street corner, had its fair share of memorable moments and events for the "O's." In 1969, they were transformed from a struggling team to winners when they beat the Minnesota Twins in the first AL Championship series. Unfortunately, they went on to lose the World Series to New York's "Miracle" Mets 4 games to 1, but revenge would come a year later.

The Orioles took out the pain of the '69 series by brushing aside the Cincinnati Reds by the same 4-1 margin for their first championship. An amazing third consecutive World Series appearance duly followed in 1971, but the O's were edged 4-3 by the Pittsburgh Pirates. Orioles' fans would have to wait till 1979 to get another taste of the World Series, again against the Pirates—but the Willie Stargell-led Pittsburgh "Family" again took a seven-game series from the O's.

When the Colts moved out of Memorial Stadium at the end of 1983 (in fact, quietly relocating to Indianapolis under the cover of darkness one night), voices started campaigning for a new baseball-only facility—funny because people on the football side of the fence always saw the stadium as a venue good for baseball, less so for football. The campaigners got their wish in 1991 when the Orioles left for new pastures at Camden Yards, leaving behind a stadium that meant so much to the community as a whole. From Independence Day fireworks celebrations to Christmas tree sales in the parking lot, the ballpark brought the town together.

Once both the NFL and MLB franchises had vacated the Memorial Stadium, it was used as a temporary home for minor-league baseball team the Bowie White Sox while their own stadium was awaiting completion, and the Baltimore Ravens, formerly the Cleveland Browns, played football for a few seasons before the stadium was eventually abandoned in 1997. It stood empty until it was finally demolished.. The memorial wall at the front of the stadium was preserved for incorporation as part of the new stadium at Camden Yards.

The opening of Oriole Park at Camden Yards touched off a baseball revolution. After three decades of constructing cookie-cutter coliseums, Baltimore reintroduced the concept of a ballpark. Nestled beside train lines in the city's inner harbor, "The Yard" was a throwback to the days of Babe Ruth, who had been born just two blocks away. Its brick facade, asymmetrical outfield, panoramic view of downtown Baltimore, and the imposing B&O warehouse—which taunts left handed hitters—reminded Americans why baseball was long regarded as the national pastime.

The rest of the baseball world took notice. Within a decade, ballparks in Cleveland, Denver, Pittsburgh, San

Left: This model gives a good overall view of Terrapin Park. *via John Pastier*

Below: General view of Memorial Stadium as the Baltimore Orioles prepare to play the Chicago White Sox in Opening Day on April 2, 1984. *MLB Photos via Getty Images*

Francisco, Arlington, Seattle, Atlanta, Milwaukee, Houston, Detroit, and San Diego would mimic Baltimore's old-time appeal.

Baseball history guided the architects, who were influenced by Ebbets Field (Brooklyn), Shibe Park (Philadelphia), Fenway Park (Boston), Crosley Field (Cincinnati), Forbes Field (Pittsburgh), Wrigley Field (Chicago), and the Polo Grounds (New York). The cozy dimensions, the steel trusses, the rustic clock on the center field scoreboard, all gave the park a classic feel.

But the park is new. It has luxury boxes (a major revenue source), microbrews, a family picnic area, and shiny bronze

Unfortunately for O's fans, the park has fared better than the Orioles who are still looking to bring a World Series to Camden Yards.

Left: Left field view of Memorial Stadium with the Baltimore Orioles on field. Photo taken in 1982. *MLB Photos via Getty Images*

Below: Full view of Memorial Stadium with the Baltimore Orioles on field in 1986. *MLB Photos via Getty Images*

Right: Fans in Camden Yards stadium watch a 1994 game between the Orioles and the Red Sox as the sun goes down. Baltimore. *Joseph Sohm/Visions of America/Corbis*

Overleaf: Game at Camden Yards on May 22, 1999. *Joseph Sohm/Visions of America/Corbis*

baseballs imbedded in Eutaw Street, which runs between the warehouse and the outfield bleachers. Just beyond the bleachers, fans can buy barbeque made by Oriole great Boog Powell, who can sometimes be found signing hot dog wrappers and ticket stubs.

The history is more than just appearance. Ruth's father owned a tavern about where center field now sits. The eight-story, red-bricked, turn of the century B&O warehouse, the park's defining feature, is more than 1,000 feet long, built in 1895 to handle long railroad freight cars, and is said to be the longest building on the East Coast. It sits 432 feet away from home plate and though Ken Griffey Jr. reached it during a home run competition before the 1993 All-Star Game, no one has yet done so during a game. The park's anchor in a revitalized downtown was a big reason that the legislature agreed to help pay for it with the sale of lottery tickets. When it was built, Maryland Governor William Donald Schaefer called the ballpark "the largest single economic development opportunity we have had in the last decade," and its success spurred other clubs to look beyond land-rich suburban areas for their stadium homes.

The move from Baltimore's old Memorial Stadium to Camden Yards "is like coming from the slums to a palace," Orioles' outfield David Segui said the week the park opened. "If we play half as good as this place looks we'll be pretty good this year."

Previous page: Night panorama of Oriole Park. *Jerry Driendl/Getty Images*

Left: Night falls over Baltimore and Oriole Park in this 2003 photograph, the out-of-town scoreboard lighting up in the fading light. Babe Ruth was born two blocks from the ballpark 75 years before Oriole Park opened in 1992. The long building past right field is a remnant from the days of the "B&O"—the Baltimore & Ohio Railroad. Built at the turn of the century the warehouse is 1,016 feet long and is used today to house the Orioles' management offices as well as restaurants and bars. Much of the success of the new park has been attributed to its location in the midst of Baltimore's bustling inner harbor. *Roger Miller*

Right: Another aerial view: note the B&O warehouse running along the open side of the ballpark. *David Sailors/Corbis*

Left: Spectators outside Oriole Park's oldest feature, the B&O warehouse. Oriole Park is a popular location, with average attendances of over 40,000 and a capacity of 48,000.
Roger Miller

Right: Pre-game introduction of the home team on April 6, 1992, the first home game of the season for the Orioles and the first official game played at Oriole Park at Camden Yards. A capacity crowd of more than 48,000 enjoyed a beautiful day at the new ballpark and a victory celebration as the Orioles beat the Cleveland Indians, 2–0.
Roger Miller

Right: Aerial view of Memorial Stadium, the home of the Orioles until replaced by the new Oriole Park at Camden Yards in 1992. Fans who had loudly voiced their dissatisfaction over the change were soon silenced by the easy access the downtown location provided and the sheer pleasure of watching a game at the new ballpark. *Roger Miller*

Left: The "Memorial Wall" at Memorial Stadium was a very large and visible concrete plaque located on the outside of the ballpark behind home plate. Its inscription read: "Dedicated as a memorial to all who so valiantly fought in the world wars with eternal gratitude to those who made the supreme sacrifice to preserve equality and freedom throughout the world—time will not dim the glory of their deeds." Before the stadium was demolished in February 2001, the wall was dismantled and preserved. Parts of it have been incorporated into a new Veteran's Memorial at Oriole Park at Camden Yards. *Roger Miller*

BIRMINGHAM, ALABAMA

The 1990s saw a big boom in what was known as "retro-ballparks." Baseball clubs were moving to new stadiums that were designed to look older than the ones they had just left, yet with all the expected modern facilities and comfort. Rickwood Field in Birmingham is not just an imitation—it's the real deal.

Touted as the closest thing baseball has to a time machine, Rickwood is the oldest ballpark still in use in the world today. Every measure has been taken to preserve the stadium, and create an authentic atmosphere of the early 20th century. All of the outfield fences have replicas of old advertisements of the time, and they have even replicated a press box on the roof of one of the stands.

The ballpark was first opened in 1910 with a capacity of just over 10,000. During its existence it has played host to both the Birmingham Barons of the southern minor leagues and the Black Barons from the Negro National League, and later of the Negro American League. The Barons moved to their new suburban Hoover Metropolitan Stadium in 1988, but an organization called Friends of Rickwood ensures pro baseball is still played at Rickwood—the annual Rickwood Classic, where the Barons play one game a season at their old stomping ground.

Right: This postcard gives an aerial view of Rickwood Stadium. *via John Pastier*

Below: The real thing. *Library of Congress*

RICKWOOD FIELD
Home of Birmingham Barons

BOSTON, MASSACHUSETTS

Fenway Park

Status: Home of the Boston Red Sox

Address: 4 Yawkey Way Boston, MA 02215

Capacity: 35,095 (opening day); 36,298 (current)

Opening day: April 20, 1912

Cost to construct: $650,000 (1912)

Architect: Osborn Engineering

Dimensions (ft):	Early	Current
Left Field:	324	310
Left Center:	379	379
Center Field:	488	420
Right Center:	380	380
Right Field:	313.5	302

Defining feature: The Green Monster wall in left field

Most expensive seat: $85

Cheapest seat: $12

World Series: 1912, 1914, 1918, 1946, 1967, 1975, 1986, 2004

All-Star Game: 1946, 1961, 1999

Home to one of the most beloved baseball teams in major-league baseball, Fenway Park may be the reason why Boston Red Sox fans have remain so loyal to their team despite—until 2004—years of frustration on the field. Instead of abandoning Feway for a state-of-the-art facility, the Red Sox fans still cram into what's known as "America's most beloved Ballpark," just as their elders have since 1912. Fenway is the oldest ballpark still in active use in the major leagues and it remains largely unchanged from its earliest days.

Fenway Park wasn't the Red Sox' first home, however. At the turn of the 20th century, Boston—then known as the Boston Pilgrims—was a founding member of the American League and played in the Huntington Avenue Grounds. The 11,500-capacity ballpark would play host to the first

ever American League-National League World Series in 1903, and crowds witnessed such legends as Cy Young, who is immortalized in a statue today on the site of the old ground.

In 1907 Boston owner John I. Taylor gave the team their current name and announced they would be moving to a new home, which he called Fenway Park after its location. After two previously scheduled games were rained out, the Red Sox finally got their Fenway tenure under way on April 20, 1912—six days after the Titanic disaster. They defeated the New York Highlanders who would later become the Red Sox' hated rivals, the Yankees.

Success would quickly arrive at Fenway, as Boston reached the World Series in their first season at the park, and they defeated the New York Giants 4-3. Three more World Series would follow for the Sox in 1915, 1916, and 1918. (The 1914 series was also held at Fenway and included a Boston team,

Left: Early view of Fenway Park exterior. *Library of Congress*

Below: Postcard view of Fenway Park interior circa 1920. *via John Pastier*

Right: Left half of Fenway Park stands circa 1912. *MLB Photos via Getty Images*

Below right: This postcard provides a view of the interior of Braves Field. *via John Pastier*

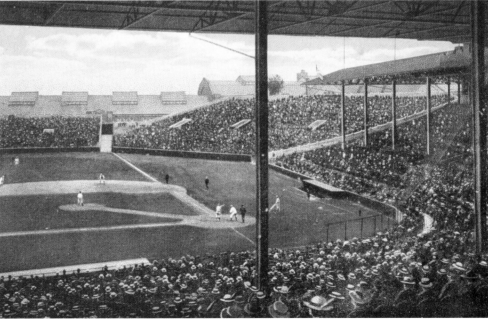

the Braves—their ballpark was still under construction.) The Red Sox won all four of the series they were involved in during those early years at Fenway, but it would be 84 years before they won another.

A small fire in 1926 destroyed the bleachers along the left field line; they were never replaced and little other damage was caused. But that would be an ominous sign of things to come as in January 1934 fire raged once again at Fenway, leaving little unharmed in its wake. This second blaze occurred in the middle of a revamping of the park by then-owner Tom Yawkey, and following the fire efforts were stepped up to fix the stadium. Three months later it was reopened.

As a result of the fire, the wooden left field wall was replaced by a metal equivalent. This would provide the basis for Fenway's signature feature—the Green Monster.

The Great Wall of China. The Wailing Wall in Jerusalem. The Green Monster in Fenway Park. Few structures in architecture, and none in baseball, are more identifiable than the 37-foot wall that separates Lansdowne Street from the outfield where Duffy Lewis, Ted Williams, and Carl Yazstremski once roamed.

A billboard for the greatness of baseball, the original wall, just 25 feet high, was probably built to keep residents in neighboring apartments from sneaking a free peak at the game. The Green Monster was expanded to its current height in 1934 and painted green in 1947. The seats built on top in 2003 have become among the most prized in baseball.

The Red Sox weren't the only team to play at Fenway, however. The Boston Redskins, who would later relocate to Washington under the same name, played NFL football there in the 1930s, and the American Football League Boston Patriots (forerunner of today's New England Patriots) played at Fenway for a few seasons in the 1960s. In a time when most classic ballparks have been shut down or destroyed, the Red Sox have resisted temptation to move to a new facility, and this was rewarded in 2004 when they defeated the St. Louis Cardinals to win their first World Series since 1918.

Today, the base of the left field wall is anchored by a manual scoreboard, which not only updates American League scores with 16-inch-high numbers (National League scores are electronic) but features two vertical strips which spell out the initials of former team owners Tom Yawkey and Jean Yawkey—TAY and JRY—in Morse code.

Left: Postwar aerial view of Fenway Park before the extensive modifications to the stands. Note no bleachers on top of the Green Monster; these were added before the 2003 season.
National Baseball Hall of Fame

Right: Huntington Avenue Grounds was the scene of the first World Series in 1903. The Boston Pilgrims were matched against the Pittsburgh Pirates and Boston won when Bill Dineen struck out the famous Honus Wagner in the seventh game. Notice the crowd clustered around the infield. *MLB Photos via Getty Images*

Right: Mounted police on crowd control outside Fenway Park in 1912. *National Baseball Hall of Fame*

Far right: A complementary pair to the last photograph. This one, some 40 years later, is a postwar view of Fenway Park that shows clearly some of the building that had taken place since 1912. *National Baseball Hall of Fame*

Right: View of the field, the Green Monster left-field wall, and spectators in the bleachers from behind home plate in the early 1990s. The Prudential Tower is at right in the background. *Getty Images*

Left: September 28, 1914, view of Fenway Park. *Library of Congress*

Overleaf: A view outside Fenway Park as fans arrive for the game between the Red Sox and the Yankees on July 25, 2003. The Yankees won 4–3. *Jerry Driendl/Getty Images*

Right: Panoramic interior view of Fenway Park from the seats above first base during the July 25, 2003 Red Sox-Yankees game. Note the bleachers atop the Green Monster. *Jerry Driendl/Getty Images*

Left: Fenway Park during the All-Star Game on June 20, 1999. *Getty Images*

Right: Looking over the diamond toward the Green Monster. *Digitalballparks.com*

Overleaf: Fenway Park in 1999. *Duomo/Corbis*

BUFFALO, NEW YORK

Dunn Tire Park

Previous name: Pilot Field

Status: Home of minor league Buffalo Bisons

Address: 275 Washington Street, Buffalo, NY 14203

Capacity: 21,050

Opening day: April 14, 1988

Cost to construct: $40 million

Architect: HOK Sport

Dimensions (ft):

Left Field: 325

Left Center: 371

Center Field: 404

Right Center: 367

Right Field: 325

Defining features: Designed to be expanded vertically to the standards of a modern major league-style ballpark, complete with food court and the largest video board in the minor leagues.

Most expensive seat: $10

Cheapest seat: $5 (youth and senior general admission)

Over the years, Buffalo's baseball team has been known as the Bisons, though there have actually been several different clubs that used that name. The first debuted in 1880 in the National League, playing games at a venue known as Olympic Park. In 1885 the team floundered and was sold—players and all—to Detroit. The very next year, a new version of the Bisons emerged in the International League. In 1889 a second Olympic Park opened at a new location at the intersection of Michigan and Cherry Streets and was built using the bleachers from the earlier version of the stadium. The venue was known as the Buffalo Baseball Park from 1907 to 1923, then was torn down and replaced with a new concrete-and-steel stadium on the same site. Named Bison Stadium, the new ballpark cost $256,000 to construct and had a seating capacity of about 13,000. A large, 60-foot scoreboard was added in 1934, and the ballpark was renamed Offermann Stadium in 1935 to honor Frank Offermann, the Bison's recently deceased principal owner and team president.

In 1960 the stadium was demolished and a new junior high school constructed on the property. The Bisons moved into nearby War Memorial Stadium, home of the American Football League's newly created Buffalo Bills, for the 1961 season. War Memorial Stadium opened in 1938 with the name Civic Stadium, but fans affectionately came to know the facility as the "Rockpile." It was a classic football bowl that offered an odd configuration for baseball (and a short right field fence), but a cozy feel that made fans feel close to the players. An earlier version of the Bills played at the stadium as part of the short-lived All-American Football Conference in the late 1940s, and then the Rockpile was used primarily for stock car racing in the 1950s.

During the 1960s, championships teams for both the Bisons and the Bills played in War Memorial Stadium. Also during this time an upper deck was built on the stadium's north stands that expanded capacity to 46,201, but the aging facility was empty by 1973. The financially struggling Bisons relocated to Winnipeg in 1971, then disbanded at the end of the season, and the Bills opened opened their own suburban Rich Stadium. In 1979 the Bisons were resurrected in the form of an Eastern League Class AA team and baseball returned to War Memorial Stadium. In 1983 the stadium was used as a filming location for the classic baseball movie, The Natural. For 1985, a new Class AAA Bison team took the field; the franchise had been relocated from Wichita. These American Association Bisons played at War Memorial Stadium until 1988 when the new Pilot Field opened, and shortly thereafter the Rockpile was demolished.

Pilot Field (now known as Dunn Tire Park) is a $40 million downtown ballpark, and with a capacity of more than 21,000 and a host of amenities it is not much of a step down from many of the modern crop of major league ballparks. The new stadium was an immediate hit and Buffalo quickly became a minor league success story as the new stadium shattered all-time minor league attendance records—and the Bisons even attracted more fans than three major league clubs. The team now plays in the International League as the Class AAA affiliate of the Cleveland Indians, and Dunn Tire Park is considered one of the best places in the country to watch minor league baseball.

Below: Buster Bison, mascot for Buffalo Bisons minor league baseball team, warming up the crowded stadium before the scrimage at Pilot Field, June 1, 1988.*Time & Life Pictures/Getty Images*

Above: This postcard provides a view of the interior of Buffalo's Offermann Stadium. *via John Pastier*

Above: An early Buffalo ballpark. *via John Pastier*

CHICAGO, ILLINOIS

Comiskey Park

Other names: White Sox Park

Status: Demolished in 1991

Location: Adjacent to (north side) of U.S. Cellular Field

Capacity: 28,800 (opening day); 52,000 (final)

Opening day: July 1, 1910

Last MLB game: September 30, 1990

Cost to construct: $750,000

Architect: Zachary Taylor Davis (original park); The Osborn Co. (expansion)

Dimensions (ft):	Initial	Final
Left Field:	363	347
Left Center:	382	382
Center Field:	420	409
Right Center:	382	382
Right Field:	363	347

Defining features: Spacious and symmetrical field almost entirely surrounded by double-deck stands. Exploding scoreboard with pinwheels.

World Series: 1917, 1918, 1919, 1959

All-Star Game: 1933, 1950, 1983

Wrigley Field

Previous names: Weeghman Park; Cubs Park

Status: Home of the Chicago Cubs

Address: 1060 West Addison Street Chicago, Illinois 60613

Capacity: 14,000 (opening day); 39,538 (present)

Opening day: April 23, 1914

First MLB game: April 20, 1916

Cost to construct: $250,000

Architect: Zachary Taylor Davis

Dimensions (ft):	Initial	Current
Left Field:	345	355
Left Center:	364	368
Center Field:	440	400
Right Center:	364	368
Right Field:	356	353

Defining features: Ivy-covered brick outfield wall. Old-fashioned, hand-operated scoreboard in center field. Intimate city neighborhood setting.

Most expensive seat: $36

Cheapest seat: $12

World Series: 1918, 1929, 1932, 1935, 1938, 1945

All-Star Game: 1947, 1962, 1990

Above and Below: The fifth game of the World Series between the Cubs and the White Sox, at West Side Grounds, Saturday, October 13, 1906. The White Sox won the series 4-2. *Library of Congress; MLB Photos via Getty Images*

With two Major League teams in the Chicago Cubs and the White Sox, there is definitely a lot of baseball history in the Windy City. The White Sox started out at South Side Park, also known as the 39th Street Grounds, in 1901. It was a primitive ballpark with a capacity of only 15,000, but it was home. Chicago's cricket team played there in the late 1800s and, at the turn of the century, White Sox owner Charles Comiskey built a wooden grandstand on the site.

The Sox would only play there for nine years, as Comiskey was intent on fulfilling his dream of giving Chicago the "baseball palace of the world." Ground was broken in February 1910, and the White Sox moved in

Right, Below right, and Below: Views of West Side Grounds, Chicago, Cubs vs. Giants, August 30, 1908. *Library of Congress*

Above: Last game and break up after it, World Championship Series, White Sox vs. Cubs, South Side Park, Sunday, October 14, 1906. *Library of Congress*

Below: World's Championship Series, Detroit vs. Chicago, October 9, 1907, West Side Grounds. *Library of Congress*

to their more capacious new home five months later. Originally named the White Sox Park, it didn't take long before it was named after Comiskey himself. Opening day ended in defeat for Chicago, which fell to the St. Louis Browns 2-0.

It wasn't long before controversy hit Comiskey. The White Sox were considered a great team, appearing in the 1906 and 1917 World Series, beating North Side neighbors the Cubs and the New York Giants by identical 4-2 counts. So stellar was the latter team's reputation that eyebrows were raised when they lost the 1919 series to the Cincinnati Reds. It transpired a year later that eight of the White Sox team had arranged to throw the series in what became known as the Black Sox scandal. Despite the players' admission, they were acquitted—but to this day are denied entry to the Baseball Hall of Fame.

It would be 40 years before the White Sox could redeem themselves, but they failed to capture the series against the Los Angeles Dodgers in 1959, and this has turned out to be their last World Series appearance until their 2005 championship. After the 1919 debacle, pride was restored to the ballpark in 1933 when it hosted the first ever All-Star game, which the American League won on the strength of Babe Ruth's performance. Comiskey would go on to host two more All-Star games, in 1950 and again in 1983.

Nearing the end of the 1980s, then-White Sox chairman Jerry Reinsdorf gave

the city an ultimatum: build a new ballpark for his team or he'd move them to Florida. The ballpark was duly built—right next door to Comiskey—and the Sox moved in April 1991. The New Comiskey Park, as it was first named, was re-christened U.S. Cellular Field in 2003.

But Chicago is by no means all about the White Sox—its other major league team, the Chicago Cubs, were around even earlier. Formed in 1876, the Cubs floated round several ballparks, using different monikers. After the turn of the century they enjoyed tremendous success, making four World Series appearances in just five years. The team won two championships, against the Detroit Tigers in both 1907 and 1908, but

lost to the White Sox in 1906 and Philadelphia in 1910

The Cubs finally settled down at what was then known as Weeghman Park. The stadium had been built two years earlier by Charlie Weeghman who wanted a ballpark for his team, the Chicago Federals, who were playing in the Federal League. The new league was designed to challenge the majors but folded after just two years. So, with an empty stadium, Weeghman and ten others bought the Cubs and moved them in. They reached the World Series again in 1918, but came up short against the Red Sox, losing 4-2.

One of the members of the Cubs ownership team was William Wrigley Jr. of

Above: Chicago Comiskey exploding scoreboard 1989. *via John Pastier*

Left: Fans at Comiskey Park. *Library of Congress*

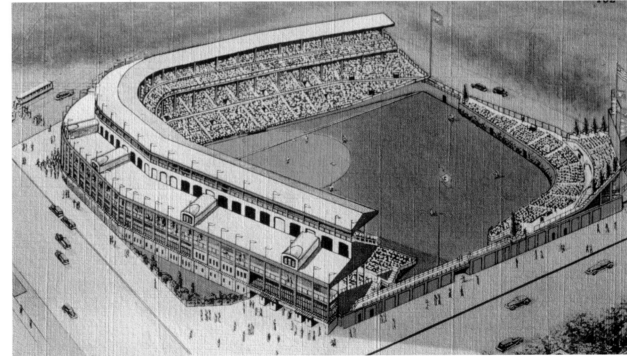

Above right: West Side Grounds, 1909, interior. *via John Pastier*

Right: Drawing of Wrigley Field after 1937–38 remodeling. *via John Pastier*

Wrigley's chewing gum fame. He bought out the club from the others, including Weeghman, in 1919, and renamed the stadium Cubs Park; it would be renamed in his honor in 1926. The Cubs have an illustrious history and Wrigley Field would witness more World Series—but never another championship. Philadelphia would haunt Chicago again in 1929 and another series loss would follow in 1932, this time a sweep at the hands of the mighty New York Yankees.

The Cubs team of this period was good, but more often than not under-performed on the grand stage. They lost two more series in the 1930s, first against the Tigers in 1935 and another to the Yankees in 1938. The Cubs returned to the World Series in 1945 and lost a seven-game set to the Tigers; it was their last trip to baseball's championship, and started several decades of mediocre play intermixed with occasional heartbreak. The 1969 Cubs appeared ready to break the string of mediocrity, only to collapse in the last days of the season. Chicago finally broke into postseason play in 1984, only to lose to the Padres. Quality Cub teams again came up short in the playoffs in 1989 and 1993, then in 2003 the team found itself just one out

from returning to the World Series. A bizarre play with a Wrigley fan interfering with a foul ball unnerved the Cubs and they let the Marlins come back for the victory. With the Red Sox and White Sox championships in 2004 and 2005, the Cubs now lead the majors—by a long shot—with the longest time since their last World Series title.

Despite this long run of futility, Cubs fans love their home ballpark, which along with Fenway Park is one of the last shrines to old-time baseball. Classic touches such as the vine-covered brick outfield wall and the old-fashioned hand-operated scoreboard make this a must-visit place for every baseball fan. Summer afternoon games at Wrigley have long been an important part of Chicago's culture. In fact, Wrigley Field was the last stadium in the major leagues to add lights, a concession to the city and nearby residential neighborhoods that had long resisted the intrusion of night games. The Cubs finally broke with tradition and played their first home game under the lights on August 9, 1988. Today, the Wrigleyville neighborhood around the stadium is one of the liveliest in the city, drawing fans to its eating and drinking establishments to cheer on the Cubs no matter what time the games are played—or how poorly the team is playing.

Left, above and below: The lights are switched on at Wrigley Field as the Cubs host the Phillies in the first night game ever at the ballpark. The lights ended a 74-year tradition of day-only baseball at the park. August 8, 1988. *Bettmann/Corbis; Jim Sugar/Corbis*

Right: An aerial view of the old and new Comiskey Parks circa 1990. *Getty Images*

Previous Pages:
Chicago White Sox play the Texas Rangers at New Comiskey Park. in 1997.
Joseph Sohm/Visions of America/Corbis

Left: For 80 years, until 1990, the home of the Chicago White Sox, Comiskey Park was also home to so many baseball greats, among them Shoeless Joe Jackson, Luke Appling, Nellie Fox, Minnie Minoso, and Luis Aparicio. The era of Bill Veeck's ownership, which began in 1959, saw such innovations as the "exploding" scoreboard, player names on the back of team jerseys, and special promotional events such as the disastrous Disco Demolition Night.
National Baseball Hall of Fame

Left: Spectator joy as the White Sox defeat the Red Sox 1-0 in the tenth inning, at Old Comiskey Park.
Time Life Pictures/Getty Images

Right: Exterior of U.S. Cellular Field on June 22, 2003. *Jerry Driendl/Getty Images*

Right: Five-year-old Brian Jones sings the national anthem with his proud father, DeNard Jones, kneeling beside him.
Time Life Pictures/Getty Images

Center right: A view from the press box at Comiskey Park during the 1959 World Series.
Time Life Pictures/Getty Images

Far right: The new owner of the Chicago White Sox, Bill Veeck, standing in a snowy Comiskey Park.
Time Life Pictures/Getty Images

Previous page: U.S. Cellular Field from press box level during the All-Star Game between the Indians and the White Sox on June 22, 2003.
Jerry Driendl/Getty Images

Right: Exterior view of Wrigley Field during the game between the Philadelphia Phillies and the Chicago Cubs on July 23, 2003.
Jerry Driendl/Getty Images

Overleaf: U.S. Cellular Field from home plate upper level
during the game between the Cleveland Indians and the White Sox on June 21, 2003. The White Sox won 4-3.
Jerry Driendl/Getty Images

154

Right: An aerial view of Wrigley Field. Easy to see why even the players refer to this classic park as the "Friendly Confines." By the time this photo was taken the bleachers and a second level of seats had been added to meet the fan demand.
National Baseball Hall of Fame

Right: Wrigley Field's center-field scoreboard during the game between the Phillies and the Cubs on July 23, 2003.
erry Driendl/Getty Images

Right: A packed Wrigley Field seen from the left-field stands. *Digitalballparks.com*

Far right: The Florida Marlins celebrate their 9–6 win over the Chicago Cubs during game seven of the National League Championship series October 15, 2003. *Brian Bahr/Getty Images*

Right: A good view of the ivy, the scoreboard, and the North Sheffield Avenue seating.
Digitalballparks.com

CINCINNATI, OHIO

Crosley Field

Previous name: Redland Field

Status: Demolished in 1972

Location: Intersection of Western Avenue and Findlay Street

Capacity: 25,000 (opening day); 29,488 (final)

Opening day: April 11, 1912

Last MLB game: June 24, 1970

Cost to construct: $225,000

Architect: Harry Hake

Dimensions (ft):	Initial	Final
Left Field:	360	328
Left Center:	380	380
Center Field:	420	387
Right Center:	383	383
Right Field:	360	366

Defining features: Inclined terrace in front of the left field fence. Site of the first major league night game.

World Series: 1919, 1940

All-Star Game: 1938, 1958

Riverfront Stadium

Previous names: Cinergy Field

Status: Demolished in 2002

Location: Adjacent to Great American Ballpark

Capacity: 52,952 (opening day); 40,008 (final)

Opening day: June 30, 1970

Last MLB game: September 22, 2002

Cost to construct: $50 Million

Architect: Heery & Heery and Finch, Alexander, Barnes, Rothschild and Pashal

Dimensions (ft):	Initial	Final
Left Field:	330	325
Left Center:	375	370
Center Field:	404	393
Right Center:	375	373
Right Field:	330	325

Defining features: Circular multipurpose stadium on the banks of the Ohio River. Astroturf playing field (replaced in 1998)

World Series: 1970, 1972, 1975, 1976, 1990

All-Star Game: 1970, 1988

Great American Ballpark

Address: 100 Main Street, Cincinnati, Ohio 45202.

Capacity: 42,059

Opening day: March 31, 2003—Pittsburgh Pirates 10, Cincinnati Reds 1

Cost to construct: $290 million

Architect: HOK Sports

Dimensions (ft):

Left Field: 328   Left Center: 379

Center Field: 404   Right Center: 370

Right Field: 325

Defining feature: "The Gap" in seats down the left field line

Most expensive seat: $225

Cheapest seat: $5

World Series: None

All-Star Game: None

Memorable moments:

2003 March 31—Former President George Bush, filling in for his son, President George W. Bush, throws out the ceremonial first pitch on the park's opening day.

2003 April 4—Sammy Sosa hits his 500th home run.

Cincinnati is one of the few cities whose major league baseball franchise hasn't packed upped and moved away—though the list of ballparks the Reds have called home is almost as long as their stay in the city!

The team first known as the Cincinnati Red Stockings started out fully professional in 1869 at the Union Grounds. They enjoyed success there and away from home with a 130-game winning streak. Cincinnati would soon leave the 4,000-seat park for a larger venue at the Avenue Grounds in 1876, the move coinciding with the team's entry into the National League as a charter member. The stay was to be brief; the ballpark was four miles away from the city center, and difficult to reach.

A brief stay at Bank Street Grounds followed, though the time was plagued by controversy. Cincinnati was kicked out of the NL in 1880 for persistently renting out their ballpark on a Sunday and selling beer during games, so the following year they joined the newly formed American Association.

The Reds left Bank Street and settled at American Park, named to show the team's

new affiliation with the AA. It had a covered grandstand and even leather-cushioned seats. Upon being reinstated to the NL in 1889, the ballpark was renamed League Park. Following a fire, a new reinforced concrete grandstand was built in 1902 with many lavish architectural flourishes, inspiring the nickname "Palace of the Fans."

But the Palace proved too small and was unexpandable, so in 1911 a new park named Redland Field was built in its place. It held 25,000 fans when it first opened, and the Reds started to enjoy the type of success that the previous three ballparks hadn't witnessed. Their first appearance in the World Series saw victory, but it was forever tainted by the "Black Sox" scandal, where members of opponents the Chicago White Sox threw the series for financial gain.

The year 1933 saw the Reds hit hard by the Depression. Just when it seemed as though the franchise might leave Cincinnati, radio tycoon Powel Crosley Jr. bought the club and the stadium was renamed in his honor the following year. Crosley Field hosted the 1938 All-Star game, won by the NL. Cincinnati's unblemished record in World Series appearances would continue in 1940 when they defeated the Detroit Tigers 4-3. It would host another midsummer classic in 1953 when the NL would again triumph 5-1.

Discussions about a new ballpark began in the late 1940s, but it wasn't until 1968 that work began on the Riverfront Stadium. It opened in 1970 and was a 53,000-capacity multipurpose venue, shared with Cincinnati's new NFL franchise, the Bengals. Immediately thrust into action, it

Above: Opening day, Pittsburgh vs. Cincinnati, Cincinnati, Ohio, April 14, 1905, attendance 18,287. *National Baseball Hall of Fame Library Archive*

Below: GE Novalux floodlights illuminate Cincinnati's Crosley Field for a night game in 1935. *Schenectady Museum; Hall of Electrical History Foundation/Corbis*

hosted the 1970 All-Star game, a 5-4 win for the NL, who must have enjoyed playing in Cincinnati by this point. That same year the Reds made it to the World Series, but were stopped in their tracks 4-1 by the Baltimore Orioles.

The 1970s were a great decade for the Reds; it was the era of the "Big Red Machine" and gave Riverfront the opportunity to host some of the most memorable games in the history of baseball. Another defeat in the World Series came in 1972, but back-to-back championships arrived in 1975 and 1976, with the Red Sox and the Yankees falling, respectively.

While never truly looking like a baseball park, Riverfront was still considered good enough to host the 1988 All-Star game, and two years later the Reds won another World Series with a 4-0 steamrolling of Oakland. In 1997 Cinergy Corporation bought the naming rights to the ballpark and rechristened it Cinergy Field. Two years

Left: General view of Crosley Field. *MLB Photos via Getty Images*

Below left: Aerial vew of Crosley Field. *MLB Photos via Getty Images*

Right: A general view of Riverfront Stadium during the World Series featuring the Cincinnati Reds and the Boston Red Sox, October 1975. *Focus on Sport/Getty Images*

Below: Exterior view of Riverfront Stadium during the 1990 World Series between the Cincinnati Reds and the Oakland Athletics. *Jonathan Daniel/Getty Images*

later the Bengals moved out. After the 2000 season a portion of the outfield stands were demolished to accommodate building of the Reds' new 42,000-seat Great American Ballpark—almost on the same site. A few important changes, including installation of grass, actually enhanced Cinergy Field for

the two years it functioned as a baseball-only park. It was demolished in 2002 after the completion of the Reds new home.

Below: World Series game played in Cincinnati in October 1940. *Bettmann/Corbis*

Right: Riverfront Stadium illuminated after dark. Its lights reflect off the surface of the Ohio River. ca. 1989. *Philip Gould/Corbis*

Left: The Great American Ball Park from home plate upper level during a National League game between the Cincinnati Reds and the Houston Astros.
Jerry Driendl/Getty Images

Overleaf: The Great American Ball Park and the Cincinnati night skyline. The suspension bridge is the Roebling Suspension Bridge, erected in 1866 as the Covington and Cincinnati Bridge and renamed after its designer John A. Roebling.
Jerry Driendl/Getty Images

Above: Aerial view of the then Riverfront Stadium. It would be renamed Cinergy Field in 1996 after Cincinnati's electric company paid $6 million for the privilege. *National Baseball Hall of Fame*

Left: Spectators aboard boats floating on the Ohio River watch as Cinergy Field is imploded on December 29, 2002, to make room for the nearby Great American Ballpark (on the right). More than 1,200lb of explosive material was used. *Mike Simons/Getty Images*

CLEVELAND, OHIO

Cleveland Municipal Stadium

Previous names: Lakefront Stadium

Status: Demolished in 1996

Location: Between downtown and Lake Erie along W. 3rd

Capacity: 78,000 (opening day); 74,483 (final)

Opening day: July 1, 1931

First MLB game: July 31, 1932

Last MLB game: October 3, 1993

Cost to construct: $3 million; $8.6 million (renovations)

Architect: Walker & Weeks; The Osborn Co

Dimensions (ft):	Initial	Final
Left Field:	322	320
Left Center:	430	395
Center Field:	470	404
Right Center:	430	395
Right Field:	322	320

Defining features: Massive, multipurpose stadium, one of the largest in MLB history. Fences inside the bleachers shortened the dimensions.

World Series: 1948, 1954

All-Star Game: 1935, 1954, 1963, 1981

Below: Good news for batters! A new fence goes up in the Cleveland Indians' ballpark April 30, 1947. It is 410 feet from the home plate, reducing the distance a batter has to sock the ball for a circuit by 60 feet. Note the old 470-foot sign in background. *Bettmann/Corbis*

Above right: Semi-professional championship game, Brookside Stadium, Oct. 10, 1915, purported attendance over 100,000. Score: White Autos 11. Omaha 6. *Library of Congress*

Below right: Cleveland Baseball Stadium: view showing crowds, September 14, 1954. *Bettmann/Corbis*

Jacobs Field

Address: 2401 Ontario Street
Cleveland, OH 44115

Capacity: 43,368

Opening day: April 4, 1994—Cleveland
Indians 4, Kansas City 3 (11 innings)

Cost to construct: $175 million

Architect: HOK Sports

Dimensions (ft):

Left Field: 325 Left Center: 370

Center Field: 405 Right Center: 375

Right Field: 325

Defining feature: Left field scoreboard

Little known ground rule: Thrown ball that enters camera pits, dugouts, or diamond suites and remains: two bases

Most expensive seat: $50

Cheapest seat: $5

World Series: 1995, 1997

All-Star Game: 1997

Memorable moments:

1995 September 8—Cleveland defeats Baltimore 3–2 to clinch the AL Central Division, its first championship in 41 years.

1995 September 30—Albert Belle hits 50th home run, most in Indians' history, until Jim Thome cracks 52 seven years later.

1997 July 8—Hometown catcher Sandy Alomar hits a seventh-inning, two-run homer to lead the AL to a 3–1 All-Star victory.

2001 August 5—Trailing the Mariners 14–2, the Tribe scores 13 unanswered runs for their greatest comeback in 76 years.

The Cleveland Indians started out at League Park. Built in 1890, it was home for Cleveland's National League side, the Cleveland Spiders. Baseball legend Cy Young pitched the first game there in 1891 and it remained an NL ballpark until 1900.

The asymmetrical ballpark was renovated in 1910 and the wooden facilities were replaced by concrete and metal, and the capacity increased from 9,000 to 21,500. In 1915 the Cleveland Spiders took on the name "Indians" and in 1920 League Park hosted the World Series. Cleveland took the championship, beating the Brooklyn Robins 5-2. Game 5 recorded two significant series firsts by Indians—Elmer Smith hit the first grand slam in the first inning, and Bill Wambsganss later recorded the first unassisted triple play.

In the late 1920s the decision was made to build a stadium on a landfill site next to Lake Erie. Disgruntled locals later said it was a ploy to bring the 1932 summer Olympics to Cleveland, but it was later revealed that Los Angeles had already been chosen.

Lakefront Stadium opened in July 1931. It was a multipurpose stadium designed to baseball and football, along with a regulation running track. The NFL's Cleveland Browns started playing at the stadium after it opened, but he Indians did not fully embrace the stadium—after playing there full-time for a year immediately after the stadium opened they reverted to only playing night and weekend games there until 1947, sharing time with League Park, which didn't have any floodlights.

Despite hosting the 1935 All-Star game, public opinion began to change towards the ballpark that was also known as the Cleveland Municipal Stadium. It was the first stadium in America to be funded by the public, so they had very forthright views. Cold winds from the lake would freeze spectators year-round. When it was hot, though, the stadium attracted swarms of flying insects. Because of its size—78,000 seats—it always seemed empty when baseball was being played there. Respectable baseball crowds of 20,000 people still looked minute, though the Browns sold out most games. These factors combined earned the stadium the nickname

Left: League Park office and ticket booth building behind right field corner. Tracks of two trolley lines visible in foreground. *via John Pastier*

Right: Part of the huge crowd at Cleveland Stadium for the 1954 All Star game, July 13, 1954. *Bettmann/Corbis*

"Mistake by the Lake" among baseball fans.

Owner Bill Veeck moved the Indians to the Cleveland Stadium permanently in 1947 and League Park was demolished in 1951. The once-prosperous area surrounding League Park is now derelict, possibly as a result. Plans are now being devised to rebuild the park, though funds could prove to be an issue.

The Indians reacted well to their new home, winning the World Series 4-2 in 1948 against the Boston Braves. The year 1954 saw Municipal host the All-Star game, won by the AL, while the Indians reached the World Series but were swept by the New York Giants 4-0. The "Mistake" wasn't doing too badly in terms of hosting prestigious events as two more All-Star games followed in 1963 and 1981, both won by the National League.

With the stadium falling into disrepair and showing its age over time, the Indians moved to Jacobs Field at the end of the 1993 season. The Browns vacated the stadium in 1995, moving to Baltimore after having a request for a new home turned down. The ballpark was eventually demolished in

Above: Upper deck of League Park, sometimes called Dunn Field, circa 1910.

Right: General view of Cleveland Municipal Stadium as the Cleveland Indians play the Texas Rangers on Opening Day April 20, 1982. *John Reid III/MLB Photos via Getty Images*

Right: Officially christened Lakefront Stadium when it opened in 1932, but more popularly known among fans of the resident Cleveland Indians as the "Mistake by the Lake," Municipal Stadium was used by the Indians until 1993. *National Baseball Hall of Fame*

Far right: After the last baseball game played in Cleveland Municipal Stadium in October of 1993, it continued in service as the home of the NFL Browns, until it was demolished in 1996 following the Browns departure for Baltimore. Now a new "Cleveland Browns" team plays in Cleveland Browns Stadium built in 1997 on the site of the original Municipal Stadium while the Cleveland Indians have played some of the best baseball in their long history at the critically acclaimed Jacobs Field since 1994. *National Baseball Hall of Fame*

1996, and the new Cleveland Browns Stadium now stands on its site after the NFL granted a new franchise to the city in 1999.

After playing for 61 years at cavernous Municipal Stadium at the edge of Lake Erie, derisively labeled the "mistake by the lake," the Indians moved into a boutique park where the blend of old and new is among the wonders of modern baseball.

Where the old stadium looked like something a child would build with an advanced erecter set, Jacobs Field was carefully sculpted to blend Indians' baseball with Cleveland's industrial roots.

The architects boast of using the city's traditional stone and brick masonry and providing direct views into the park from two street-level plazas to further integrate it with the city. Critics have credited the lattice work on the exterior for reflecting the bridges that cross the Cuyahoga River and the light standards for mimicking the industrial city's smokestacks. The result is an urban structure that is an integral part of Cleveland's downtown renaissance.

While the old stadium offered little more than a baseball diamond and seats, the Jake is a feast for the eyes. An appealing panorama of downtown Cleveland, if such a thing is possible, rises over the outfield, as does a 120-foot tall, 222-foot wide scoreboard, the largest freestanding scoreboard in the majors. The left-field scoreboard is reachable only by the likes of Mark McGwire, who did it off Orel Hershiser on April 30, 1997. Seats are angled to face the action at the plate.

Some elements resemble other parks. The 19-foot tall left-field fence, is referred to as the "mini-green monster." The bleachers compare to Wrigley's. Like most old parks, the playing field is anything but symmetric. Dead center field is not as deep as deepest left center. There is a triple deck in right. Home plate was transplanted from the old Municipal Stadium.

The new park is named after Richard Jacobs, who bought the Indians in 1985 and paid for the stadium's naming rights. The new home has suited the Indians well. Perennial losers, the Tribe won five consecutive division titles from 1995 to 1999. The stadium was sold out for a record 455 consecutive games, which would have been unimaginable at its old home.

Left: Bernie Williams—#51 of the New York Yankees—leaps up to catch a home run hit and misses the ball during the game against the Indians at Jacobs Field on May 26, 2001. The Yankees defeated the Indians 12–5. *Tom Pigeon /Allsport via Getty Images*

Right: General view of the stadium during the opening day game at Jacobs Field April 8, 2002. The Indians won 9–5. *Tom Pidgeon/Getty Images*

COLUMBUS, OHIO

Cooper Stadium in Columbus is a rare treat for baseball fans—a ballpark built in the 1930s still in use today. Now home to the Triple A Columbus Clippers, a New York Yankees' farm club, it was built in 1931 and it opened in 1932. Columbus Red Birds owner Branch Rickey had the facility built on cheap farmland he purchased during the Depression. It was named the Red Bird Stadium upon its opening.

The Red Birds roosted there for 23 seasons before moving to Omaha in 1955, and Columbus was about to face the reality of a summer without baseball—a first for the city in the 20th century. Fortunately, a group of local businessmen was able to bring the Jets to Columbus for 1955 and the stadium was renamed Jets Stadium for their 15-year tenure.

The idea of one blank summer must have seen like a walk in the park when Columbus endured six baseball-less years after the Jets left after the 1970 season, and the already-crumbling stadium fell into disuse. In 1977 Franklin County Commissioner Harold Cooper, the man who had helped bring in the Jets, used tax dollars to renovate the stadium and brought the Clippers in.

The stadium was the first minor-league ballpark to have artificial turf, but this proved to be unpopular with the fans, and was replaced with real grass in 2000. On the Clippers' arrival the stadium reverted to the generic Franklin County Stadium, but was renamed in 1984 in tribute to Harold Cooper and his efforts to keep baseball in Columbus.

Right: Red Bird postcard—night view aerial. *via John Pastier*

Left: Postcard showing Red Bird interior. *via John Pastier*

COOPERSTOWN, NEW YORK

Doubleday Field

Status: In use primarily for youth and amateur baseball leagues

Address: Main Street and Chestnut Street, Cooperstown, NY

Capacity: 9791

Opening day: original wooden structure, September 26, 1920; present brick and steel structure, May 6, 1939

Cost to construct: N/A

Architect: N/A

Dimensions (ft):

Left Field: 296

Left Center: 336

Center Field: 390

Right Center: 350

Right Field: 312

Defining features: The stadium has great charm, a traditional feel, and a beautiful setting.

Most expensive seat: Most games are free to watch or have a nominal cost.

Baseball's great creation myth is that it was single-handedly invented by Abner Doubleday in a Cooperstown cow pasture in 1839. It was based on the uncorroborated testimony of a childhood friend of Doubleday, and promulgated in 1907 by the Mills Commission, which had been set up in 1905 to establish the game's origins. Commenting on this, history professor David Q Voigt writes: "Ever since then, sports historians have repeatedly and futilely assailed the Doubleday account, arguing that Abner Doubleday never visited Cooperstown in 1839, that his diaries contain no reference to the game, and that the form of baseball he supposedly invented too closely resembles the game [of] the early 1900s."

Despite the lack of any connection to the game's origins, Cooperstown still retains its role as an important spiritual center of baseball. In part, this is true because the town is home to the National Baseball Hall of Fame and Museum, but Doubleday Field

does its part to keep enthusiasm for the game alive. Today, the field hosts around 350 games per year between mid-April and mid-October, ranging from youth baseball to senior leagues—any team can play so long as they pay the village a few hundred dollars. The stadium is also the home of the Oneonta Tigers of the New York-Penn League, though they only play there once a season. And since 1940, Doubleday Field has hosted the annual Hall of Fame Game, MLB's only in-season exhibition, and part of the Hall of Fame's induction festivities.

Above and Below: Two views of Doubleday Field's original 1920 wooden grandstand sometime prior to 1939. *National Baseball Hall of Fame*

Overleaf, left: Doubleday Field entrance portal in the 1950s. *Getty Images*

Far left and Overleaf, right: Doubleday Field's steel grandstand. *National Baseball Hall of Fame*

DENVER, COLORADO

Right: An overview of Coors Field during a Colorado Rockies game in the 1990s. *Chase Swift/Corbis*

Mile High Stadium

Previous names: Bears Stadium

Status: Demolished in 2002

Location: Along Eliot Street on site partially occupied by Invesco Field

Capacity: 76,098 (baseball)

Opening day: 1948

First MLB game: April 9, 1993

Last MLB game: August 7, 1994

Cost to construct: $25 million (renovations)

Architect: N/A

Dimensions (ft):

Left Field: 335

Left Center: 363

Center Field: 423

Right Center: 400

Right Field: 375

Defining feature: Football stadium with moveable stands allowing conversion for baseball

World Series: none

All-Star Game: none

Coors Field

Address: 2001 Blake Street

Denver, CO 80205

Capacity: 50,544

Opening day: April 26, 1995—Colorado Rockies 11, New York Mets 9 (14 innings)

Cost to construct: $215 million

Architect: HOK Sports

Dimensions (ft):

Left Field: 347 Left Center: 390

Center Field: 415 Right Center: 375

Right Field: 350

Defining feature: Row of purple, mile-high seats

Most expensive seat: $45

Cheapest seat: $1

World Series: None

All-Star Game: 1998

Memorable moments:

1995 October 1—The Rockies beat the Giants 10–9 to win a spot in the National League playoffs in just their third season.

1999 May 19—The Reds beat the Rockies 24–12 in the third highest scoring game since the turn of the century.

1998 July 7—The American League beats the National League 13–8 in the highest scoring All-Star game in history.

2003 April 10—First baseman Todd Helton snags a line drive off the bat of Cardinal Orlando Palmeiro, setting in motion the Rockies first triple play.

Mile High Stadium in Denver only hosted two years of Major League Baseball in its 53 years, but it had a colorful history. It was built using the money of a rich local family, the Howsams, in 1948 for Denver's local minor-league team, the Denver Bears.

Originally named the Bears Stadium, the baseball team it housed played in the now-defunct Western League. In later years the Bears played in the Triple A American Association and became one of the most popular teams in minor league history. On opening day, the stadium had around 17,000 seats, but Bob Howsam always dreamed of a major league team occupying the stadium. Expecting the imminent arrival of a franchise in the late 1950s, he expanded it to nearly 35,000 seats. When informed that he would have to wait for a team, he was left with a huge stadium that was only being used for minor-league baseball.

In came the Denver Broncos, a franchise from the upstart American Football League that was awarded to the city in 1960. Fan support for the Broncos was limited at first, but after their popularity began to soar in the 1960s, Howsham sold the stadium to Denver and another tier was added in 1968, creating a capacity of more than 50,000. After this renovation the stadium was renamed the Mile High Stadium, noting the fact that Denver, at 5,000 feet above sea level, is nicknamed "The Mile High City."

By 1975 stadium capacity had hit the 75,000 mark, and the next two years were spent creating what would undoubtedly be the main feature of the stadium. The East Stands, which held 21,000 seats, were designed to "float" so they could be moved outwards for baseball games, changing the shape of the playing field so the facility was able to accommodate both sports. Meanwhile, the Bears were setting minor league attendance records; Mile High still stands as the largest venue in minor league baseball history. In 1984 the team changed its name to the Denver Zephyrs, though they continued to play at the Class AAA level.

In 1993 Denver finally received the major league franchise it had craved so long. The new team, named the Colorado Rockies, displaced the Zephyrs to New Orleans and inherited the largest-capacity

reminiscent of Ebbets Field, and anchor a newly bustling downtown neighborhood.

Inside, the triple deck structure features small foul areas, an asymmetric field, and seats with sight lines geared toward the infield. A heating system under the field melts snow quickly, and its drainage system can clear away five inches of rain in a matter of hours.

The absence of an upper deck in left field provides fans along the first base and right field side a spectacular view of the Rocky Mountains. The stadium's designers passed up the chance to offer a panoramic view of downtown Denver so the sun would not be in batters' eyes, though the skyline is still visible from the top of the Rockpile, a 2,300-seat center field bleacher section where many tickets are held until game day, and kids and seniors can get in for just $1.

The park was originally designed to be even more intimate, seating just 43,000. But the huge popularity of baseball in nearby Mile High Stadium, where the Rockies played their first two years, persuaded the owners to add another 6,000 seats.

stadium in the major leagues, 80,000-seat Mile High Stadium; it would set and still holds the all-time seasonal attendance record. The Rockies would leave for brand-new baseball-only Coors Field in 1995, and the Broncos would stay until 2000; Mile High was demolished the following year.

The purple seats on the 20th row of Coors Field's upper deck tell the story of this ballpark. It is there that the elevation reaches 5,280 feet, exactly one mile above sea level. At that altitude balls fly further. Curve balls break less sharply. And that,

more than any other feature, has defined the Rockies' home.

Coors Field, the first park in the National League to be constructed exclusively for baseball since Dodger Stadium 33 years earlier, is by no means a small park. Its center field fence is a deep 415 feet, and left center juts out nine feet deeper. Yet the dimensions are deceptive. According to a team estimate, a ball hit 400 feet at sea-level Yankee Stadium would travel 440 feet in mile high Coors Field. The thin air contributed to a record-setting 1999 season,

when teams combined for an average of 15 runs and four home runs each game.

The incredible offense, the classic charm of the old-fashioned park, and the views of the Rocky Mountains in the distance, have made Coors Field among the best attended parks in baseball history.

The deep red brick and Colorado sandstone exterior makes Coors Field look like it has always been located in Denver's lower downtown, on a spot where a train depot once stood. The classic architecture and old fashioned corner front clock are

Left: A view toward the diamond and downtown Denver taken during a game between the Atlanta Braves and Colorado Rockies on June 18, 1995. A row of purple seats in the upper deck mark the elevation at exactly one mile above sea level.
Nathan Bilow/Allsport via Getty Images

Right: A view over the diamond toward the Rocky Mountains: Coors Field has wonderful views from its substantial stands.
Jonathan Daniel/Allsport via Getty Images

Left: July 1998 photo of the Colorado Rockies playing the Pittsburgh Pirates. *Joseph Sohm; ChromoSohm Inc./Corbis*

DETROIT, MICHIGAN

Below: Paul Molitor of the Minnesota Twins bats during a game at Tiger Stadium in 1997. *MLB Photos via Getty Images*

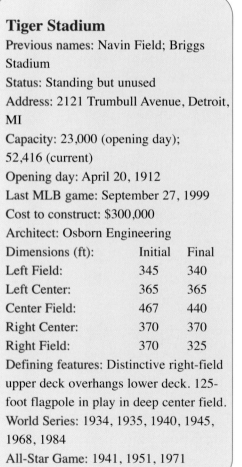

Tiger Stadium

Previous names: Navin Field; Briggs Stadium

Status: Standing but unused

Address: 2121 Trumbull Avenue, Detroit, MI

Capacity: 23,000 (opening day); 52,416 (current)

Opening day: April 20, 1912

Last MLB game: September 27, 1999

Cost to construct: $300,000

Architect: Osborn Engineering

Dimensions (ft):	Initial	Final
Left Field:	345	340
Left Center:	365	365
Center Field:	467	440
Right Center:	370	370
Right Field:	370	325

Defining features: Distinctive right-field upper deck overhangs lower deck. 125-foot flagpole in play in deep center field.

World Series: 1934, 1935, 1940, 1945, 1968, 1984

All-Star Game: 1941, 1951, 1971

When the Detroit Tigers prepared to play their first ever game — in 1901 in the American League against Milwaukee — they were playing in a ballpark that was already five years old, and on a site that would become steeped in baseball history for more or less the next century. That first game at Bennett Park had already been postponed a day due to the weather, but when it did come about it certainly wasn't short of excitement. After entering the ninth inning trailing 13-4, the

Below: Eastern League opening game, Rochester–Newark, April 21, 1910. *Library of Congress*

Tigers ended up winning 14-13 in front of a 10,000 crowd — a sign of successful times to come.

The old stadium was built in 1896 and was named after Charlie Bennett, the Detroit catcher in the late 1800s who lost both legs in a train accident just two years before the ballpark was opened. The Tigers would experience many a bittersweet moment there, appearing in three consecutive World Series starting in 1907, and losing on all three occasions — twice to the Cubs, and to the Pittsburgh Pirates in 1909.

After the painful losses, Tigers owner Frank Navin believed they needed a state-

of-the-art stadium, and perhaps a change of scenery. So in the winter of 1911, a new stadium was built, replacing the wooden structure with concrete and steel. It held 23,000 people and was named after Navin himself.

It opened the same day as Boston's Fenway Park, April 20, 1912, rain again delaying the Tigers opening game at a new ballpark. An interesting feature was the 125-foot flagpole in play in center field — the tallest in-play obstacle in major league history. A second tier was added to the stands behind home plate in 1924, bringing the capacity up to 30,000.

Above: World Series at Bennett Park, October 11, 1909. *Library of Congress*

Below: World Series, Chicago vs. Detroit, Bennett Park, October 12, 1907. *Library of Congress*

Tigers' fans had to wait until 1934 for a World Series at Navin Field — and again they suffered defeat, edged in seven games by the St. Louis Cardinals. Retribution and more importantly success would come the next year with a 4-2 series margin against the Chicago Cubs, who hadn't won a championship since beating the Tigers for the second time back in 1908.

After Navin died the same year, the new man in charge decided to renovate the

ballpark. Walter Briggs presented a new capacity of 36,000 to the fans in 1936 and, after double-tiered stands were built in the outfield in 1938, the stadium began to take on its memorable shape. With seats for 53,000 spectators and the new name of Briggs Stadium, it also welcomed the NFL's Detroit Lions, who would stay there until 1974.

The revamped ballpark saw the Tigers lose 4-3 in the 1940 World Series to the Cincinnati Reds. It then went on to host the 1941 All-Star game, despite being one of the few ballparks in the major leagues not to have floodlights. This omission was corrected in 1948, by which time they were the last team in the AL to outfit its stadium for night baseball.

Right: View of the first game of the 1934 World Series between the Detroit Tigers and the St. Louis Cardinals at Navin Field, October 3, 1934. The Cardinals won the game, 8–3. *Getty Images*

Below right: A general view of Tiger Stadium. *MLB Photos via Getty Images*

Below: A grounds crew resods the infield at Navin Field with 2,000 feet of new grass in anticipation of hosting the 1935 World Series while the Detroit Tigers are on the road, Detroit, Michigan, September 4, 1935. *Getty Images*

Comerica Park

Address: 2100 Woodward Ave.

Detroit, MI 48201

Capacity: 40,120

Opening day: April 11, 2000 — Detroit Tigers 5, Seattle Mariners 2

Cost to construct: $300 million

Architect: HOK Sports

Dimensions (ft):

Left Field: 346 Left Center: 402

Center Field: 422   Right Center: 379

Right Field: 330

Defining feature: Scoreboard tigers Little-known ground rule: Ball passing through or under the bullpen fence: two bases

Most expensive seat: $60

Cheapest seat: $5

World Series: None

All-Star Game: 2005 (scheduled)

Memorable moments:

2000 April 11 — Fans endure 34-degree temperatures to watch the Tigers beat Seattle in the park's first game.

2000 August 23 — Swarms of flying ants send fans fleeing.

2000 October 1 — Shane Halter plays all nine positions on the final game of the season, the fourth major leaguer to do so.

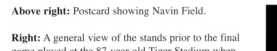

Above right: Postcard showing Navin Field.

Right: A general view of the stands prior to the final game played at the 87-year old Tiger Stadium when the Detroit Tigets hosted the Kansas City Royals on September 27, 1999. 6,873 games were played at the corner of Michigan and Trumbul streets. The Tigers won the game 8–2. *Getty Images*

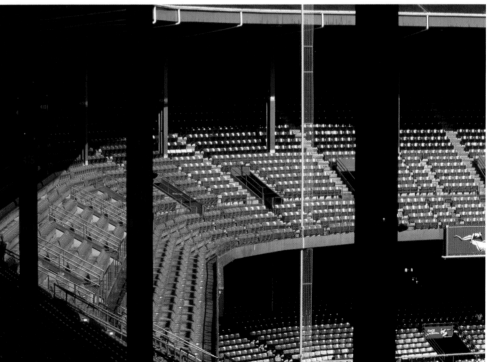

Success in the World Series was achieved again in 1945, again against the Cubs. Briggs Stadium hosted the All-Star game again in 1951 after a 10-year wait, the NL triumphing in what would be Joe DiMaggio's last midsummer classic.

The year of 1961 saw John Fetzer assume ownership of the Tigers and the ballpark was once again renamed, this time after the team itself. Tiger Stadium was extensively refurbished in the 1980s, and was commercialized with huge exterior beer

View of the exterior of Tiger Stadium.
Getty Images

nonsense, old-fashioned ambiance of Tiger Stadium which sat on the well-worn intersection of Michigan and Trumbull, a corner where baseball was played for more than a century. Comerica Park's Ferris wheel (carriages are shaped like baseballs), its multi-colored water fountain that shoots "liquid fireworks," the air-conditioned bar, enormous state-of-the-art scoreboard, and the lack of a single pillar to block the view, would have been unthinkable at Tiger Stadium.

Yet Comerica Park works to celebrate the city's rich baseball history.

Oversized sculptures cast in stainless steel along the center field wall show six Tiger greats in classic poses: Ty Cobb sliding spikes up, Willie Horton swinging, Al Kaline making a one-arm grab, along with Charlie Gehringer, Hank Greenberg and Hal Newhouser. Kaline's glove is positioned so that some day, some shot to deep center might just get caught.

The park's brick and steel construction and asymmetric dimensions mimic old parks, as does the dirt patch from the pitchers mound to home plate, a staple of turn-of-the-century fields. Originally the center-field flagpole was in play, just like at Tiger Stadium, though the fences were moved in and the flagpole now sits beyond the fence.

The park also frames a spectacular view of downtown Detroit, which has worked hard to keep baseball in the city.

signs in the 1990s. It witnessed two Detroit World Series victories—in 1968 over St. Louis and again in 1984 over San Diego. There was also one more All-Star game, in 1971, before the Tigers' move to Comerica Park in September 1999. The ballpark still stands, but is seldom used.

It is ironic that Detroit's baseball team moved from a place called Tiger Stadium. It is at Comerica Park that tigers roam.

Large tiger statues greet visitors outside. The perimeter is lined with tigers holding baseballs (actually lights) in their mouths. Two enormous tigers are positioned at either side of the scoreboard, who roar when the home team hits a home run. A merry-go-round featuring 30 hand-painted tigers entertains children along the first base side. There are even tiger claw marks scratched into concrete pillars around the park.

Comerica Park is a far cry from the no-

Left: Tiger Stadium taken on the occasion of the last game—Kansas City versus Detroit on September 27, 1999. *National Baseball Hall of Fame*

Far left: Comerica Park Entrance with Comerica Park Tigers by Michael Keropian. *Richard Cummins/Corbis*

HOUSTON, TEXAS

Below: General view of the playing field of the Astrodome Stadium on April 7, 1965—two days before the Astros, formerly the Colts, inaugurated their new stadium with an exhibition game against the New York Yankees. *Bettmann/Corbis*

Right: Fisheye view of the Astrodome taken during the exhibition game betweenNew York yankees and the Houston Astros. *Bettmann/Corbis*

Astrodome

Status: In use, but not for major league baseball

Address: 8400 Kirby Drive, Houston, TX

Capacity: 42,217 (opening day); 54,816 (current)

Opening day: April 12, 1965

Last MLB game: October 9, 1999

Cost to construct: $35 million; $65 million (1989 expansion)

Architect: Hermon Lloyd & W.B. Morgan and Wilson, Morris, Crain & Anderson

Dimensions (ft):	Initial	Final
Left Field:	340	325
Left Center:	375	375
Center Field:	406	400
Right Center:	375	375
Right Field:	340	325

Defining features: First indoor baseball stadium. First stadium to use artificial grass—"Astroturf."

World Series: None

All-Star Game: 1968, 1986

Minute Maid Park

Aka: Enron Field 2000-2002

Address: 501 Crawford Street

Houston, TX 77002

Capacity: 40,950

Opening day: April 7, 2000—Philadelphia Phillies 4, Houston Astros 1

Cost to construct: $248 million

Architect: HOK Sports

Dimensions (ft):

Left Field: 315   Left Center: 362

Center Field: 435   Right Center: 373

Right Field: 326

Defining feature: Centerfield hill

Most expensive seat: $40

Cheapest seat: $5

World Series: none

All-Star Game: 2004

Memorable moments:

2001 July 18—Jeff Bagwell hits for the cycle as Houston beats St. Louis 17–11.

2001 October 4—Barry Bonds ties Mark McGwire's single season home run record, hitting No. 70 into the second deck.

Houston was finally awarded a National League franchise, the Houston Colt .45s, that started play in 1962. The selling point for Houston's bid was a model of a domed stadium, the first of its kind. The only problem was it wasn't built yet!

The Colt .45s needed a place to play ball, and a stopgap stadium was deemed the logical solution. Work got under way on a 33,000-seat temporary ballpark, which was ready in April 1962. Open single-tiered stands ran from home plate down the left and right field lines. Additional, smaller stands were placed in both left and right field, with a scoreboard in center.

Despite never really being "home," the new facility was named Colt Stadium. Actually watching or playing a game there, however, was hard work. Due to the openness of the park and the notorious Texas weather, the heat was immense, even at night, much like at Turnpike Stadium in Arlington. On one

Sunday game, about 100 Colts fans had to be treated for heat-related symptoms in the first-aid room.

After just over two years at the Colt Stadium, the team was ready to move to their nearby new home, the Astrodome. Once vacated, Colt Stadium was used mainly for storage, and owner Roy Hofheinz had it painted gray, so people wouldn't see it blemish the Astrodome in aerial shots. After a minor-league Mexican team bought the stadium in the late 1960s, the temporary structure was shipped off to Mexico, where it was reconstructed for a minor league team. The stadium has since moved again, to Tampico, Mexico, where it sits today.

To coincide with their relocation, the Colt .45s were renamed the Astros and moved into their new indoor ballpark in 1965. Hailed as the "Eighth Wonder of the World," the 42,000-seat Houston Astrodome was the first of it's kind. Never before had major-league baseball been played indoors. Originally named the Harris County Domed Stadium, but with the name never sticking, the Astros won their opening game against the New York Yankees — an exhibition, but a victory nonetheless.

Air-conditioned so heat problems were now a thing of the past, the dome was built for the city as a whole, for other sports. The Astros were joined in 1965 by the University of Houston football team and National Football League Houston Oilers.

Although initially planted with real grass, the field soon adopted artificial Astroturf—not as a name gimmick but because the grass was dying in the indoor environment. The clear roof panes designed to give the grass light were painted a translucent white after players complained of being blinded by the glare when trying to track fly balls.

The Astrodome witnessed two All-Star games. The first was in 1968, when the NL won a low scoring game 1-0. Traditionalists didn't like having the midsummer classic indoors, but despite that Houston was chosen again in 1986 and 46,000 people watched the AL win 3-2. Unfortunately the Astros could never treat the Dome to a World Series during their 34-year tenure, though the team finally reached baseball's championship in 2005, ultimately getting swept by the Chicago White Sox.

The Oilers departed for Tennessee in 1996 after a dispute over a new stadium, and the Astros bided their time until 1999, when they moved into Minute Maid Park. The most important contribution the Astrodome has made in its existence happened after the Astros had left. In 2005 the Dome housed victims of Hurricane Katrina that ravaged New Orleans, and also aided victims of another hurricane, Rita, that attacked Texas later in the year.

Left: Aerial view of Enron Field and downtown Houston. *Bob Daemmrich/Corbis*

To appreciate the Astros' new home, think of the Houston Astrodome. Minute Maid Park is the opposite. The Astrodome was a dark, completely enclosed, oversized gymnasium where power hitters went to die. Minute Maid Field is light, open, thoroughly unique, and conducive to scoring runs. Even when the retractable roof is closed, 50,000 square feet of glass panels allow patrons to gaze upon the Houston skyline or tropical storms passing above.

In its time, the Astrodome represented an amazing architectural achievement, allowing Houston fans to watch their team despite the swampy heat and mosquitoes of summer. Over time, it came to represent everything that modern baseball parks try to avoid.

Now, the Astros play in a state-of-the art structure where the roof alone cost about twice what it took to build the Astrodome. This is no cookie-cutter gymnasium. Its most unusual quirk, Tal's Hill —named after team president Tal Smith —is a grassy knoll in dead center field, that rises at a 20 degree angle to a height of about five feet, prompting the most graceful centerfielders to watch their feet as they chase down deep fly balls. On the left side of the incline is a flagpole, which is in play as at the old Tiger Stadium.

The left field bleachers are close, just 315 feet away, and protrude into the outfield, creating funny bounces and fantastic views. A one-of-a-kind porch

Left: A view of the Houston Astrodome during a game between the Chicago Cubs and the Houston Astros on August 29, 1996. The Cubs won the game 4–3. *Getty Images*

Right: Houston Astrodome opening night of April 9, 1965, playing the Yankees in an exhibition game in front of President Lyndon B. Johnson. *National Baseball Hall of Fame*

Left: Aerial view of the Houston Astrodome, photographed in 2000.
Paul S. Howell/Getty Images

Right: The Houston Astrodome was the home of the Astros for 35 years 1965–2000.
National Baseball Hall of Fame

hangs out over the outfield action, where walls come in several different shapes and heights. Small foul territories bring fans close to the field.

The park's signature feature is a 57-foot, 24-ton, 1860s steam locomotive, which chugs down an 800-foot track along the left field roof when the Astros do something special. Trains are a motif throughout the stadium. Most fans enter through the 1911 vintage Union Station, which forms the park's main entrance. The scoreboard is baseball's biggest, and explodes in celebration of every Astros' home run.

The park opened as Enron Field, after the Houston-based energy conglomerate which paid $100 million for 30 years of naming rights. At the park's opener, with soon-to-be President Bush on hand, Enron President Ken Lay threw out the ceremonial first pitch. Two years later, the energy conglomerate had gone bankrupt amid scandal. The large Enron sign remained on the park until the Astros bought back the naming right. Months later, they sold the rights to Minute Maid.

Far left: Minute Maid Park—view toward first base from third base. *Digitalballparks.com*

Left: This photograph of Minute Maid Park affords a view of the 57-foot, 24-ton full-size replica steam loco that runs on an 800-foot track above left field. The park has a strong railway connection: the main entrance is the 1911 Union Station. *Digitalballparks.com*

INDIANAPOLIS, INDIANA

Indianapolis had a quasi-major league team and ballpark in 1914, when the Hoosiers played in the upstart Federal League. Their home was Washington Park, a 20,000-seat venue with outfield dimensions of 375 - 400 - 310. The Hoosiers excelled, winning the pennant with an 88-65 record, thanks to 25-game winning pitcher Cy Falkenberg and right fielder Benny Kauff, who led the league with a .370 average. Despite all this, attendance was poor, and the team moved to Newark, N.J., in 1915.

Sixteen years later, one of the finest minor league parks of the century was built on Washington Park's site. Perry Stadium, designed by Osborn Engineering and opened in 1931, was home to the Indianapolis Indians. As well as housing the Indians, 15,000-seat Perry Stadium also played a part in encouraging Negro League baseball. Both the Indianapolis ABCs and Clowns played there during the 1930s and 1940s. The Clowns were remembered as the Harlem Globetrotters of baseball. They used humor to get people to notice them, and then fielded solid baseball sides to keep the fans interested.

The stadium was renamed Victory Stadium in 1942 in an attempt to show support for U.S. forces in the World War II. Many people assume it was to celebrate victory, but at that early date there was nothing, as yet, to celebrate.

The facility was renamed once more, in 1967, to honor major league player and Indianapolis native Owen Bush, who eventually became the Indians' president. The Indians moved out in 1996 and the venue was converted for use as a dirt auto racing track for a time, but now stands vacant.

Left: Enron Field became Minute Maid Park for the 2003 season after an accounting scandal bankrupted the Houston-based energy conglomerate. This photograph shows off well Tal Hill at Minute Maid Park; note also the flagpole, which is in play. *National Baseball Hall of Fame*

Right: Postcard showing interior of Washington Park.

WASHINGTON BASEBALL PARK, INDIANAPOLIS, IND.

KANSAS CITY, MISSOURI

Municipal Stadium

Previous names: Muehlebach Field;
Ruppert Stadium; Blues Stadium
Status: Demolished in 1976
Location: Intersection of 22nd Street and
Brooklyn Avenue
Capacity: 16,000 (opening day); 35,561
(final)
Opening day: July 3, 1923
First MLB game: April 12, 1955
Last MLB game: October 4, 1972
Cost to construct: $400,000; $2.5 million
(renovation)
Architect: Osborn Engineering

Dimensions (ft):	Initial	Final
Left Field:	350	369
Left Center:	408	408
Center Field:	450	421
Right Center:	382	382
Right Field:	350	338

Defining features: Double-deck grandstand
built for 1955 season. Children's petting
zoo and picnic area behind right field fence.
World Series: none
All-Star Game: 1960

Kauffman Stadium

Previous names: Royals Stadium
Status: Home of the Kansas City Royals
Address: 1 Royal Way Kansas City,
Missouri
Capacity: 40,793
Opening day: April 10, 1973
Cost to construct: $43 million
Architect: HOK Sports
Dimensions (ft):
Left Field: 330
Left Center: 385
Center Field: 410
Right Center: 385
Right Field: 330
Defining features: A 12-story-high
scoreboard, shaped like the team's crest
with a crown on top, and a 322-foot-wide
"water feature" both stand above the
outfield.
Little-known ground rule: Batted
or thrown ball that hits tarpaulin area cover
is in play.
Most expensive seat: $27
Cheapest seat: $7
World Series: 1980, 1985

It was local girl Dorothy who claimed "there's no place like home"—and, while Kansas City baseball has had two, they've both been memorable. The first ballpark in the city was originally known as Muehlebach Field when it opened in 1923, and it was home to minor league side the Kansas City Blues. The park cost $400,000 and its one-tiered, mostly covered grandstand served its purpose in housing 17,500 potential Blues fans.

The Blues were bought by the New York Yankees in 1937 as a farm team, and the stadium was immediately named Ruppert Stadium in homage to the Yankees owner. The name would outlast the man, but only by four years, and in 1943 the park was renamed as the more appropriate Blues Stadium.

The Kansas City Monarchs had also played at the ballpark since it opened. They were known as the Negro League's answer to the New York Yankees, and were the longest-running Negro National League franchise. They appeared in back-to-back Negro World Series in 1924 and 1925—both against the Hilldale Daisies, winning the first time but losing the following year. They would leave the stadium in 1955.

Near the end of 1954 Kansas City got the news it had always wanted: major league baseball was coming. The Philadelphia Athletics were relocating for the 1955 season and in preparation the city ballpark's grandstand was enlarged, creating a new capacity of 30,000. By opening day, the ballpark was called Municipal Stadium and the Kansas City "A's" began to bring the stadium some memorable moments.

A's owner Charles Finley was renowned for pushing the league's boundaries, most famously creating "Pennant Porch," an area of bleachers that considerably shortened the distance in right field, making the home-run distance shorter and mocking Yankee Stadium, but the league requested he revise it.

Unique features of Municipal Stadium didn't stop at Finley's use of bleachers—behind right field there was a picnic area and even a small zoo, containing the A's mascot Charlie O the mule. During the period of two All-Star games per year, the ballpark held the first of the 1960s double header, with the NL coming out on top 5-3.

The 1960s were somewhat eventful for the ballpark. In 1962 the American Football League's Kansas City Chiefs moved in, staying until 1971. Two years later the Beatles played a concert at the stadium as part of their first-ever U.S. tour, a result of Finley offering them $150,000 for the appearance.

In 1967, despite the offer of a new stadium, Finley decided to move the A's to Oakland, California, but the major leagues were looking to expand, and awarded Kansas City a new AL franchise. The Kansas City Royals were born and played at Municipal until 1973.

The Royals moved into the 40,000-seat Royals Stadium—originally meant for the A's—the same year. The park's defining feature was a 12-story-high scoreboard, shaped like the team's crest and even with a crown on top. There was no doubting whose home it was now. The year it opened the stadium hosted its only All-Star game to date—the 40th anniversary spectacular—which was won 7-1 by the NL.

It would take until 1980 for the Royals to experience the World Series, but they failed to capitalize on the opportunity, losing 4-2 to the Phillies from the city that brought Kansas City the Athletics, Philadelphia. A second appearance wouldn't take as long, and this time the Royals captured the "Interstate 70 series" against cross-state rival St. Louis Cardinals with a hard-fought seven-game victory.

The stadium was renamed Kauffman Stadium in 1993 after Ewing Kauffman, the man who helped bring the Royals to Kansas, and their only owner. He died just a month later. In 1995 the Astroturf that had been there since the ballpark opened was replaced by real grass. The stadium is still used today by the Royals.

If baseball stadiums are urban cathedrals, then Kauffman stadium is a rogue church.

There is no Waveland Avenue or Lansdowne Street hugging the fence at Kauffman Stadium, just freeway and farmland.

Below: The opening ceremony for the New Royals Stadium on April 10, 1973, took place under lights before the first game—between the Royals and the Texas Rangers. The game was a sellout, but temperatures in the 30s kept the crowd down. *Bettmann/Corbis*

Overleaf, left: View of the playing field of the Royals Stadium during game between Kansas City and the Minnesota Twins in May 1973. *Bettmann/Corbis*

Kauffman Stadium.
National Baseball Hall of Fame

Far left: General view of action during a game between the Red Sox and the Royals at Royals Stadium. *Getty Images*

Left: The Truman Sports Complex comprises the Royals Stadium (lower) and Arrowhead Stadium, home of the NFL Kansas City Chiefs. *National Baseball Hall of Fame*

Right: Night game at Royals Stadium. *National Baseball Hall of Fame*

Approaching from the West, one could drive hundreds of miles without seeing lights as bright as the standards atop the stadium, which draw insects from acres around.

Yet it is orthodox baseball they worship inside, as devout as anywhere else. At a time when other cities were building multi-sports complexes, the Royals was the only franchise to build a baseball-only stadium during the 60s, 70s, and 80s. The site lines and seats all point toward the action. Grass replaced artificial turf in 1995, the fences were moved in, and the walls lowered.

Known for most of its life as Royals Stadium, it was renamed in honor of Ewing M. Kauffman who purchased the expansion team for Kansas City in 1968. If you want to date a color photo of Kauffman Stadium look at the seats. By the end of 2000, all of the red seats had been replaced by new blue ones. Intentionally located at the junction of I-70 and I-435, passersby can catch glimpses inside the park as they drive by.

If there is any monument to the era in which it was built, it is the 12-story high scoreboard, containing 16,320 lights, with a huge Royals crown on top, a Midwest version of Anaheim's Big A. The park's signature feature is a 322-foot wide water fountain spectacular—the largest privately funded waterworks in the world—which occupies the space that bleachers normally would, offering water-filled entertainment between innings.

LOS ANGELES, CALIFORNIA

L.A. Wrigley Field

Status: Demolished in 1966

Location: Intersection of 42nd Place and Avalon Boulevard

Capacity: 22,000 (opening day); 20,457 (final)

Opening day: September 29, 1925

First MLB game: April 27, 1961

Last MLB game: October 1, 1961

Cost to construct: N/A

Architect: Zachary Taylor Davis

Dimensions (ft):

Left Field: 340

Left Center: 345

Center Field: 412

Right Center: 345

Right Field: 338.5

Defining feature: Designed to copy Wrigley Field, home of the Chicago Cubs, including an ivy-covered outfield wall.

World Series: none

All-Star Game: none

L.A. Memorial Coliseum

Status: Still in use, but not for baseball

Address: 3939 S. Figueroa Street, Los Angeles, CA 90037

Capacity (baseball): 93,000 (1958); 94,600 (1959-1961)

Opening day: October 6, 1923

First MLB game: April 18, 1958

Last MLB game: September 20, 1961

Cost to construct: $954,000

Architect: Donald and John Parkinson

Dimensions (ft)	Initial	Final
Left Field:	250	251.6
Left Center:	320	320
Center Field:	425	420
Right Center:	440	380
Right Field:	301	300

Defining feature: Built for football, was the largest stadium ever used for major league baseball. Tall screen fence in left field compensated for short distance.

World Series: 1959

All-Star Game: 1959

Dodger Stadium

Other names: Chavez Ravine (when used by Angels)

Status: Home of the Los Angeles Dodgers

Address: 1000 Elysian Park Avenue, Los Angeles, CA 90012

Capacity: 56,000

Opening day: April 10, 1962

Cost to construct: $23 million

Architect: Captain Emil Praeger

Dimensions (ft):	Initial	Current
Left Field:	330	330
Left Center:	380	385
Center Field:	410	395
Right Center:	380	385
Right Field:	330	330

Defining features: Beautifully landscaped and immaculately maintained. Stunning views of downtown, the Elysian Hills, and the San Gabriel Mountains

Most expensive seat: $75

Cheapest seat: $6

World Series: 1963, 1965, 1966, 1974, 1977, 1978,1981, 1988

All-Star Game: 1980

Several ballclubs have called Los Angeles their home over the years. The Pacific Coast League's Los Angeles Angels were based in the city between 1925 and 1957, and played their home games at L.A. Wrigley Field. This ballpark replaced the 15,000-seat Washington Park, which was in use between 1903 and 1925. The American League's California Angels had a brief stay at the former stadium, which had been named after the chewing gum magnate William Wrigley, playing their first game there on April 27, 1961, and their last the following October 1. Thereafter the team moved to the newly built Dodger Stadium (called Chavez Ravine by the Angels), where they remained until 1965. Thereafter the franchise moved to Orange County—eventually becoming Los Angeles Angels of Anaheim—leaving the Dodgers in sole occupancy of their eponymous stadium

The Los Angeles Dodgers, who have played in the National League's West Division since it was formed in 1969, came into existence in 1957. At that time, Brooklyn Dodgers' owner, Walter

Left: An aerial view of Dodger Stadium in 1996. *William Boyce/Corbis*

Below: *Washington Park around 1911. Library of Congress*

O'Malley, successfully negotiated to move his New York team to the West Coast and had also chosen, while flying in a helicopter, the 300-acre Chavez Ravine site for the ballclub's new stadium. The team moved west the following year and for the next three seasons, 1958-1961, the Dodgers played their home games at the 92,000-plus capacity L.A. Memorial Coliseum, a stadium originally built for football and later host to the 1932 Olympics, until the building work on Chavez Ravine was completed. The team won the 1959 World Series during their four-season stay at the Coliseum; they played their last game there on September 21, 1961.

The Chavez Ravine stadium finally opened on April 10 of the following year, when the Dodgers played there for the first time (against the Cincinnati Reds) in front of a 56,000-strong crowd. They continue to play their baseball there to the present day.

Between April 17, 1962, and September 22, 1965, the Dodgers shared the stadium with the Los Angeles/California Angels, but when the American Leaguers moved out the venue become more commonly known as Dodger Stadium. It is widely viewed as being extremely friendly toward pitchers—and very much less so to batters.

The westward migration of the Dodgers was a huge blow to New York, and the loss was compounded when the West Coast Dodgers won the 1959 World Series, beating the Chicago White Sox 4-2. Led by famed manager Walter Alston and pitching ace Sandy Koufax, the Dodgers soon added two more World Series titles to their rich legacy: In 1963 they defeated the New York Yankees 4-2 and in 1965 took a seven-game series from the Minnesota Twins.

The Dodgers remained a quality team, but failed in their next four opportunities to take baseball's championship. They were swept in 1966 by the Orioles, lost to the

229

Oakland A's 4-1 in 1974, and the Yankees avenged their 1963 defeat with identical 4-2 margins in both 1977 and 1978. The Dodgers returned to their winning ways in the World Series the following decade. Managed by Tommy Lasorda, they took two titles. The first came in 1981 after yet another six-game series against their old enemy, the Yankees. Seven years later the Dodgers took revenge on the Oakland A's for their mid-1970s defeat, notching a 4-1 series victory.

The Dodgers have enjoyed tremendous success since their move to Los Angeles. In addition to their nine World Series appearances since 1959, the team has logged five other playoff appearances—in 1983, 1985, 1995, 1996, and 2004. Given the Dodgers success on the field since 1959, it is hardly surprising that they have had some outstanding ball players on their roster. Several former Los Angeles Dodgers are now enshrined in the Hall of Fame. Among the notables are: Sandy Koufax, who holds the season records for most games won (27 in 1966) and most strikeouts (382 in 1965); outfielder Duke Snider; pitchers Don Drysdale and Don Sutton; and managers Walter Alston and Tommy Lasorda.

Right: Dodger Stadium December 28, 2000. *Mike King/Corbis*

Below: The interior of Adelanto, home of the High Desert Mavericks of the California League from 1991. Built in the Mojave Desert outside Los Angeles, it has a capacity of 3,808.

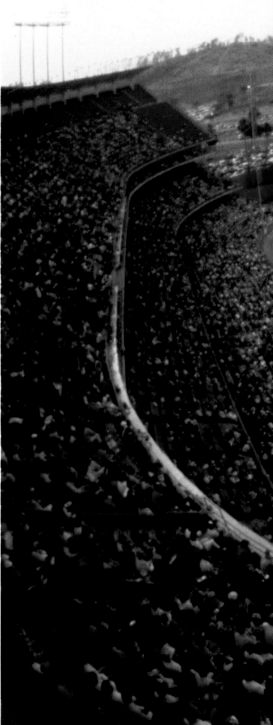

Left: The Dodgers' were a New York team, playing at Ebbets Field seen here during the 1956 World Series. Ebbets Field is arguably where baseball became the national pastime. For 45 years, the stadium between Brooklyn's Bedford and Flatbush neighborhoods defined what it meant to go the ballpark. From its brick arched exterior to its ornate domed rotunda, many of today's stadiums reflect its memory. Seats were close to the field. The outfield wall framed a uniquely shaped field. Its trademark Shaefer Beer billboard flashed an "H" for hits and an "E" for errors. Clothier Abe Stark invited players to hit his advertisement on the outfield fence for a free suit, something he never needed to pay up. It was here that Jackie Robinson broke the color barrier in 1947, where television broadcast its first game, where the Dodgers won nine pennants, and where owner Walter O'Malley broke Brooklyn's heart by taking his team to Los Angeles. In its final years, O'Malley complained that the stadium was falling apart, and he searched for a new home. He was not satisfied with the plot of land offered to him in Queens where the Mets would end up several years later. He left Brooklyn for the west after the 1957 season. See the New York section for further details. *National Baseball Hall of Fame*

Left: Dodger Stadium looks today much as it did when it opened in 1962. *National Baseball Hall of Fame*

Right: A postcard of the CalifornianWrigley Field.

This picture: L.A. Memorial Coliseum. *Getty Images*

Right: External view of the stadium, showing some of the 3,400 trees planted in the 300-acre site. Dodger Stadium has parking facilities for 16,000 automobiles. *Digitalballparks.com*

Far right: Fireworks go off during the national anthem before the game between the Los Angeles Dodgers and the Colorado Rockies on opening day at Dodger Stadium on April 9, 2007. *Getty Images*

MEMPHIS, TENNESSEE

Tim McCarver Stadium

Previous names: Blues Stadium;
Chicks Stadium

Status: Demolished in 2005

Location: Mid-South Fairgrounds,
next to the Liberty Bowl

Capacity: 8,800 (1999)

Opening day: 1963

Last game: 1999

Cost to construct: N/A

Architect: N/A

Dimensions (ft):

Left Field: 323

Left Center: N/A

Center Field: 398

Right Center: N/A

Right Field: 325

Defining features: The stadium had an
artificial turf infield and a grass outfield.
Renamed in 1978 to honor McCarver,
Memphis-born baseball player and sports
broadcaster.

Baseball in its amateur form came to Memphis in the 1860s, but things began to really develop with the advent of the Southern League in 1885. Memphis took the pennant in 1894. Fifteen years later the league crumbled and Memphis was without baseball until the creation of the Southern League in 1901. Memphis won that league's title in 1903 but thereafter the team, variously known as either the Egyptians or Turtles, was largely mediocre.

Memphis baseball improved in 1914 when a local businessman, Russell Gardner, purchased a controlling interest in the club, which he renamed the Chickasaws or "Chicks" after the Native American tribe. Gardner left the day-to-day running of the club in the hands of his son-in-law Thomas Watkins and success finally came in 1921. The capacity of their home ballpark, Russwood Park was doubled to 11,500 and the fans saw the Chicks win the league by the wide margin. Watkins remained at the helm until 1940, then sold his controlling interest in the club and retired from baseball

The Chicks became a farm club for the Chicago White Sox the following year, but the latter pulled out of the relationship in 1956. The team remained in the Southern League until the league was disbanded after 1961. Ironically the Chicks' Russwood Stadium had burned down in April 1960 and, following the league's demise, Memphis was to be without a baseball team until the arrival of what had been a Texas League franchise in 1968. The Memphis Blues, who played at Tim McCarver Stadium, were born as a farm club for the New York Mets but they only stayed until 1973, although they did win the Texas League Chmpionship in 1969. The Memphis Chicks returned in 1978 and won the Southern League in 1990. In 1998 the city joined the Pacific Coast League as the Memphis Redbirds, the affiliate of the St. Louis Cardinals. The Redbirds spent just that one season playing at the Tim McCarver Stadium and moved into the state-of-the-art but retro-looking Autozone Park for the 2000 season and promptly won the Pacific Coast League.

Right: The New York Giants seen at Memphis on April 6, 1922. The photo shows the bleachers—then a segregated area. *Bettmann/Corbis*

MIAMI, FLORIDA

Dolphins Stadium

Previous names: Joe Robbie Stadium;
Pro Player Stadium

Status: Home of the Florida Marlins

Address: 2269 NW 199th Street, Miami, FL

Capacity: 47,662 (baseball, opening day);
42,531 (current)

Opening day: August 16, 1987

First MLB game: April 5, 1993

Cost to construct: $115 million;
$10 million (renovations)

Architect: HOK Sport

Dimensions (ft):	Initial	Current
Left Field:	335	330
Left Center:	363	357
Center Field:	410	404
Right Center:	373	373
Right Field:	345	345

Defining features: Double-deck stadium,
with upper deck usually closed for baseball.
Left field wall nicknamed "The Teal
Monster."

Most expensive seat: $85

Cheapest seat: $8

World Series: 1997, 2003

All-Star Game: none

A major league franchise didn't arrive in Miami until 1993, but south Florida has a long baseball history. The first minor league team to call the city home was the Class D Miami Hustlers, which played in 1927 and 1928. Next up came the Miami Wahoos (or Seminoles), which competed in Class D from 1940 to 1942.

The arrival of the Miami Sun Sox in 1949, an affiliate of the Brooklyn Dodgers, improved the city's baseball fortunes. Sun Sox owner Manual Alemau built a new ballpark, Miami Stadium, which also opened in 1949. The stadium was large, with a capacity of nearly 14,000, and quite distinctive. The single-level grandstand was topped with a curving white roof that arched over most of the seats. In addition to minor league ball, the stadium was used for spring training and exhibition games—first by Dodgers, and later by the Baltimore Orioles, who occupied the ballpark until 1990. Abandoned and derelict, it was torn down in 2001. Late in its history, Miami Stadium was renamed Bobby Maduro Stadium to honor the "Father of Cuban Baseball" and a legendary player and team owner in his home country.

The Sun Sox had one of the greatest teams in minor league history in 1952, but disbanded just two years later. For five years starting in 1956 a Class AAA team called the Miami Marlins played in the International League, then another Marlins—this time in Class A—started playing in Miami Stadium in 1962. Over the years these Marlins were affiliated with the Phillies and the Orioles. The team was eventually renamed the Miracle, moved out of Bobby Maduro Stadium, and in 1992 moved to Fort Meyers.

Miami won a hard-fought battle for a major league expansion franchise in 1991 and the Florida Marlins debuted on April 5, 1993, by defeating the Dodgers in front a sellout crowd at Joe Robbie Stadium. From that start the team has gone on an amazing roller-coaster ride, achieving both stunning highs and unfortunate lows—low enough that MLB probably regrets awarding the franchise to south Florida.

Many of the team's problems have revolved around stadium issues, even though the Marlins have played all their home games in a relatively new facility now known as Dolphins Stadium. Opened in 1987 for the city's NFL team, and first named for then-owner of the Dolphins Joe Robbie, the football-oriented stadium was built with accommodating baseball in mind. After Robbie's death, Wayne Huizenga bought the Dolphins and a half share in the stadium, in 1990, and started renovations to even better suit the facility to baseball. His efforts paid off and he soon had the Marlins playing in the stadium.

Dolphins Stadium is large—most argue too big for baseball—and located far from downtown, but it is colorful, comfortable, and a decent place to watch a game. The outfield has a quirky wall contour and a tall blue-green left field fence nicknamed "The Teal Monster." Sadly, Miami fans have never embraced the team, and most blame the isolated, open-air stadium, which exposes fans to the region's hot and rainy climate.

Huizenga, a legendary businessman, knew there were problems from the start, so he invested in top players with the hope of winning quickly to generating interest from a new buyer. He got his wish when the 1997 Marlins reached the playoffs as a wild card team and went on to take the World Series from the Indians. Huizenga then embarrassed MLB by dismantling the team and slashing payroll; the 1998 Marlins won only 54 games—but his strategy paid off when John Henry bought the franchise in January 1999.

For a time Henry worked to get a new stadium for the Marlins. In addition to its weaknesses for baseball, the Marlins lease was set to expire in 2010 and Huizenga wanted MLB out of his football stadium. With no progress and a deteriorating financial situation, MLB stepped in to help resolve what was quickly becoming a major headache. In 2002 the league worked out an agreement for Henry to sell the Marlins to Jeffrey Loria and purchase a majority stake in the Boston Red Sox. Loria seemed confident that he could both field a good team and get himself a new stadium. He succeeded on one of those goals when the Marlins amazingly won their second World Series in 2003, defeating the Yankees 4-2.

The team stayed competitive for two more seasons, but attendance remained mediocre and Loria admitted that he was losing considerable money. In late 2005 stadium talks seemed to break down for good, and MLB gave Loria permission to relocate the team. Portland and Las Vegas were viewed as the top candidates, though Marlins fans held out hope that this development might encourage Miami to get serious about a new ballpark.

Above: Miami's Maduro Stadium.

Above and Below: Two postcards of Miami Stadium.

Left: This photograph shows the San Diego Padres game against the Florida Marlins at Dolphin Stadium on May 6, 2007. The Padres won 3–1. *Doug Benc/Getty Images*

Far left: A general view of Dolphin Stadium taken before the game between the Philadelphia Phillies and Florida Marlins at Dolphin Stadium on April 6, 2007. *Doug Benc/Getty Images*

MILWAUKEE, WISCONSIN

County Stadium

Status: Demolished in 2001

Location: Adjacent to Miller Park

Capacity: 36,011 (opening day);
53,192 (final)

Opening day: April 6, 1953

Last MLB game: September 28, 2000

Cost to construct: $5 million

Architect: Osborn Engineering

Dimensions (ft): Initial   Final

Left Field: 320   315

Left Center: 376   377

Center Field: 377   377

Right Center: 355   362

Right Field: 320   315

Defining feature: Bernie Brewer (mascot) chalet, slide, and beer mug behind center field bleachers. First "suburban-style" stadium, built surrounded by parking lots.

World Series: 1957, 1958, 1982

All-Star Game: 1955, 1975

Milwaukee gained one of the original American League franchises in 1901 in the form of the original Brewers, who briefly played at the city's small Lloyd Street Grounds. After finishing last in the new league's first season, they moved to Missouri and became the St. Louis Browns. Milwaukee then suffered through a half century without major league baseball.

Finally, the National League's Boston Braves migrated west for the 1953 season and became the Milwaukee Braves. The team played its first game (an exhibition against the Red Sox) in Milwaukee on April 6 of that year in brand-new County Stadium, the first new ballpark opened in the second

Below: Milwaukee County Stadium. *National Baseball Hall of Fame*

Miller Park

Address: One Brewers Way
Milwaukee, WI 53214

Capacity: 42,400

Opening Day: April 6, 2001—Milwaukee Brewers 5, Cincinnati Reds 4

Cost to construct: $400 million

Architect: HKS, Inc. (Dallas), NBBJ (L.A.), Eppstein Uhen Architects (Milwaukee)

Dimensions (ft):

Left Field: 344   Left Center: 370

Center Field: 400   Right Center: 374

Right Field: 345

Defining feature: Bernie Brewer

Most expensive seat: $75

Cheapest seat: $1

World Series: None

All-Star Game: 2002

Memorable moments:

2001 April 6—President Bush throws out the ceremonial first pitch, and the Brewers rally behind Richie Sexson's eighth-inning home run to beat the Cincinnati Reds in Miller Park's debut.

2002 May 23—Dodger outfielder Shawn Green hits four home runs, seven RBI, scores six runs and sets a major-league record with 19 total bases.

half of the 20th century. Milwaukee had started building the stadium in 1950 with the goal of attracting a major league team, and the plan succeeded.

Also in 1953, the NFL's Green Bay Packers—headquartered then, as today, in the league's smallest city, 120 miles north of Milwaukee—started playing some of their "home" games at County Stadium. Their goal was to build fan support in the state's largest city. With attendance soaring for both baseball and football, additional grandstands were double-decked for the

1954 season, pushing capacity to more than 43,000.

After the Braves' glory years of 1957 (including a World Series victory over the Yankees) and 1958, attendance waned and the team started studying a move to Atlanta. The Braves played their final game at County Stadium on October 3, 1965, and moved south. Milwaukee was stunned; serious baseball fans in the city still sting from this slight four decades later.

Despite their short time in Milwaukee, six future Hall of Famers played for the

team during the era, including three stars who played for most of the team's Milwaukee history—outfielder Hank Aaron, third baseman Eddie Mathews, and lefty pitcher Warren Spahn. The other three Cooperstown inductees spent shorter periods with the Braves: Red Schoendist, Enos Slaughter, and Phil Niekro. In 1957 Spahn won the Cy Young Award, Aaron was voted Most Valuable Player, and pitcher Lew Burdette was the World Series MVP. Milwaukee Braves pitchers also tossed four no hitters: Spahn in 1960 and 1961,

Above: A view of a game during the 1958 World Series at Milwaukee County Stadium. *Time & Life Pictures/Getty Images*

Burdette in 1960, and Jim Wilson in 1960.

It took only five years after the Braves' departure for major league baseball to return to the city. The Milwaukee Brewers emerged on April 1, 1970, when a consortium of businessmen led by a local automobile dealer, Bud Selig (currently the commissioner of MLB), bought the Seattle Pilots. The team was in the middle of spring training, preparing for only its second season, and had just six days to switch cities and change its identity. The new Brewers name seemed an obvious choice in a city that is sometimes called the "Beer City." The team first played in the American League's West Division, transferred to the East Division in 1972. It remained there until 1994, when the team joined the newly formed Central Division. When MLB expanded and realigned for the 1998 season, the Brewers voluntarily switched to the National League's Central Division and remain there to this day.

The Brewers played their first game at County Stadium on April 7, 1970, losing to the California Angels 12-0. The Brewers record over the three decades they occupied County Stadium was far from great. The lone exception was the 1982 team, which captured the pennant from the California Angels 3-2, before losing an exciting seven-game World Series to the Cardinals. Four of the stars from that AL Championship team have been inducted in the Hall of Fame: pitchers Rollie Fingers and Don Sutton (both relatively short-term Brewers), and infielders Robert Yount and Paul Molitor. The latter two were Brewer stalwarts for many years, and both men were honored by the team by having their uniform numbers retired—19 in the case of Yount and 4 for Molitor.

The Brewers left County Stadium after their last game on September 28, 2000, and moved next door into the modern Miller

Far right: Milwaukee Borchert.

Right: View of County Stadium from RF post during the game between the Chicago White Sox and Milwaukee Brewers, April 26, 1995. *Time & Life Pictures/Getty Images*

Below right: County Stadium from behind homeplate during introductions before game of White Sox Brewers game. *Time & Life Pictures/Getty Images*

Overleaf, left: A view of the entrance to Miller Park before the game between the Milwaukee Brewers and the Cincinnati Reds on May 17, 2003. The Brewers defeated the Reds 8–6. *Jonathan Daniel/Getty Images*

Overleaf, right: Milwaukee County Stadium from behind the right field foul post. *Milwaukee Journal/National Baseball Hall of Fame*

Park, which features a retractable roof. The team has yet to approach the success of the 1957-1958 Braves or the 1982 Brewers in their new stadium, but after the Selig family sold the franchise to Mark Attanasio in September 2004 fans started hoping for a brighter future.

Miller Park is the major leagues' latest retractable dome stadium, this one built in a unique fan shape, in which the 12,000-ton roof pivots around a point near home plate, covering more than 10 acres, and able to open and shut in just over 10 minutes.

The convertible structure not only means year-round climate control in a northern climate where April and September are pushing the baseball envelope, it also strikes

wonder in the upper Midwest cheeseheads, who shattered attendance records in the park's first year. During the opening season, fans stuck around after the game on nice summer nights to watch the roof close to the symphonic sounds of Johann Strauss' "Blue Danube Waltz."

The stadium took almost five years to build, opening a year late after a tragic crane accident in 1999 killed three steel workers, and added $100 million to the project's cost.

The roof stands more than 30 stories high at its peak, adding an imposing new landmark to Milwaukee's modest skyline. The Brewers claim on their internet site, rather oddly, that the stadium weighs the equivalent of 62.5 million bowling balls, and that it would take 4.66 billion baseballs to fill it top to bottom.

Architects boast that the roof's steel mirrors the bridges over the Menomonee River, though the height of the walls and the omnipresence of the dome has led fans to complain that it feels like an indoor stadium even when the roof is open.

Patrons in County Stadium got to watch the project from their seats, as it was built just beyond centerfield in what was a parking lot. It includes a manual scoreboard and seats close to the field in the vain of other recent parks. Brewer Hall of Famer Robin Yount helped design the park's dimensions, which includes a quirky outfield with unique slants and angles.

Outside is a classic brick facade, with statues of Yount and Hank Aaron.

The Brewers transplanted some of their most distinctive traditions from County Stadium, including Bernie Brewer, who used to slide down an enormous, several-story high slide into a beer stein, and now does the same onto a platform in left field. Humans dressed in sausage costumes race around the bases in the middle of the sixth inning. And huge parking lots facilitate Wisconsin's obsession with tailgate parties.

Outside, eight names have been immortalized on a "Walk of Fame," that encircles the ballpark plaza, including Aaron, Yount, Rollie Fingers, Cecil Cooper, Paul Molitor, Allan H. (Bud) Selig, Harry Dalton and Bob Uecker.

The stadium offers $1 "Ueker seats," named after the well known Brewer's broadcaster, obstructed by roof pivots and located in the upper deck terrace, but still one of the best deals in baseball.

Far left: Miller Park during the game between the Milwaukee Brewers and the Cincinnati Reds on May 17, 2003. The Brewers defeated the Reds 8–6. *Jonathan Daniel/Getty Images*

Left: Mascot Bernie Brewer of the Milwaukee Brewers looks on from "Bernie's Dugout" during the game against the Cincinnati Reds on May 17, 2003. *Jonathan Daniel/Getty Images*

MINNEAPOLIS, MINNESOTA

Metropolitan Stadium (Bloomington)

Status: Demolished 1985

Location: Current site of the Mall of America; a metal floor plaque in the mall marks the site of home plate.

Capacity: 18,200 (opening day); 45,919 (final)

Opening day: April 24, 1956

First MLB game: April 21, 1961

Last MLB game: September 30, 1981

Cost to construct: $8.5 million

Architect: Osborn Engineering

Dimensions (ft): Initial (MLB)		Final
Left Field:	329	343
Left Center (short):	365	360
Center Field:	412	402
Right Center (short):	365	370
Right Field:	329	330

Defining features: First ballpark built in a truly suburban area. Triple-decked stands behind the infield only.

World Series: 1965

All-Star Game: 1965

Hubert H. Humphrey Metrodome

Status: Current home of Minnesota Twins

Address: 501 Chicago Avenue, Minneapolis, MN 55415

Capacity: 45,423 (Twins official number; other sources disagree)

Opening day: April 3, 1982

Cost to construct: $68 million

Architect: Skidmore, Owings & Merrill

Dimensions (ft): Initial		Current
Left Field:	344	343
Left Center:	385	385
Center:	407	408
Right Center:	367	367
Right Field:	327	327

Defining features: Air-supported fiberglass fabric roof with snow-melting ducts to prevent a collapse. Right field wall—nicknamed the "Hefty Bag"—is 23 feet tall and covered in plastic.

Most expensive seat: $44

Cheapest seat: $6

World Series: 1987, 1991

All-Star Game: 1985

Right: An overview of the Hubert Humphrey Metrodome during a Minnesota Twins–Toronto Blue Jays game in 1998. An audience of 40,096 watched the Blue Jays defeat the Twins 6 to 4. *Joseph Sohm/Visions of America/Corbis*

Built on a plot of derelict farmland with the dream of bringing major-league baseball to Minneapolis, Metropolitan Stadium in Bloomington was opened in 1956. Upon completion it already had three tiers that stretched from third to first base, and was hailed as the best in the minor leagues.

The stadium's first team was the AA Minneapolis Millers. While only entertaining minor-league baseball, the Met had a capacity of 18,000 when it opened. Minneapolis dreamed of attracting a major league franchise, so in 1957 the capacity was raised to 21,000.

The next year the Washington Senators played an exhibition game at the Metropolitan; owner Calvin Griffith liked the area and announced the Senators would be relocating. In anticipation, the capacity was raised to 30,000, and in 1961, when the Senators finally moved in and were renamed the Minnesota Twins, another 10,000 seats were added.

The NFL came to Bloomington in 1961 in the form of the Minnesota Vikings. Within five years they had constructed a new grandstand that made the Metropolitan a 45,000-seat stadium in exchange for reduced rent. Baseball benefited and the Met hosted the 1965 All-Star game, won by the NL. Within the next 20 years the stadium began to show signs of wear and tear, and in 1982 both the Twins and the Vikings moved downtown to the Metrodome. Three years later the

Metropolitan Stadium was demolished and the gigantic Mall of America now occupies the site. True baseball fans eagerly seek out the metal plaque in the floor (found in the Camp Snoopy amusement park) that commemorates the location of home plate.

The Metrodome helped solved one of the Twins' problems caused by being located in Minnesota—it rendered cold (or even snowy) spring and fall weather harmless. Beyond that benefit, many Twins fans found little to like about the new dome. The first game was played in the stadium on April 3, 1982, and spectators quickly learned about one of its primary flaws—it's extremely loud. The new park also drew jeers for the turf used in its first few years, which made balls bounce like they were made from rubber. And the tall, plastic-covered right field wall (which hides a bank of retractable football seats) has long been the source of jokes—"Big Blue Baggy" and "Hefty Bag" are among it nicknames.

The Twins played in the American League's West Division from 1969 to 1993 and then moved to the Central Division in 1994. Though one of baseball's classic, cash-strapped "small market" teams, the Twins have enjoyed tremendous success since moving to Minneapolis. They have won seven division titles—1969, 1970, 1987, 1991, 2002, 2003, and 2004—and appeared in three World Series. They lost their first series, in 1965 to the Dodgers, but won their next two, taking seven-game sets

from the St. Louis Cardinals in 1987 and the Atlanta Braves in 1991.

Among history's top Twins are: Harmon Killebrew, who holds the record for most home runs hit in a season (49 in both 1964 and 1969) and carew (475); Rod Carew, with the highest batting average for a season (.388 in 1977) and career (.334); pitcher Jim Kaat, who holds both the most games won in a season (25 in 1966) and a career (189). Three Twins are in the Hall of Fame—Killebrew, Carew, and Kirby Puckett. Five players have had their numbers retired by the team. In addition to Killebrew (3), Carew (29), and Puckett (34), Tony Oliva (6) and Kent Hrbek (14) were also honored.

The recent history of the team has taken some odd twists. In the midst of playing

some of their best baseball, but dogged by weak attendance and financial problems, the Twins were targeted in 2001-2002 by MLB for elimination (along with the Montreal Expos). The players union fought to stop the action, and the Twins were safe for the time being. The team continued its winning ways during and after the crisis, and its ownership stepped up efforts to get a new stadium. In 2005, the Twins and Hennepin County came to an agreement for building a 42,000-seat, open-air, downtown ballpark. The $444 million stadium was supposed to be ready for the 2009 Twins opener.

Above: Drawing of Nicollet Park entrance.

Right: Minnesota Twins #32 Dave Winfield in action during his 3000th hit, September 14, 1993. *Time & Life Pictures/Getty Images*

Left: Sign at the Metrodome. *Richard Cummins/Corbis*

Above and Right: The dome of the Hubert H. Humphrey Metrodomeroof is an air-supported structure supported by positive air pressure. As these photos show, it can be deflated by outside causes—snow buildup, punctures, and once varying air pressure due to a severe storm. The fiberglass fabric is covered with Teflon—reputed to be the largest application of Teflon anywhere. *Bettmann/Corbis*

Left: The exterior of the Metrodome during the 1999 season. *MLB Photos via Getty Images*

Right: Metropolitan Stadium. *National Baseball Hall of Fame*

The Metrodome and downtown Minneapolis at night. *Richard Hamilton Smith/Corbis*

267

MONTREAL, QUEBEC, CANADA

Jarry Park

Other names: Parc Jarry

Status: Still standing, used as a professional tennis venue

Address: 285 Rue Faillon West, Montreal, Quebec

Capacity: 28,456 (MLB opening day)

Opening day: April 14, 1969

Last MLB game: September 26, 1976

Cost to construct: N/A

Architect: N/A

Dimensions (ft):	Initial	Final
Left Field:	340	340
Left Center:	368	368
Center:	415	420
Right Center:	368	368
Right Field:	340	340

Defining features: Plain, utilitarian stadium, entirely single-tiered. Built as temporary home for the Expos until a new facility was built.

World Series: none

All-Star Game: none

Olympic Stadium

Status: Still standing, not used by MLB

Address: 4549 Avenue Pierre de Coubertin, Montreal, Quebec H1V 3N7

Capacity: 43,739 (baseball)

Opening day: April 15,1977 (first Expos game)

Last MLB game: September 29, 2004

Cost to construct: $1 billion (Canadian)

Architect: Roger Taillibert

Dimensions (ft):

Left Field: 325

Left Center: 375

Center Field: 404

Right Center: 375

Right Field: 325

Defining feature: The 575-foot leaning towerused to retract the original roof is the world's tallest inclined structure.

World Series: none

All-Star Game: 1982

On September 29, 2004, the Montreal Expos played their final game at Olympic Stadium and then relocated to Washington, D.C. (becoming the Nationals), leaving Canada with just one remaining franchise, the Toronto Blue Jays. The Expos suffered through 35 mostly mediocre years in the National League East, but most people will only remember the team's bizarre final years. In 2002 MLB purchased the team with the express purpose of eliminating the franchise. A dispute with the players union prevented the league's plans, so they changed strategies. Starting in 2003 the team played some of its games in San Juan, Puerto Rico's, Hiram Bithorn Stadium, which drew bigger crowds than Montreal. Meanwhile, MLB started studying new, permanent locations for the team; Washington's selection was announced hours after the last Montreal game.

The Expos began their career in the majors by playing at outdoor Jarry Park from 1969 to 1976. This plain-but-serviceable stadium was built as a temporary venue for the team until a permanent stadium was constructed. In 1977 the Expos moved to Olympic Stadium, which had been tailor-made for the 1976 Montreal Summer Games, then modified for baseball. Olympic Stadium is generally regarded as one of the worst MLB stadiums in history, and it was continually plagued with problems. The stadium was supposed to feature a retractable roof—suspended from a 522-foot leaning tower that hovered overhead—when it hosted the Olympics, but the tower remained unfinished until 1988. The roof never functioned as promised. It remained closed after 1992, was removed for one season (1998), and then replaced with a permanently closed roof.

The Expos enjoyed little success over their three-and-a-half decades in Montreal. There were no World Series titles and they claimed just one division title, in 1994—fittingly, the year that the playoffs and World Series were called off thanks to the player's strike. The Expos seemed dogged by bad luck. In 1991, for example, they had to play a handful of their home games on the road after one of Olympic Stadium's 55-ton roof beams fell onto the playing field.

Though the Expos had little team

Right: A game at the crowded Montreal Stadium—also known as Delorimier Downs and Hector Racine Stadium—on February 8, 1934. *Getty Images*

success, they nevertheless had some talented players on their roster. The lone Hall of Famer who entered Cooperstown as an Expo is slugging catcher Gary Carter, who played for Montreal 1974-1984 and 1992. (Not surprisingly, he is probably best remembered for leading another team—the Mets—to the 1986 World Series victory over the Red Sox.) The Expos retired Carter's uniform number (8), an honor that they bestowed on just three other players— Rusty Staub (10), Andre Dawson (10), and Tim Raines (30). Another Hall of Famer, Tony Perez, played for the Expos 1977-1979, though he entered the Hall as a Cincinnati Red. Frank Robinson, one of the game's all-time greats, never played for the Expos but is permanently linked to the team by serving as its last manager.

Several other former Expos enjoyed noteworthy success. Slugger Vladimir Guerrero holds three team records: home runs in a season (44 in 2000), season batting average (.345), and career batting average (.322). Among Expo pitchers, Ross Grimsley holds the record for season wins (20 in 1978), Pedro Martinez has the season strikeout record (305 in 1997), and Steve Rogers is the career leader in both wins (158) and strikeouts (1,621).

Right: A game at Montreal Stadium in the 1950s.
Getty Images

Previous page, left: Biodome and Montreal Olympic Stadium in 1999. *Alan Schein Photography/Corbis*

Previous page, right: Montreal Stade Olympique interior 1989.

Below and Far left: Two views of the exterior of the Olympic Stadium. Built for 1976 Summer Olympics, the Montreal Expos played their first regular season game here in 1977. Aside from its cavernous interior, the building's most distinctive feature is its leaning tower. At just over 550 feet, it is the world's tallest inclined structure. *National Baseball Hall of Fame*

NASHVILLE, TENNESSEE

Herschel Greer Stadium

Status: Home of minor league
Nashville Sounds

Address: 534 Chestnut Street Nashville,
TN 37203

Capacity: 10,700

Opening day: 1978

Cost to construct: N/A

Architect: N/A

Dimensions (ft):

Left Field: 327

Left Center: 354

Center Field: 354

Right Center: 53

Right Field: 327

Defining feature: The stadium's scoreboard
is shaped like a guitar.

Most expensive seat: $10 (reserved)

Cheapest seat: $6 (general)

The city of Nashville has baseball roots going back to the late nineteenth century, when a team called the Americans became a founding member of the Southern League in 1885. The team underwent several name changes over the next 15 years or so—the Blues, Tigers, and Seraphs—but failed to win anything and second place was about the best the fans had to cheer. In 1901 a team from the city helped found the new Southern Association and would stay around for the next 61 years. The new club was known as the Volunteers, or "Vols" for short, after Tennessee's nickname the "Volunteer State." The Vols called Sulpher Dell Park, which was substantially remodeled in 1927, home.

The new team was good from the start, winning pennants in its first two seasons and in 1908 and 1916. Starting in 1938 the Vols were affiliated with the Brooklyn Dodgers, and two years later started a tremendous run of success. The 1940 championship team is recognized as one of the greatest in minor league history. They followed up with four straight playoff championships, the 1948 regular-season crown, and the 1949, 1950, and 1953 pennants. Sadly, Nashville lost baseball after the 1961 season when the Southern Association folded.

The city went without baseball for a year, and then had a one-year flirtation with the South Atlantic League in 1963. The new version of the Vols finished last in their only year of play. This city had no minor league team until 1978, when the Nasville Sounds joined the Southern League after it expanded from eight to ten clubs. The team moved into Herschel Greer Stadium, a facility named after a local businessman who had worked to bring baseball back to the city. In 1980-1981 the team, now affiliated with the New York Yankees, won the Larry MacPhail Trophy for the most outstanding minor league club. They took the 1980 regular season title with a 97-46 record, but lost the playoffs to Memphis. The Sounds remained with the Southern League until 1985, when they joined the Class AAA American Association. When this league split in 1997, they joined the Pacific Coast League, where they play their baseball today. The Sounds are currently the farm club for the Milwaukee Brewers.

NEW YORK, NEW YORK

Hilltop Park

Status: Demolished in 1914

Location: In Manhattan, west of Broadway between 165th and 168th streets; current site of Columbia-Presbyterian Medical Center

Capacity: 15,000 (seated)

Opening day: April 3, 1903

Last game: October 5, 1912

Cost to construct: $300,000

Architect: N/A

Dimensions (ft):

Left Field: 365

Left Center: N/A

Center Field: 542

Right Center: N/A

Right Field: 400

Defining feature: The official capacity could double because there was standing room for 15,000 in the outfield.

World Series: none

Polo Grounds (fourth version)

Status: Demolished in 1964

Location: Manhattan in area bounded by Harlem River, Eighth Avenue, Harlem River Drive, and West 159th Street. Site of Polo Grounds Towers apartments.

Capacity: 16,000 (opening day); 54,555 (final)

Opening day: June 28, 1911

Last MLB game: September 18, 1963

Cost to construct: $300,000

Architect: Osborn Engineering

Dimensions (ft):	Initial	Final
Left Field:	277	279
Left Center:	451	455
Center Field:	433	483
Right Center:	445	449
Right Field:	256	258

Defining features: Almost entirely closed (except center field) double-decked stadium. Overhanging left field deck (by 21 feet) made for easy home runs. Deep center field fence.

World Series: 1905, 1911, 1912, 1913, 1917, 1921, 1922, 1923, 1924, 1933, 1937, 1951, 1954

All-Star Game: 1934, 1942

Ebbets Field

Status: Demolished in 1960

Location: 55 Sullivan Place, site of Ebbets Field Apartments

Capacity: 18,000 (opening day); 31,000 (final)

Opening day: April 9, 1913

Last MLB game: September 24, 1957

Cost to construct: $750,000

Architect: Clarence Randall Van Buskirk

Dimensions (ft):	Initial	Final
Left Field:	419	351
Left Center:	423	351
Center Field:	450	389
Right Center:	350	344
Right Field:	350	297

Defining feature: A stunning 80-foot circular rotunda

World Series: 1916, 1920, 1941, 1947, 1949, 1952, 1953, 1955, 1956

All-Star Game: 1949

Yankee Stadium

Status: Home of the New York Yankees

Address: E. 161 Street and River Avenue, Bronx, NY 10451

Capacity: 58,000 (opening day); 57,545 (current);

Opening day: April 18, 1923

Cost to construct: $2.5 million (original); approx. $100 million (1974-76 rebuilding)

Architect: Osborn Engineering; Prager-Kavanaugh-Waterbury (renovations)

Dimensions (ft):	Initial	Current
Left Field:	281	318
Left Center:	460	399
Center Field:	490	408
Right Center:	429	370
Right Field:	295	314

Defining features: The 15-foot copper facade put up to decorate the stadium's third deck. Monument Park that original stood in fair territory in dead center, with statues and plaques honoring former players and managers.

Most expensive seat: $110

Cheapest seat: $12

World Series: 1923, 1926, 1927, 1928, 1932, 1936, 1937, 1938, 1939, 1941, 1942, 1943, 1947, 1949, 1950, 1951, 1952, 1953, 1955, 1956, 1957, 1958, 1960, 1961, 1962, 1963, 1964, 1976, 1977, 1978, 1981, 1996, 1998, 1999, 2000, 2001, 2003

All-Star Game: 1939, 1960, 1977

Left: Opening day for Brooklyn Stadium—that would become Ebbets Field. Rival teams line the diamond as the band plays and a procession nears the home plate where it will sing the national anthem. *National Baseball Hall of Fame*

Right: The Dodgers played their last game at Ebbets Field on September 24, 1947, before moving to the west coast. The stadium was demolished in 1960. *National Baseball Hall of Fame*

Shea Stadium

Status: Home of the New York Mets

Address: 123-01 Roosevelt Avenue, Flushing, NY 11368

Capacity: 55,601

Opening day: April 17, 1964

Cost to construct: $25.5 million

Architect: Praeger-Kavabaugh-Waterbury

Dimensions (ft):	Initial	Current
Left Field:	341	338
Left Center:	371	371
Center Field:	410	410
Right Center:	371	371
Right Field:	341	338

Defining features: The Mets Magic Top Hat behind center field fence has a red apple rising out of it when a Mets' player hits a homer. Noisiest outdoor ballpark because of nearby LaGuardia Airport.

Most expensive seat: $60

Cheapest seat: $5

World Series: 1969, 1973, 1986, 2000

All-Star Game: 1964

Manhattan Field & Harlem River in 1901. *Library of Congress*

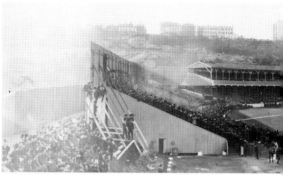

A general view of the stands at the Polo Grounds in the early 1900s. *MLB Photos via Getty Images*

If Cooperstown is the official home of baseball, then New York City must be its powerhouse. Although several teams have called the city home, the cream of the crop is undoubtedly the Yankees, currently of the American League's East Division. They began life as the Baltimore Orioles in 1901, moved to New York as the Highlanders in 1903, and emerged with their current name in 1913. As the Yankees, the team's record is unparalleled and simply awe inspiring. They have captured thirty-nine American League pennants, and been the World Series champions no fewer than 26 times—three times in the 1920s, four times in the 1930s,

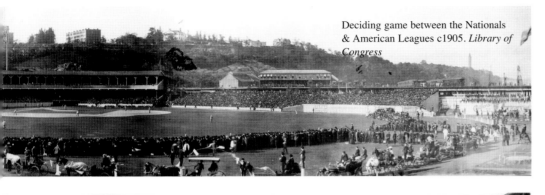

Deciding game between the Nationals & American Leagues c1905. *Library of Congress*

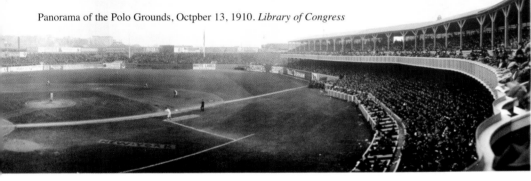

Panorama of the Polo Grounds, Octpber 13, 1910. *Library of Congress*

Polo Grounds, October 13, 1910. *Library of Congress*

Above: Players survey the damage to the Polo Grounds after the 1911 fire. *Library of Congress*

six times in the 1950s, twice in the 1960s, twice in the 1970s, three times in the 1990s, and their most recent victory in 2000. Fourteen of these wins were achieved under just two Hall of Fame managers, who were responsible for seven wins each, Joe McCarthy and Casey Stengel.

The team has had several homes in New York. As the American League Highlanders, they played for a decade or so at Hilltop Park, a quickly built facility with a single-deck, roofed grandstand. The park gave the team the nickname Hilltoppers, though as early as 1905 newspapers started referring to them as the Yankees. The Highlanders shared the ballpark with their bitter rivals, the New York Giants, after the latter's Polo Grounds burned down near the beginning of the 1911 season. After the Polo Grounds were rebuilt, the Giants returned the favor

Left: The Polo Grounds in 1887. *Getty Images*

Right: A game between Boaston and New York, 1910. *Library of Congress*

Above: A crowded Polo Grounds for the first game of the 1912 World Series. *Library of Congress*

Below: Standing room only for this 1911 game. *Library of Congress*

This picture: September 16, 1951: the Yankees play the Indians. Mickey Mantle is at bat; Bob Feller pitches with catcher Jim Hegan behind the plate. The Yankees outscored the Indians 6–1, putting themselves back into first place in the American League.
Bettmann/Corbis

Right and Far right:
Two views of the Polo Grounds, from center field; the color postcard dates from around 1940. *National Baseball Hall of Fame; Mark Rucker/Transcendental Graphics, Getty Images*

Polo Grounds, New York City, Home of the New York Giants.

Above left: The Polo Grounds during a 1912 World Series game between the New York Giants and the Boston Red Sox. The Red Sox won the series 4–3. *MLB Photos via Getty Images*

Left: Over 34,000 fans pack the Polo Grounds to watch the sixth and last game of the 1923 World Series. The Yankees defeated the Giants in their own stadium, 6 to 4, to win the series 4 to 2, October 15, 1923. *Bettmann/Corbis*

Above: The Polo Grounds in 1913. *Lake County Museum/Corbis*

starting in 1913, and the Yankees played there until 1923, when their Yankee Stadium opened.

Because of it age, and the team's great success, Yankee Stadium is more steeped in baseball history than any other ballpark, and when it opened it was impressive—and huge for its era. It was the first three-tiered ballpark and a 15-foot copper façade decorating the third deck became one of the stadium's signature features. Centerfield was enormous, and with deep left nicknamed "Death Valley" because of its distance from home. Starting in 1932, a number of monuments and plaques to former players and managers were erected—in play—in center, creating an area that became known as Monument Park.

And the Yankees had no shortage of great players. As their championship record indicates, the Yanks could probably create two full line-ups—with well-stocked bullpens—with the thirty-plus Hall of Famers that have played for them over the years. Among these are some of the game's truly legendary names, gifted ballplayers

such as Yogi Berra, Joe DiMaggio, Whitey Ford, Lou Gehrig, Mickey Mantle, and of course Babe Ruth (the stadium is sometimes called "The House That Ruth Built"). Two of the team's current stars, infielders Derek Jeter and Alex Rodriguez, are likely to join them.

In 1973, colorful current owner George Steinbrenner purchased the team, and he immediately embarked on a major renovation project on the stadium—one so extensive that it forced the Yankees to play their home games at the Mets' Shea Stadium during 1974 and 1975 (and which prompted the new nickname "The House That Steinbrenner Built"). Parts of Yankee Stadium were completely demolished and rebuilt, and posts and columns were

Above: The Polo Grounds in the early 1930s. *Getty Images*

Above right: Highlight of the charity baseball carnival staged by the New York Yankees, Giants and Brooklyn Dodgers at the Polo Grounds, on September 24, 1931, was the odd contests held by the diamond stars. Babe Ruth (above) established a new world's mark for fungo batting when he drove a ball 422 feet. This broke the mark of 419 feet made by Big Ed Walsh. *Bettmann/Corbis*

Right: Baseball superstar Willie Mays—then recently traded from the San Francisco Giants to the New York Mets for minor league pitcher Charlie Williams and $50,000 in cash—surveys Shea Stadium from the press box May 11, 1972. *Bettmann/Corbis*

Above: An exterior view
of Shea Stadium.
Digitalballparks.com

Left: The Shea playing
area from above the plate.
*Photofile/National
Baseball Hall of Fame*

Left: In an era of cookie-cutter parks, Shea Stadium was distinctive not for its architectural features, but for its location below the flight path of New York's La Guardia airport With an average of 1,000 flights a day, even the players sometimes wore earplugs.
National Baseball Hall of Fame

Right: Shea Stadium from the upper deck during the game between the Philadelphia Phillies and the New York Mets on July 13, 2003. The Mets won 4–3. The stadium had been designed to be expanded. However, when plans were drawn up to add seats but cover the stadium with a dome, they had to be scrapped because the engineers said the stadium could collapse under the weight. *Jerry Driendl/Getty Images*

Overleaf: Shea Stadium at dusk during the July 13, 2003 game between the Phillies and the Mets. *Jerry Driendl/Getty Images*

Above: A exterior view of Shea Stadium, circa 1960. *Getty Images*

removed to eliminate obstructed views, and new seats were installed. The aging facility needed the facelift—but in the process, many fans were disappointed by some of the changes. In particular, the removal of the distinctive copper façade on the upper deck,

and the relocation of Monument Park behind the outfield fence, drew the ire of Yankee purists. Nonetheless, the upgrade added at least three decades to the stadium's life, which sadly is about to end. The team has announced plans to build a new Yankee Stadium right next door, and it should be ready for play in April 2009.

For much of their history, the Yankees' great rivals were the New York Giants, who began life as the New York Gothams in 1883, but took their more famous name in 1885. By 1889 they had moved to Coogan's Bluff, where there were two ballparks. The northern one, Brotherhood Park, was confusingly the home to the New York

Giants of the Players League, while the southern one, the Polo Grounds, was home to the Giants of the National League. The former team went bankrupt and the surviving Giants moved into Brotherhood Park for the 1891 season, renaming it the Polo Grounds. It burned down in 1911 and the Giants shared Hilltop Park with the

Yankee Stadium during a game in the 1930s.
MLB Photos via Getty Images

Yankee Stadium, New York Cit

© 1923 by Irving Underhill

Above: Yankee Stadium 1923. *Lake County Museum/Corbis*

Yankees for a short while before moving back to the rebuilt version of the Polo Grounds.

This fourth edition of the Polo Grounds became one of the game's sacred ballparks. When it opened on June 28, 1911, the Polo Grounds were still under construction and only contained 16,000 seats; by the end of the season double-decked grandstands lined most of the playing field and the capacity was 34,000. Eventually the park looked from the outside like a giant horseshoe. Hitters loved the Polo Grounds because of its short measurements down the foul lines, with the overhanging left field upper deck especially susceptible to home runs. On the other hand, the distant center field fence was nearly unreachable at 450 feet. The park remained relatively unchanged right up until the day that the Giants departed for San Francisco in 1957.

The Giants couldn't match the Yankees' tally of trophies but while in New York they were still one of baseball's elite teams. They won the National League pennant fifteen seasons—six times between 1900 and 1920, four times in the 1920s, three times in the 1930s, and twice in the 1950s. The Giants went on to win the World Series five times, in 1905, 1921, 1922, 1933, and 1954. Among

Yankee Stadium. *Joseph Sohm/Visions of America/Corbis*

Right: Yankee Stadium as the bleachers fill with fans prior to the start of World Series game one between the Brooklyn Dodgers and the New York Yankees on September 30, 1947. *Olen Collection/ Diamond Images/Getty Images*

Far right: A panoramic view of the baseball diamond taken during a game between the Texas Rangers and the Yankees on April 12, 2000. The Yankees defeated the Rangers 8–6. *Al Bello/Allsport via Getty Images*

Left: Yankee Stadium during the Mets-Yankees game on June 27, 2003. The Yankees won 6-4. *Jerry Driendl/Getty Images*

Left and Far left: Two aerial views of Yankee Stadium. The first (left) was taken on September 9, 1928 and shows the Yankees playing the Phillies. The second photograph (far left) shows a 1960s view. *National Baseball Hall of Fame*

Overleaf, left: Another view of Yankee Stadium during the game against the Texas Rangers on April 12, 2000. *Al Bello/Allsport via Getty Images*

Overleaf, right: An exterior view of Yankee Stadium and its proud declaration of 26 World Championships. The structure in the shape of a baseball bat was erected in front of the stadium in 1976. For fans, it's a popular meeting point. Its real function is to serve as an exhaust chimney for the stadium's boilers. The design is modeled after a Louisville Slugger, just like that used by Yankee Sluggers to win those 26 World Championships. *National Baseball Hall of Fame*

their World Series losses, the four at the hands of the Yankees in 1923 (4-2), 1936 (4-2), 1937 (4-1), and 1951 (4-2)—were the most infuriating. The New York Giants also fielded a host of Hall of Famers at one time or another—21 in all, including legendary names such as Christy Matthewson, Carl Hubbell, Mel Ott, and Willie Mays.

The third team to call New York home was actually the first chronologically: the Brooklyn Dodgers, who began life in 1884 as the Trolley Dodgers. Baseball in

Brooklyn can be traced back as far as 1845, but when the first incarnation of Washington Park was opened in 1884 it soon became the sport's recognized home. Two more parks of the same name were built on the land where George Washington's Continental Army had fought the battle of Long Island, but in the six years between versions II and III, Brooklyn played baseball at Eastern Park. Their third stint in Washington Park would be their longest, and their last, playing in the National League. But soon the team was

bound for a new ballbark, Ebbets Field

Dodgers fans held great affection for Ebbets Field. On the opening day of its final season, overcrowding caused the police to arrive and the game was called off. Now all that remains of the old ground is one of the outfield walls that the Dodgers used to hit balls over. It runs along a regular street—so regular that most people who pass do not even know it used to be a ballpark.

Charles Ebbets, the Dodgers owner at the time of the stadium's construction,

Above left: Bob Feller pitching to Joe DiMaggio at a Cleveland–Yankee game in 1946. Feller pitched a no-hit game. *Bettmann/Corbis*

Above: Spectators leave Yankee Stadium after the first game of the World Series, October 5, 1949, following a bottom of the ninth inning home run from Tommy Henrich which won the game for the Yankees. The Yankees went on to win the series, defeating the Brooklyn Dodgers four games to one. *Getty Images*

eventually gained control of land on which a garbage dump stood, buying different sections from what was thought to be 40 different people. He set about transforming

Above: Lou Gehrig with Joe DiMaggio and Bill Dickey. *Bettmann/Corbis*

Above right: The Brooklyn Dodgers play the Cincinnati Reds during the 1939 season. *MLB Photos via Getty Images*

it into a new home for Brooklyn baseball. In April 1913, 25,000 fans packed his self-named ballpark to see the Dodgers beat the Yankees 3-2.

The stadium would become the site of many firsts. On August 26, 1939, the Dodgers played the Reds in the first ever televised baseball game. A year earlier Larry MacPhail had attempted to introduce yellow baseballs but, unlike the concept of live sports on television, they didn't catch on and were abandoned after just three games. In April 1947 Jackie Robinson became the first black man to play in the majors, and today the Brooklyn Dodgers Hall of Fame is housed at the school named after him, formerly known as Crown Heights.

Memorable moments would continue at Ebbets Field. In 1949 it hosted the All-Star game in which the AL came out victorious thanks to Yankee Joe DiMaggio. This was also the first All-Star game to feature black players. Though the team captured nine pennants over the years in Brooklyn, the only World Series the Dodgers won while playing at Ebbets Field was in 1955 when they narrowly beat the Yankees 4-3—avenging previous losing series to their Bronx rivals.

Walter O'Malley gained ownership of the club at the beginning of the 1950s and by 1957 he was lobbying for a new stadium, which the Borough of Brooklyn declined to fund. As a result, O'Malley made the decision to move the Dodgers to Los Angeles. They played their last game at Ebbets Field—and indeed in Brooklyn—on September 24, 1957, and the stadium was destroyed three years later, leaving fans devastated. The apartment blocks that now stand on the site still bear the Ebbets Field name, though they were reportedly renamed after Jackie Robinson in 1972, the year of his death.

The only other major league team currently calling the city home is the New York Metropolitans or "Mets," who have been around since 1962 and have been playing in the National League's Eastern Division since 1969. They entered the league as an expansion team in 1962 and played at the old Polo Grounds. Even though managed by the legendary Casey Stengel, the Mets were easily one of the worst teams in the history of baseball. The Mets made their swansong at the Polo Grounds on September 18, 1963, and transferred to the new Shea Stadium in 1964.

Shea was a showpiece in its day, with five tiers of seats—all pointed to the center of the field—and moveable stands that would allow easy conversion for football. Elaborate plans were unveiled to add a dome, but engineering studies ruled out the conversions. In fact, the park has changed little over the years, and has remained a good place to watch a game, with one drawback—noise. Busy LaGuardia Airport and brings in a steady stream of howling jets throughout every game.

As bad as the Mets were at the beginning, they turned things around in a big way in 1969. That year, the "Miracle Mets" came from far behind to catch the Cubs late in the season, knocked off the Braves in the playoffs, then stunned the favored Baltimore Orioles in the World Series 4-1. The team returned to baseball's championship in 1973, 1986, and 2000. In 1986 they defeated the Red Sox in seven games, but they lost crosstown series to the Yankees in 1973 and 2000.

Dyckman Oval

Like Rickwood Field in Birmingham, Dyckman Oval was instrumental in helping develop Negro League baseball in the 1920s and 1930s. Originally named after the wealthy Dyckman family, the 4,500-seat park also housed motorcycle races and even wrestling as well as giving Negro players the chance to play pro ball.

One of the teams that played at the Oval was the New York Cuban Stars, named after the origins of their owner, Alejandro Pompez, who had alleged links to organized crime. He was in charge for the duration of the Negro National League, and was also NNL Vice-Chairman. The Cubans played in the Eastern Colored League, and were considered formidable opponents throughout the 1910s. When the ECL folded in 1928 they went on to play in the American Negro League, and later as an independent team. In 1930 Pompez added floodlights to the Oval, but four years later the team vacated the ballpark to play at the Polo Grounds, and became a farm team to the New York Giants after the end of the Negro Leagues. Now an apartment block stands on the site of the ballpark.

Right: Ebbets Field, a classic fireproof stadium. *MLB Photos via Getty Images*

Below: An aerial view showing the Brooklyn Dodgers playing the St. Louis Cardinals at Ebbets Field on January 1, 1939. *Time & Life Pictures/Getty Images*

Above: Ebbets Field during the first inning of the second World Series game October 5, 1956. *Bettmann/Corbis*

Right: Babe Ruth sits wrapped in a blanket in the dugout at Ebbets Field prior to an exhibition game with the Brooklyn Dodgers.

Left: Buffalo Bisons and Brooklyn Tip Tops between 1908 and 1925. *Library of Congress*

NEWARK, NEW JERSEY

Ruppert Stadium

Previous names: Davids Stadium;
Newark Ballpark; Bears Stadium

Status: Demolished in 1967

Opening Day: 1926

Last game: 1949

Capacity: 19,000

Cost to construct: $500,000

Architect: N/A

Dimensions (ft):

Left Field: 305

Left Center: N/A

Center Field: 410

Right Center: N/A

Right Field: 305

Defining feature: The stadium was built
next to a garbage dump and games were
sometimes delayed because of smoke from
burning garbage.

Newark was never home to a major league team, but during the first half of the 20th century, the New Jersey city was home to two of history's greatest baseball teams. Minor league baseball came to Newark in 1902 when the Newark Indians were formed as charter members of the Class AAA Eastern (later International) League. The team changed its name to the Bears in 1917, went through some rough years, and then was forced to moved to Providence, Rhode Island, in 1925. Charles Davids rescued the team and brought it back to Newark for the 1926 season. He built the team a new stadium in the Meadowlands that he named after himself, but he went broke and lost the team two years later.

In 1931 the team was purchased by legendary New York Yankees owner Colonel Jacob Ruppert. The Bears became a farm club and training ground for many future Yankee stars. In addition, Newark's ballbark, Davids Stadium, was renamed Ruppert Stadium. The 1937 Bears were a powerhouse, winning the pennant by 25-1/2 games; the team is considered by many to be the greatest minor league team of all time.

The Bears shared Ruppert Stadium with another legendary team—the Newark Eagles—between 1936 and 1948. The Negro League Eagles were the brainchild Effa Manley, the first woman to own and operate a professional baseball team, and wife to a successful Newark businessman, Abe, who financed the purchase. The team was established in Brooklyn during 1935 and took its name from a local newspaper. The Eagles briefly played at the Brooklyn Dodgers' Ebbets Field, but in 1936 Manley purchased the Newark Dodgers' franchise and moved the Eagles to New Jersey.

The team fielded some outstanding players during its thirteen seasons in the league, including future Hall of Famers Ray Dandridge, Leon Day, Larry Doby, Monte Irvin, and Willie Wells. The team's crowning moment came in 1946 when they took the Negro World Series, beating the Kansas City Monarchs in a seven-game series. Many of their best players, including Doby and Irvin, had just returned from military service in World War II.

However, the writing was on the wall for the Negro National League by the late 1940s. The color bar to the major leagues was fast disappearing and the team's best players were increasingly being poached by the majors—without compensation, much to the Manleys' frustration. Doby was the first African-American to break through the American League color barrier when he joined the Cleveland Indians. Monte Irvin followed Doby into the majors, leaving the Eagles for the New York Giants. The Manley's could see the writing on the wall and made the decision to fold the team in 1948.

The Newark Bears, meanwhile, departed Ruppert Stadium shortly after the Eagles. After the 1950 campaign, the Bears were sold to the Chicago Cubs, which decided to move the team to Springfield, Massachussetts. Left without a tenant, Ruppert Stadium was eventually demolished in 1967. The Newark Bears were revived in 1998 as part of the independent Atlantic League, playing their games in the new Bears & Eagles Riverfront Stadium.

OAKLAND, CALIFORNIA

McAfee Coliseum

Previous Names: Oakland Coliseum;
Oakland-Alameda County Coliseum;
UMAX Coliseum; Network Associates
Coliseum

Status: Current home of the Oakland As

Address: 7000 Coliseum Way, Oakland,
CA 94621

Capacity: 50,000 (opening day);
48,219 (current)

Opening day: April 17, 1968

Cost to construct: $25.5 million;
$200 million (renovations)

Architect: Skidmore, Owings & Merrill

Dimensions (ft):	Initial	Current
Left Field:	330	330
Left Center:	378	375
Center Field:	410	400
Right Center:	378	375
Right Field:	330	330

Defining features: Mostly three-tiered
stadium dominated by a massive center
field grandstand added for football.
Pitcher's park with large foul territory.

Most expensive seat: $36

Cheapest seat: $9

World Series: 1972, 1973, 1974, 1988,
1989, 1990

All-Star Game: 1987

The major league franchise now known as the Oakland Athletics—or the "As"—has made westward migration over its 100-plus years of existence. The club, first known as the Philadelphia Athletics, was a founding member of the American League. The team stayed in Philadelphia from 1901 to 1954 and then were sold and moved west to Missouri to become the Kansas City Athletics. In 1960 the team was sold again, this time to the flamboyant Charlie Finley, who initially tried to move the team to Dallas-Fort Worth. The league turned him down but eventually allowed the team to move to California.

The Oakland Athletics made their debut in 1968 at Oakland Coliseum, which had been built with the hopes of attracting baseball and football teams. It was successful on both fronts, with the AFL's Oakland Raiders playing in the stadium starting in 1966. The first incarnation of the stadium was circular in shape and almost entirely surrounded by a three-tiered grandstand. The stadium was located adjacent to a freeway and partly sunken into the ground. The ballpark was first considered an adequate place to watch a game, but starting in the early 1970s was nicknamed "The Mausoleum," even when the team was exciting and winning a string of pennants. The Raiders abandoned the stadium and Oakland in 1981, moving to Los Angeles.

In 1995 the Raiders were lured back to Oakland, but it meant that changes were in store for what had become known as Oakland-Alameda County Coliseum. To add seats for football, the outfield bleachers were replaced with a four-tier grandstand. In addition, the $200 million renovation added luxury suites, two giant video boards, and other "amenities" that some baseball fans lamented. Construction also forced the As to play some of their 1996 home games in Las Vegas.

In addition to structural changes, the stadium became a poster child for identity crisis in the naming rights era. Initially renamed UMAX Coliseum in 1997 after UMAX Technologies bought the naming rights, a legal dispute led to the original name being restored a year later. The naming rights were sold again in 1998, to Network Associates, which gave its name to the stadium. When that company changed its name to McAfee in 2004, the coliseum followed suit to its current moniker.

Despite the changes with the stadium, and a long-time lack of financial muscle the As have filled the Oakland ballpark with some outstanding teams.

Their golden age was undoubtedly the early 1970s, when Oakland fielded one of the greatest teams in baseball history. The As dynasty captured three straight World Series: 1972 over the Cincinnati Reds (4-3), 1973 over the New York Mets (4-3), 1974 over the Los Angeles Dodgers (4-1). They bookended those world championships with additional AL West division titles in both 1971 and 1975.

The A disappeared off the radar screen for the next fifteen years or so, before fans enjoyed a revival of team fortunes between 1988 and 1990. The team again appeared in three straight World Series in that span, winning just once, a sweep of cross-bay rival San Francisco Giants in 1989. This was the memorable series that was disrupted by the devastating Bay Area earthquake that occurred right before the start of Game 3, forcing a twelve-day delay. When the series resumed, Bay Area fans understandably didn't have much interest in baseball.

A decade of underachievement followed but the turn of the new century saw signs of life in the team. The well-managed franchise became a model for other small market teams when it outsmarted richer teams to take division titles in 2000, 2002, and 2003—but, much to their fans obvious disappointment another World Series has eluded the team.

A number of Hall of Famers have played in Oakland at one time or another, but four Cooperstown inductees made their biggest marks while As: Dennis Eckersley, Rollie Fingers, Jim "Catfish" Hunter, and Reggie Jackson. Other leading players include Mark McGwire who holds both the records for most home runs in a season (52 in 1996) and most home runs in a career (363). The As pitcher who recorded the most wins in a season was Bob Welch (27 in 1990), while Catfish Hunter holds the career wins record of 131. Vida Blue recorded the season and career strikeout records—301 (in 1971) and 1,315, respectively.

Above: A wide shot of the Oakland-Alameda County Coliseum during the World Series on October 1972. *Focus on Sport/Getty Images*

Left: Oakland-Alameda County Coliseum. *National Baseball Hall of Fame*

OMAHA, NEBRASKA

Rosenblatt Stadium

Previous names: Omaha Municipal Stadium

Status: Used for minor league baseball and the College World Series

Address: 1202 Bert Murphy Avenue, Omaha, NE 68107

Capacity: 10,000 (opening day); 24,700 (current)

Opening day: April 25, 1949

Cost to construct: $770,000 (original) $35 million (renovations)

Architect: Leo A. Daly Co. (renovations)

Dimensions (ft)

Left Field: 332

Left Center: 375

Center Field: 408

Right Center: 375

Right Field: 332

Defining features: Pressbox/skybox addition behind home plate and above the grandstand. John Lajba's 1991 "Road to Omaha" sculpture outside the ballpark celebrates the College World Series.

Most expensive seat: $10

Cheapest seat: $6

Professional baseball has a long history in Nebraska's largest city, dating back to the 1879 Green Stockings. In 1949, the class A Cardinals moved in to the newly built Omaha Municipal Stadium, where they played until 1955. They were replaced by the St. Louis Cardinals top farmteam, which became the American Association's AAA Omaha Cardinals. The relationship did not last for long and the Cardinals moved out after the 1959 season. Baseball returned in 1961 when the Los Angeles Dodgers sent their AAA club out to Omaha but their stay lasted for two seasons.

The Omaha Municipal Stadium was renamed the Johnny Rosenblatt Stadium in 1964 to recognize the outstanding efforts of the former mayor who, among others, had worked so hard to bring the College World Series to the city. In fact, the College World Series gave Omaha the impetus to steadily increase the capacity of the city's stadium from an original 10,000 to the current total of more than 24,000, which makes it the largest minor league stadium in the U.S. Renovations have become a regular feature, with $7 million spent on Rosenblatt in 2002 alone. One change of particular note took place in 1994 when the old wooden pressbox was replaced with a new structure that also incorporated skyboxes. The attractive addition—which seems to hover over the grandstand on stilt-like girders—completely changed the look of the stadium.

Minor league baseball matters took a turn for the better in 1969 when the Kansas City Royals AAA baseball team moved to Omaha and, as the Omaha Royals, went on to nurture such talents as George Brett, Frank White, and Willie Wilson. The Royals briefly became the Omaha Golden Spikes in 1998 but reverted back to Royals by popular demand in time for the beginning of the 2002 season. The various Omaha teams have played in the Western League (1948-1954), the American Association (1955-1959, 1961-1962, and 1969-1997), and the Pacific Coast League from 1998 to the present.

Below: A College World Series game between Cal State Fullerton and USC at Rosenblatt Stadium in 1995. Cal State won the game, 11-5. *Getty Images*

PAWTUCKET, RHODE ISLAND

McCoy Stadium

Status: Used for minor league baseball

Address: Ben Mondor Way, Pawtucket, RI 02860

Capacity: 10,031

Opening day: June 6, 1946

Cost to construct: N/A

Architect: N/A

Dimensions (ft):

Left Field: 325

Left Center: 375

Center Field: 400

Right Center: 375

Right Field: 325

Defining feature: Dugouts are actually at ground level, built into the wall of the grandstand.

Most expensive seat: $9

Cheapest seat: $4

Pawtucket had been home to professional baseball since 1892 but only continuously since 1970. For much of the past, the town's association with minor league baseball has been sporadic and the early days saw various teams come and go, beginning with the Secrets of the New England League. They lasted just one season (1892) and were followed by the Maroons (1894-1895 and 1897-1899) and the very brief Phenoms (1896). Pawtucket did not see the return of baseball, albeit extremely briefly, until 1908 when the Colts arrived from the Class C Atlantic Association—but the team disbanded after just nine games. Next came the Rovers of the Class C Colonial League (1914) but they bowed out the following year.

The hiatus lasted for more than three decades until 1946, when the Class B New England League's Slaters made their debut and played at the then-recently built McCoy Stadium, which had been named in honor of Pawtucket's former mayor, Thomas P. McCoy. Pawtucket was again left without baseball in 1950, when the league folded. The Cleveland Indians came to the rescue, moving their AA Eastern League team to Pawtucket in 1966, but that team left after the 1967 season. Finally, baseball settled in Pawtucket for the long term in 1970 when McCoy Stadium became home to the Boston Red Sox's AA affiliate playing in the Eastern League. Three years later the Sox' AAA affiliate moved to the town and they have remained there ever since, playing in the International League.

It's been a bumpy ride over the years. The team won the Governor's Cup in their inaugural year, but went bankrupt in 1976. The team was saved thanks to the intervention of retired businessman Ben Mondor, who set about revitalizing both the club (the stadium was usually less than a third full when he took over) and McCoy Stadium. The ballpark is well liked by fans. The grandstand arcs elegantly around home plate, giving fans great views and keeping them very close to the action. In a twist on normal design, the dugouts are built into the grandstand at ground level. Renovations completed in 1999 added 3,000 new seats and a roof covering many of the existing seats.

In recent years the Pawtucket Red Sox have prospered. They took the International League East Pennant in 1991, 1994, and 1996, and the International League North title in 2003. They also won the Governor's Cup for the second time in 1984, defeating the Maine Guides 3-2. Two Hall of Famers have played for the team, Dennis Eckersley and Wade Boggs.

PHILADELPHIA, PENNSYLVANIA

Baker Bowl

Previous Names: National League Park, Huntingdon Street Baseball Grounds

Status: Demolished in 1950

Location: In area bounded by West Lehigh Avenue, North 15th Street, West Huntingdon Street, and North Broad Street

Capacity: 18,000 (early); 18,800 (final)

Opening day: May 2, 1895

Last MLB game: June 30, 1938

Cost to construct: $80,000

Dimensions (ft):	Initial	Final
Left Field:	335	341
Left Center:	N/A	
Center:		408
Right Center:	300	300
Right Field:	272	280

Defining features: Small dimensions of playing field, including short right field wall with a 40-foot-high fence. Called "The Hump" because it was built on ground raised over a railroad tunnel.

World Series: 1915

All-Star Game: none

Shibe Park

Previous name: Connie Mack Stadium

Status: Demolished in 1976

Location: Area bounded by West Somerset Street, North 21st Street, West Lehigh Avenue, and North 20th Street

Capacity: 23,000 (opening day), 33,608 (final)

Opening day: April 12, 1909

Last MLB game: October 1, 1970

Cost to construct: $300,000

Architect: William Steele and Sons

Dimensions (ft):	Initial	Final
Left Field:	378	334
Left Center:	409	362
Center:	481	410
Right Center:	368	356
Right Field:	360	329

Defining feature: The stadium's French Renaissance brick-and-arch facade and the Beaux Arts cupola/tower over the main entrance.

World Series: 1910, 1911, 1913, 1914, 1929, 1930, 1931, 1950

All-Star Game: 1943, 1952

Veterans Stadium

Status: Demolished in 2004

Location: Packer Street and Pattison Avenue, just off I-76

Capacity: 56,371 (opening day), 66,744 (1985)

Opening day: April 4, 1971

Last MLB game: September 28, 2003

Cost to construct: $50 milllion

Architects: Hugh Stubbins; George Ewing; Stonorov & Haws

Dimensions (ft):

Left Field: 330

Left Center: 371

Center Field: 408

Right Center: 371

Right Field: 330

Defining features: Largest seating capacity in the National League for most of its history. Poor quality artificial surface.

World Series: 1980, 1983, 1993

All-Star Game: 1976, 1996

Citizens Bank Park

Address: Pattison Avenue, Philadelphia

Capacity: 43,000

Opening Day: April 12, 2004. Cincinnati Reds 4, Philadelphia Phillies 1

Cost to construct: $346 million

Architect: Ewing Cole Cherry Brott (ECCB) and HOK

Dimensions (ft):

Left Field: 329

Left Center: 370

Center Field: 401

Right Center: 370

Right Field: 330

Defining feature: Electronic Liberty Bell set off by home run

Most expensive seat: $40

Cheapest seat: $15

Philadelphia has been home to several major league teams, most notably the American League Athletics, who were around from 1901 to 1954, and the National League Phillies, a franchise that has played in the city since 1883. The Athletics first played at Columbia Park, but under owner Ben Shibe they moved to Shibe Park, which was designed by manager Connie Mack, in 1909. Shibe Park was a showplace, especially on the outside, and at that point probably the most glorious ballpark in America. The park had a brick and stone French Renaissance-style façade, and a Beaux Arts tower over the main entrance. Inside, the field dimensions were initially huge (500 feet in center), but changes over time reduced these to more reasonable measurements. In 1925 the park changed dramatically when a left field grandstand was constructed, and all of the grandstands were double-decked. After 1940, the ballpark remained largely unchanged until it closed—except that the name was changed to Connie Mack Stadium to honor the Athletics long-time manager.

The Athletics had a fine record during their early years in Philadelphia. They won the AL Pennant no less than eight times by 1930, and went on to win the World Series in 1910, 1911, 1913, 1929, and 1930—all under Mack. Nine players and Mack himself

Left: Drawn by the prospect of seeing Lynwood (Schoolboy) Rowe shatter the American League record of sixteen straight wins, a crowd of 33,000 turned out for the doubleheader here between the Athletics and Detroit, and saw Rowe fail in his attempt as the teams split on the day's work. The Tigers won the first game, and fell before the shoots of Marcum in the second, with Rowe on the mound. This scene at the Park was snapped in the eighth inning of the first game Goslin scored, on Greenberg's hit, putting Bogel on second. Detroit won 12–7 in the first, and lost 13–5 in second. August 29, 1934. *Bettmann/Corbis*

Right: Entrance to Shibe Park, Philadelphia. *Library of Congress*

were inducted into the Hall of Fame. Mack never could get the team back to the series after 1930, and eventually retired in 1950 (at the age of 88!) with the still-standing career mark of wins by a skipper—3,776. The Mack-less Athletics moved to Kansas City after the 1953 season.

The Philadelphia Phillies have been in the National League, under one name or another, since 1883, when they were known as the Quakers. For much of their first 93 years, the Phillies were underachievers, managing just two pennants, in 1915 and 1950, and no World Series titles. The Phillies began play at the remodeled National League Park in 1895, later called Baker Bowl, built of concrete and steel and recognized as the first modern (and relatively fireproof) ballpark. The Baker Bowl was also noteworthy For its tiny right field, 279 feet down the line and only partly offset by a a tall wall (originally 40 feet, later expanded to about 53 feet). During the 1930s the stadium started to deteriorate and the Phillies abandoned it after the 1938 season in favor of sharing Shibe Park. After the Athletics moved west, the Phillies found themselves the sole tenants of Connie Mack Stadium.

By 1961 the Phillies, along with the NFL's Philadelphia Eagles, started lobbying for a new multipurpose stadium. It took a decade to finally complete the huge Veterans Stadium, which ultimately came to viewed as one of the worst stadiums in baseball. In particular, players groused about the terrible Astroturf on

Left and Right: Shibe Park. *Both National Baseball Hall of Fame*

Far right, above: Members of the Washington Senators stand in the dugout as they wait for the start of the first game of the season against the Philadelphia Athletics, April 14, 1931. At left, team manager Walter Johnson (1887–1946) squats down with a bat in his hands. The Senators lost the game 5–3. *Getty Images*

Far right, below: A postcard showing the stands and interior of the Baker Bowl.

the field, which was notorious for its uneven surface and bad bounces. Despite these drawbacks, Veterans seemed to offer exactly the change of scenery the Phillies needed to improve their play.

Starting in 1976 the Phillies won the East Division three straight years, and later added four more division titles—in 1980, 1981, 1983, and 1993. Over that stretch the team played in the 1980, 1983, and 1993 World Series, winning only the first, defeating the Royals in six games. As the 1990s progressed, the Phillies fortunes sank and Veterans Park started to show its age; plans for a new venue emerged. The Phillies played their first game at their new retro-style stadium, Citizens Bank Park, in April 2004, with most fans agreeing that it was a big improvement over Veterans Stadium.

Right: Veterans Stadium in 1989. *Joseph Sohm/Visions of America/Corbis*

Below: The Philadelphia Phillies play the Houston Astros at Philadelphia's Veteran's Stadium, to a crowd of 46,000 on September 12, 1993.

Philadelphia has had the best of ballparks, and the worst of ballparks. Now it has the newest. Citizens Bank Park, scheduled to open in time for the 2004 season, is Philadelphia's edition of a throwback park, said to mimic stately Shibe Park, which was opened before World War I, and Baker Bowl, where the Phillies began playing baseball in the time of Mark Twain.

It is located across the street from Veterans Stadium, the run down cookie-cutter arena where the Phillies spent the last 30 years. The new park was tilted 45 degrees clockwise, in order to frame a panorama of downtown Philadelphia over its center-field wall. It has a natural grass infield and dirt basepaths, as compared to the artificial turf and small sliding pits in the Vet. It contains 20,000 fewer seats, and a concourse that allows fans to watch the action while they are walking around. The seats behind the plate are 10 feet closer than at the old stadium, and about half the seats are located below the concourse.

The outfield was loosely modeled after Shibe Park, which was best remembered for its enormous French Renaissance facade. Red steel, brick, and stone give the exterior a classic feel, and its main entrances are framed by light standards for a grand approach. Rising 50 feet above first, home, and third are glass towers which are illuminated at night.

The field's distinctive shape, with a little lip in left field, is expected to create entertaining bounces. The architects conducted extensive wind studies, measuring ball trajectories and wind velocities which led them to conclude that Citizens Bank Park will be neither a hitter's nor a pitcher's park.

The center-field concession area is dedicated to Philly Hall of Famer and broadcaster Richie Ashburn. Greg "the Bull" Luzinski, who enjoyed many years of glory at the Vet, serves BBQ in Ashburn Alley, as Boog Powell does for Oriole fans at Baltimore's Camden Yards.

A statue of Connie Mack, the great Philadelphia A's player and manager has been brought over from the Vet. And inside the park, bronze statues honoring Phillies legends Mike Schmidt, Steve Carlton, Robin Roberts and Richie Ashburn celebrate the Phillies' past. A lot of emotional farewells were paid to the Vet in its final days, but the field at Citizens Bank Park was declared ready to go after the 2003 season amid high expectations

Left: The Vet's unique rounded rectangular shape has been the setting for two All-Star Games (1976, 1996) and three World Series (1980, 1983, and 1993).*National Baseball Hall of Fame*

Right: Philadelphia Phillies pitcher Randy Wolf delivers the first pitch to Cincinatti Reds D'Angelo Jiminez in the new Citizens Bank Ballpark, April 12, 2004. *Tim Shaffer/ Reuters/Corbis*

PHOENIX, ARIZONA

Bank One Ballpark

Address: 401 E. Jefferson Street, Phoenix, AZ 85004

Capacity: 49,033

Opening day: March 31, 1998—Colorado Rockies 9, Arizona Diamondbacks 2

Cost to construct: $354 million

Architect: Ellerbe Becket

Dimensions (ft):

Left Field: 330

Left Center: 374

Center: 407

Right Center: 374

Right Field: 334

Defining features: Right field swimming pool.

Most expensive seat: $60

Cheapest seat: $1

World Series: 2001

All-Star Game: None

Memorable moments:

2001 November 4—Luis Gonzalez hits a bases-loaded single to score Jay Bell, capping a two-run, ninth-inning comeback to beat the Yankees 3–2 in the seventh game of the World Series.

Bank One Ballpark is a monument to the power of air conditioning. The very qualities that make the Phoenix area such a popular destination for Cactus League games in the spring make it downright unbearable for baseball in the summer, when the average high temperature tops 100 degrees for three consecutive months.

The "BOB" cooled things down with 8,000 tons of air conditioning equipment, capable of creating enough cold air to chill 2,500 homes, and bring temperatures down by 30 degrees in three hours.

The unique retractable roof allows sunlight to shine on the natural turf, while keeping the oppressive desert heat from baking the grandstands. Nine million pounds of structural steel, using the same technology as a drawbridge, can open and close in less than five minutes, and can move into a variety of partially open positions.

With the climate under control, the BOB can focus on baseball. More than 80 percent of the seats are located between the foul poles, and there is no upper deck in the outfield. Natural turf and an old-fashioned dirt path connecting the pitchers mound to home plate, give the park more of a classic feel than might be expected under a dome.

The stadium is cluttered with advertisements, among other distractions. Its most unique feature is the swimming pool and hot tub located just beyond the right field fence about 415 feet from home plate, where bathing suit clad patrons can buys tickets for a swim and a unique outfield view. Chicago's Mark Grace was the first to plunk a ball into the pool in May of 1998, a feat that has since been duplicated dozens of times.

Outside, Bank One Ballpark more resembles an airplane hanger than a baseball stadium. The red brick and green structural steel are said by the architects to blend into Phoenix's surrounding warehouse district, but the huge baseball murals on the side give it the look of a basketball or hockey arena.

Inside, the Diamondbacks boast a quarter mile of concession stands, and enough entertainment to draw 3.6 million fans its opening year. The park hosted the World Series in only its fourth year, beating the Yankees in a dramatic, come-from-behind, ninth-inning rally in game seven.

Right: General Manager Jerry Colangelo of Arizona Diamondbacks throws the ceremonial first pitch before his team plays against the San Diego Padres during Opening Day at Bank One Ballpark April 1, 2002. The Diamondbacks won 2–0. *Donald Miralle/Getty Images*

Left: Entrance to Bank One Ballpark. The $354 million cost of the structure was split between the Diamondback owners (32 percent) and public funding that came from a quarter-cent sales tax in Maricopa County. *Allsport via Getty Images*

Far left: March 31, 1998: a view of batting practice before a game between the Diamondbacks and the Colorado Rockies at Bank One Ballpark. The Rockies defeated the Diamondbacks 9–2. *Allsport via Getty Images*

PITTSBURGH, PENNSYLVANIA

Exposition Park

Status: Demolished some time after 1915

Location: Between current sites of PNC Park and Heinz Field

Capacity: 16,000

Opening day: April 19, 1890. (Players League)

Last MLB game: Oct 2, 1915 (Federal League)

Cost to construct: N/A

Architect: N/A

Dimensions (ft):

Left Field: 400

Left Center: N/A

Center: 450

Right Center: N/A

Left Center: 400

Defining feature: Built along the Allegheny River and prone to flooding

World Series: 1903

Forbes Field

Status: Demolished in 1972

Location: University of Pittsburgh campus; Posvar Hall is on the former site of the infield

Capacity: 25,000 (opening day); 35,000 (1970)

Opening day: June 30, 1909

Last MLB game: June 28, 1971

Cost to construct: No reliable data available

Architect: Charles Leavitt Jr.

Dimensions (ft):	Initial	Final
Left Field:	360	365
Left Center:	390	395
Center:	422	435
Right Center:	390	380
Right Field:	376	300

Defining features: One of the first concrete and steel ballparks. Small third deck called "The Crow's Nest." Spacious, asymmetrical playing field.

World Series: 1909, 1925, 1927, 1960

All-Star Game: 1944, 1959

Three Rivers Stadium

Status: Demolished in 2001

Location: 600 Stadium Circle, Pittsburgh, PA

Capacity: 50,500 (opening day), 58,729 (1990)

Opening day: July 16, 1970

Last MLB game: October 1, 2000

Cost to construct: $55 million

Architect: Osborn Engineering, Deeter Ritchy Sipple, Michael Baker

Dimensions (ft):	Initial	Final
Left Field:	340	335
Left Center:	385	375
Center:	410	400
Right Center:	385	375
Right Field:	340	335

Defining features: Colorful seating. Inner fence to shrink outfield dimensions. Statues of Roberto Clemente and Honus Wagner outside the stadium.

World Series: 1971, 1979

All-Star Game: 1974, 1994

PNC Park

Address: 115 Federal Street

Pittsburgh, PA 15212

Capacity: 38,365

Opening day: April 9, 2001—Cincinnati Reds 8, Pittsburgh Pirates 2

Cost to construct: $262 million

Architect: HOK Sports

Dimensions (ft):

Left Field: 325   Left Center: 389

Center Field: 399   Right Center: 375

Right Field: 320

Defining feature: Roberto Clemente Bridge

Most expensive seat: $210

Cheapest seat: $9

World Series: None

All-Star Game: None

Memorable moments:

2001 June 27—Pirates Manager Lloyd McClendon steals first base, literally, after being ejected from the game for disputing a call at first base. Play is resumed after a replacement base is located and installed.

2001 July 28—Brian Giles hits a grand slam to cap a two-out, seven-run rally in the bottom of the ninth inning to beat the Astros 9–8.

2002 July 6—Houston's Daryle Ward becomes the first player to hit a home run into the Allegheny River over the park's right field wall, a shot estimated at 479 feet.

Washington Senators' outfielder Goose Goslin at bat against the Pittsburgh Pirates, during the 1925 World Series. *Bettmann/Corbis*

The Pittsburgh Pirates, a team with five World Series titles under their belt to date, have been around in one form or another since 1887, when they joined the National League as the Alleghenys. The played under that name until 1891, when they became the Pirates. When MLB created divisions, the "Bucs" (short for Buccaneers) played in the National League East from 1969 to 1993, and then joined the new Central Division in 1994.

The team's first significant home was Exposition Park (1891-1909), which was located on the north shore of the Allegheny River (which flooded the stadium several times) across from downtown. The ballpark had a covered single-tier grandstand extending from first to third base and uncovered bleachers the remaining distance down the foul lines. Additional fans frequently stood in right field.

In 1909 the Pirates moved to Forbes Field, built on a former ravine in Oakland, the city's cultural and educational center two miles from downtown. Following the lead of Philadelphia's Shibe Park, Forbes was constructed of concrete and steel. The stadium featured a three-tier grandstand behind the infield, and was one of the first ballparks to feature roof boxes. The Pirates must have liked their new home because that year they won the World Series for the first time by beating the Detroit Tigers in seven games. The Pirates enjoyed other successes while at Forbes Field, winning three more

Left: Exposition Park, August 23, 1904. *Library of Congress*

Below: Exterior of Forbes Field, c1909. *Library of Congress*

pennants—in 1925, 1927, and 1960—plus World Series titles in 1925 (beating the Washington Senators, also in seven games) and in 1960, when they defeated the New York Yankees in another seven-game series.

Forbes Field was expanded to 35,000 in 1925 and a new press box was built in 1938, but afterward the stadium did not change much. In 1958 the University of Pittsburgh bought the ballpark for the property on which it sat. The stadium started to crumble and Pittsburgh began construction on multipurpose Three Rivers Stadium. The last game was played at Forbes in June 1970, it was demolished the following year, and now its site is home to the university library and dormitories.

Three Rivers Stadium—built at the point where the Allegheny and Monongahela rivers joined to form the Ohio—seemed to do wonders for the Pirates and the 1970s was a decade of triumph. They were division champs six out of ten years, and World Series champs in 1971 and 1979, defeating the Baltimore Orioles in seven games both times. The stars of these two teams are both Hall of Famers: Outfielder Roberto Clemente (tragically killed in a 1972 plane crash) and Willie "Pops"

Left: View of the stands at Exposition Park during a 1903 World Series game between the Pittsburgh Pirates and the Boston Americans. The Americans won the series 5–3. *MLB Photos via Getty Images*

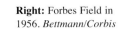

Right: Forbes Field in 1956. *Bettmann/Corbis*

Stargell, charismatic leader of 1979's "We Are Family" team.

Other than three straight division titles between 1990 and 1993, the Pirates have fared poorly in the last quarter century, a small-market team struggling to compete in a big-money sport. Three Rivers Stadium remained serviceable, but as a "cookie cutter" stadium it was not very charismatic and offered little to attract fans already losing interest in their mediocre team. The Pirates started asking for a new stadium to help improve their fortunes and in 2001 they got their wish. PNC Park—a retro-style stadium with great views of the Pittsburgh skyline—has much more appeal than Three Rivers, though with 38,365 seats is the second smallest venue in MLB.

At first glance, PNC Park looks like something out of a child's baseball fantasy. The outfield wall reveals sweeping views of the Allegheny River, the Depression-era Roberto Clemente bridge, river boats, and downtown Pittsburgh. The stadium's simple two-deck construction and limited seating make it perhaps the most intimate park in the major leagues. Old fashioned light standards add to the historic feel, while a huge scoreboard updates every game in baseball. Fans can arrive by riverboat, or by walking across the picturesque suspension bridge from downtown, which is closed to vehicles on game days.

If Camden Yards began the retro park revolution in 1992, Pittsburgh's PNC Park perfected it nine years later. Located on the north bank of the Allegheny River between the Roberto Clemente and the Fort Duquesne bridges, the park was built to show off Pittsburgh, where baseball has been played since the days when steel was produced for locomotives, not automobiles.

Located only blocks from where Three Rivers Stadium once stood, PNC Park is everything the old stadium wasn't—natural, intimate, and inviting. PNC is the first major-league park with just two decks to be built since Milwaukee County Stadium a half a century before it. As a result, it highest seat is just 88 feet from the field. Nearly three-quarters of the seats are on the field level. Fenway is the only major-league park with a smaller capacity.

Though many touches are borrowed from Forbes Field, where the Pirates played for 61 years, the view more resembles Exposition Park, which opened in 1882, and featured a view of barges floating down the Allegheny and Monongahela Rivers, not to mention smokestacks in the background.

The field dimensions are unique, with a nook in deep left that is 10 feet deeper than straight-away center. The outfield fences vary in height, ranging from just six feet in left field to 21 feet in right, honoring Clemente who wore No. 21.

The waters of the Allegheny are 443 feet, four inches from home plate, considerably further than McCovey Cove in San Francisco, but reachable on rare occasion by the game's most powerful left handed hitters. As in San Francisco, there is a walkway between the water and the park that gives fans views of the city and river, and a free look inside the park.

PNC Park relies on dark blue Pennsylvania steel, rather than the green more familiar in other new stadium. The distinctive light standards are modeled after those at Forbes Field.

Outside, a statue of Honus Wagner which first stood outside Forbes Field, and later Three Rivers, is at the home plate entrance. The Roberto Clemente statue was moved to the foot of his bridge, and a new Willie Stargell statue greets visitors at the left field entrance.

Left: The 1935 Pittsburgh Crawfords of the Negro Leagues pose for a team photo in front of their team bus and their home park. Brick-fronted Greenlee Field was one of the few ballparks built with Black capital for Negro Leagues use. The Crawfords are considered the greatest black baseball team of all-time. The team included players such as Josh Gibson, Oscar Charleston, Cool Papa Bell, Judy Johnson and Leroy "Satchel" Paige. *MLB Photos via Getty Images*

Right: Three Rivers Stadium stands across the Alleghany River from Three Rivers Point State Park in a 1986 view. *Mark E. Gibson/Corbis*

Above: Forbes field during the first game of the 1960
World Series between Yankees and Pirates.
Hy Peskin/Time Life Pictures/Getty Images

Left: On May 25, 1935, Babe Ruth hit the last home run of his major-league career in Forbes Field. The blast cleared the right-field wall, then cleared the screen and finally cleared the doubledeck grandstands. The historic shot (a first of that distance in Forbes Field) was approximately eighty-six feet high and at least three-hundred feet away from home plate. *National Baseball Hall of Fame*

Right: View over the Forbes Field diamond. Known for its sheer size, the park was abandoned in favor of Three-Rivers Stadium, a cookie cutter park built at a cost of $40 million. *Time Life Pictures/Getty Images*

FORBES FIELD (1909–70)

Forbes Field was among baseball's first luxury stadiums. Built beside one of the city's most upscale neighborhoods, it boasted elevators, electric lights, telephones, and even toilets for its patrons. The field was distinguished by its sheer size, which spread 376 feet to right field and 462 to dead center. The distance from home plate to the backstop was well over 100 feet, about double today's standard, frustrating generations of foul ball hitters.

The park was named after John Forbes, a general in the British Army who captured Fort Duquesne during the French and Indian War. Home to Honus Wagner, Ralph Kiner and Roberto Clemente, its most storied moment came in the bottom of the ninth inning during the final game of the World Series between the Pirates and the Yankees, when Bill Mazeroski hit a series ending ball high over the left-field wall. Part of the outfield wall remains on the University of Pittsburgh campus where the stadium once stood. The park was abandoned in 1970, in favor of ultra-modern, Three Rivers Stadium.

Left and Below: Three Rivers Stadium was knocked down on February 11, 2001. Built where the Allegheny, Monongahela, and Ohio Rivers come together, a cookie-cutter stadium resembling those in Philadelphia, Cincinnati, and St. Louis, Three Rivers was home to the Pirates as well as the NFL Steelers. *Time Life Pictures/Getty Images*

Right: PNC Park in 2001. *Getty Images*.

Left: Statue of Honus Wagner (1874–1955)—the "Flying Dutchman"—one of the Hall of Fame's five original inductees in 1936. He was a long-time Pirates' shortstop, hit over 300 for 17 consecutive seasons for a lifetime average of .329. Wagner was one of the first baseball stars to have his signature on a Louisville Slugger.
National Baseball Hall of Fame

Below: PNC Park in Pittsburgh, Pennsylvania during the game between the New York Mets and the Pittsburgh Pirates on April 1, 2001.
Jamie Squire/Allsport via Getty Images

Right: Aerial of PNC Park looking over the Allegheny River.
National Baseball Hall of Fame

Left: An aerial view of
Forbes Field.
*Charles "Teenie"
Harris/Corbis*

PORTLAND, OREGON

PGE Park

Previous names: Multnomah Field;
Multnomah Stadium; Civic Stadium

Status: Currently used for minor league
baseball

Address: 1844 S.W. Morrison, Portland,
OR 97205

Capacity: 28,000 (original); 23,105
(current)

Opening day: October 9, 1926 (football
game)

Cost to construct: $502,000 (original);
$38.5 million (renovation)

Architect: A. E. Doyle (Multnomah Field)

Dimensions (ft):

Left Field: 317

Left Center: N/A

Center Field: 405

Right Center: N/A

Right Field: 320

Defining features: Sunken stadium built 40
feet below ground level. Spacious, single-
tier grandstand mostly covered with roof.
Attractive arched façade on exterior.

Most expensive seat: $13

Cheapest seat: $8

Baseball in the city stretches back to back to 1890 and its first success was in 1891, when the Portland Gladiators beat Spokane to win the Pacific Northwest League pennant—but the league folded in 1892. Another Gladiators team played in the revived Pacific Northwest League in 1898. In 1901, the Portland Webfoots began play in another incarnation of the PNL, and also began playing at the new Vaughn Street Park. In 1904, the Portland Browns became a charter franchise in the Pacific Coast League, but showed little promise at first. Matters began to improve..." at the end of the 1904 season, when Judge W. W. McCredie purchased the team. They were rebranded as the Giants, but this title was dropped in favor of the Beavers in 1906— and they promptly took the Pacific Coast League pennant. The team went on to win the pennant again in 1910, 1911, 1913, and 1914.

The McCredies sold the club after the end of the 1921 season and the Beavers then went through a succession of owners over the following decades. During the next 50 years or so the team won just three championships—in 1932, 1936, and 1945—

and spent most seasons languishing in the second division. They left Vaughn Street Park in 1956 and moved to Multnomah Field, a stadium that had been built in 1926 and used for a wide range of sports and other public activities between 1928 and 1955. In 1967 the name was changed to Civic Stadium; two years later it became the first outdoor baseball field to install artificial turf.

The franchise was moved to Spokane at the end of the 1972 season and Civic Stadium was used by the Portland Mavericks, who played in the A Northwest League between 1973 and 1977. The Pacific Coast League increased to 10 clubs in 1978 and the Spokane Beavers paid a large fee to the Northwest League to return to Portland and join the expanded PCL. This incarnation of the team survived through to 1993, when the franchise moved again, this time to Salt Lake City. During this period, the Beavers won the Pacific Coast League championship in 1983 and the Northwest Division title in 1993. There then followed a year without baseball in Portland, but the city returned to the Northwest League in 1995. After the 2000 season a group of

investors from Portland bought the Albuquerque Class AAA franchise and Pacific Coast League baseball returned to the city for the third time in 2001. The revived Portland Beavers play at what is now known as PGE Park, which underwent a dramatic $38.5 million renovation the year they returned.

SAN DIEGO, CALIFORNIA

Qualcomm Stadium

Previous names: San Diego Stadium; Jack Murphy Stadium

Status: Current home of NFL San Diego Chargers

Address: 9449 Friars Road, San Diego, CA 92108

Capacity: 50,000 (opening day), 67,544 (final)

Opening day: August 20, 1967

First MLB game: April 8, 1969

Last MLB game: September 28, 2003

Cost to construct: $27.75 milllion

Architect: Gary Allen (Frank L. Hope & Associates)

Dimensions (ft):	Initial	Final
Left Field:	330	327
Left Center:	375	370
Center Field:	420	405
Right Center:	375	370
Right Field:	330	327

Defining features: The only stadium where a foul ball caught in either bullpen could not be seen by umpires and most players.

World Series: 1984, 1998

All-Star Game: 1978, 1992

Petco Park

Address: 100 Park Boulevard, San Diego CA 92173

Capacity: 46,000

Opening day: April 8, 2004. San Diego Padres 4, San Francisco Giants 3 (10 innings)

Cost to construct: $449 million

Architect: HOK Sports

Dimensions (ft):

Left Field: 334

Left Center: 367

Center Field: 396

Right Center: 387

Right Field: 322

Defining feature: Left field Western Metal Supply Co. Building

Major league baseball came to San Diego with the arrival of the Padres in 1969 and they have graced the National League's West Division from that date. They have played the most of their home games at what was originally known as the San Diego Stadium, a 1960s undertaking that was very much inspired by Jack Murphy, the sports editor of the San Diego Union. He began a personal campaign in the middle of the decade to find a top-ranking home for the National Football League's Chargers and a yet-to-be-named baseball expansion team.

The public's response was overwhelmingly positive to the proposal and the "small" matter of finding some $28 million of public money to finance the new stadium was no barrier to a 72 percent "yes" vote in a referendum on the matter in 1965. A 166-acre site was selected in Mission Valley and construction work began. The Padres played their first game there on April 8, 1969, and the team called the ballpark home for the next three decades.

The stadium was renamed in honor of Jack Murphy in 1980, but was rechristened Qualcomm Stadium seventeen years later after an $18 million donation by the company helped to fully enclose the ballpark. The Padres original lease ran out at the end of the 1999 season, but it was extended to September 28, 2003, when they played their last game at the stadium. In the meantime, San Diego was trying to build a new downtown ballpark. Construction on the facility stopped for a time in 2000 thanks to a lack of money caused by political problems; the opening was delayed by two years. The Padres finally moved into state-of-the-art Petco Park near the city's waterfront and took the field for their first game at the 42,500-seat stadium on April 8, 2004.

The Padres have not exactly set major league baseball on fire over their history. It took until the mid-1980s for the team to enjoy their first taste of success. In 1984 they took their first division title and NL pennant, but fell to the Tigers in five games in the World Series. It took until 1998 for the Padres to again advance to baseball's championship, but once there they were swept by the New York Yankees.

Attendance ebbed and flowed during the team's tenure at their first stadium, but the overall trend was generally positive. Seating capacity at Jack Murphy/Qualcomm grew to 51,319 in 1983, reached 58,671 the following season after new seats were added to several areas, and peaked at 67,544 in 1997. Petco Park is smaller, with only 46,000 seats.

Five Hall of Famers have played in San Diego, but only two entered Cooperstown as a Padre—outfielder Dave Winfield, who was inducted in 2001 and Tony Gwynn. Four players have had their numbers retired by the team, including the incomparable Tony Gwynn (19), who holds the Padres' highest season (.394) and career (.338) batting averages. The others are Winfield (31), Steve Garvey (6), and pitcher Randy Jones (35), who also holds the record for most wins in a season (22 in 1976)

Baseball was played in downtown San Diego before there really was a downtown. More than a 130 years later, the bustling city center is home to the nation's newest downtown stadium, just blocks from the spot of the first sandlot games.

PETCO Park is a "retro" stadium with a distinctly Southern California look. Surrounded by jacaranda trees, water walls, natural stone, and a stucco exterior, the park offers panoramic views of downtown skyscrapers, Mission Bay, Balboa Park, and the arid mountains that surround the city.

Its trademark feature is a left-field warehouse, the turn-of-the-century Western Metal Supply Co. building. Though far smaller than Camden Yard's B&O warehouse, it directly abuts the field, creating an irresistible target for right handed hitters. The left corner of the building holds the left-field foul pole, and each of its four floors contains outdoors seating and a unique perspective on the game.

Unlike the Padres' old home at Qualcomm Stadium, also known as Jack Murphy Field, PETCO Park was built exclusively for baseball. The park is intimate, with 20,000 fewer seats than Qualcomm, three decks rather than four,

Left: The then recently completed San Diego Stadium, which could seat 50,000 and was convertible between football to baseball configurations, seen on April 4, 1967. *Getty Images*

Below: Jack Murphy Stadium, home of the San Diego Chargers, during a game in 1987. *Getty Images*

seats located much closer to the field, and all angled toward the pitchers mound. The park boasts a capacity of 46,000, though there are only 42,000 seats, reflecting a range of standing room options for fans who can see the ballgame from the concourse and a variety of porches and terraces, in addition to the center field "Park at the Park," a grass park and picnic area for about 2,500 fans.

The unusual (and already ridiculed) name comes from the San Diego-based retailer of pet supplies, which bought the naming rights reportedly for $60 million over 22 years.

Outside, where the early sandlot games were played, the ballpark is anchor to a larger downtown redevelopment project, with plans for a new library, museum, and apartments.

Left, Far left and Pages 358–361: Views of PETCO Park during the home opener between the San Diego Padres and the San Francisco Giants on April 8, 2004. The Padres defeated the Giants 4-3.
MLB Photos via Getty Images

SAN FRANCISCO, CALIFORNIA

Seals Stadium

Status: Demolished in 1959

Location: Intersection of 16th and Bryant streets, current site of a supermarket and other stores

Capacity: 16,000 (opening day); 22,900 (final)

Opening day: April 7, 1931

First MLB game: April 15, 1958

Last MLB game: September 20, 1959

Cost to construct: N/A

Architect: N/A

Dimensions (ft):

	Initial	Final
Left Field:	340	361
Left Center:	375	364
Center Field:	400	400
Right Center:	397	397
Right Field:	385	350

Defining feature: The playing field lacked a warning track, with the outfield grass running right up to the fence.

World Series: none

All-Star Game: none

Candlestick Park

Other names: 3 Com Park; Monster Park

Status: Still used for NFL football

Address: 02 Jamestown Avenue, San Francisco, CA 94124

Capacity: 43,765 (opening day), 57,546 (final, for baseball)

Opening day: April 21, 1960

Last MLB game: September 30, 1999

Cost to construct: $15 million; $16.1 million (renovations)

Architect: John Bolles

Dimensions (ft):

	Initial	Final
Left Field:	330	335
Left Center:	397	365
Center Field:	420	400
Right Center:	397	365
Right Field:	330	328

Defining feature: The stadium's exposed location led to the worst weather in baseball—cold, windy, and sometimes foggy.

World Series: 1962, 1989

All-Star Game: 1961, 1984

A T & T Park

Aka: Pac Bell Park (2000–03)

Address: 801 Third Street, San Francisco, CA 94107

Capacity: 41,059

Opening day: April 11, 2000—Los Angeles Dodger 6, San Francisco Giants 5

Cost to construct: $319 million

Architect: HOK Sports

Dimensions (ft):

Left Field: 335	Left Center: 364
Center Field: 404	Right Center: 420
Right Field: 307	

Defining feature: McCovey Cove

Most expensive seat: $75

Cheapest seat: $10

World Series: 2002

All-Star Game: None

Memorable Moments:

2000 May 1—Barry Bonds hits the first regulation game ball into McCovey Cove, off Rich Rodriguez of the NY Mets.

2001 October 5—Bonds hits home runs No. 71 and 72 against the Dodgers, passing Mark McGwire's single season record. At four hours and 27 minutes, it is the longest nine inning game in major-league history. Two days later, Bonds hits No. 73, sending two fans to court over the ball's possession.

2002 August 9—Bonds joins Hank Aaron, Babe Ruth and Willie Mays as the only players to hit 600 home runs.

This picture: Seals Stadium opened in 1931. *Time & Life Pictures/Getty Images*

San Francisco was home to the Pacific Coast League's Seals and Missions, who played at Seals Stadium from its opening in 1931 until September 1957, shortly before major league baseball came to the city. Seals Stadium was a fairly nondescript steel-and-concrete stadium located near downtown. It had a single-tier grandstand that extended down both foul lines, plus a small bleacher section in right field.

San Francisco became home to the Giants in 1958, when the New York Giants (1885-1957) migrated from the East Coast to the West in 1957—the same year that the Brooklyn Dodgers made the same journey but to Los Angeles, giving the new California Giants an immediate, and natural, rival. Both teams have played in the National League's West Division since 1969. The Giants have graced three venues since their move to San Francisco. They started off at Seals Stadium—forcing the stadium's namesake minor league team to move out—but only played there for two seasons before moving to the Candlestick Park, famous among music fans for hosting the last Beatles concert on August 29, 1966. Among baseball fans, Candlestick's reputation is decidedly mixed.

Candlestick was a relatively attractive park next to San Francisco Bay. The semicircular double-deck grandstand was open to the water; it was a beautiful place to watch baseball on a warm sunny day—which rarely happened. The ballpark was the coldest, windiest in the majors,

and it was often beset by fog. It was a terrible place for a stadium. Candlestick started to fall apart within years after opening, then the city invested $16.1 million to modify and enlarge the park to also host football's 49ers. The double-decking fully enclosed the stadium, which some thought would improve conditions for baseball. They were wrong—it was still cold and often foggy, and the winds now swirled unpredictably instead of howling straight into the ballpark.

Despite its shortcomings, the Giants played at Candlestick for the better part of four decades before relocating to the Pacific Bell Park, which some argue is one of the best parks in baseball. The brick-clad, retro-style ballpark is located near downtown and was built entirely with private funds. The Giants played their first game there on April 11, 2000, losing to long-time rivals Los Angeles Dodgers 6-5. At the start of the 2004 season the stadium was renamed SBC Park.

The San Francisco Giants have never matched the success of their New York predecessors, but they had some quality teams in their years at Candlestick Park. They captured the West Division title on three occasions (1971, 1989, and 1997), and appeared in two World Series: They went down to the New York Yankees 4-3 in 1962 and were swept by their cross-bay rivals in Oakland. The latter series was disrupted when the Bay Area was hit by destructive earthquake just minutes before Game 3

Above, Below, Left and Far left: Views of Seals Stadium on April 1, 1958, which saw the San Francisco Giants first game—against the Los Angeles Dodgers. *All Time & Life Pictures/Getty Images*

Left: The opening game at Candlestick Park, April 1, 1960. *Time & Life Pictures/Getty Images*

This picture: 2004 view of Candlestick Park. *MLB Photos via Getty Images*

Overleaf, left and right: 2004 views of Candlestick Park. *Both MLB Photos via Getty Images*

started at Candlestick. The ballpark sustained minor damage in the quake, and the series was stalled for twelve days before resuming to understandably lackluster interest from fans.

The move to Pacific Bell/SBC Park seems to have rejuvenated the Giants. They took the West Division in 2000 and 2003, and advanced to the World Series as a wild card in 2002. The team was still searching for that elusive MLB championship after going down to the Anaheim Angels 4-3. The San Francisco fans have enjoyed watching several stars play for the Giants over the years. Five Hall of Famers spent significant parts of their careers playing next to the bay: Orlando Cepeda, Willie Mays, Willie McCovey, Juan Marichal, and Gaylord Perry. In recent years, Giant fans have enjoyed watching slugger Barry Bonds earn five MVP awards and launch an assault on the baseball record books. In 2001 Bonds hit 73 round-trippers to take baseball's single-season mark, and even though his reputation was tainted by a steroid scandal, he still has a shot at breaking Hank Aaron's career home run tally, passing 750 in 2007.

There is much that is appealing about the Giants' new home. The park is small and its dimensions intimate. The sight lines are engineered exclusively for baseball. The field is asymmetrical with a 25-foot high brick wall just 309 feet from home plate, the closest foul pole in the majors. The view beyond the outfield is as beautiful an urban landscape as can be imagined.

But for all its charms, nothing compares to the childishly irresistible anticipation that a powerful left handed hitter might clear the 25-foot brick wall in right field, and plop a home run into the water named after the Giants' Hall of Fame first baseman Willie McCovey. The Giants have such a hitter, and SBC is unmistakably the park that (Barry) Bonds built. Just as the Yankees erected a short right-field fence in 1923 for their star left hander, Babe Ruth, the Giants built SBC for Bonds, the marquee power hitter of his time. As the 2004 season opened, only four players had "gone Bay," but Bonds himself has done it 27 times, thrilling capacity crowds who were just warming up after four decades at frigid Candlestick Park.

Just as fans gather on Chicago's Waveland Avenue for the chance at a home run ball, sailors, kayakers, and other boaters fill McCovey Cove during Giants games, their eyes fixed on the right field fence. The location is so close that when the Yankees Jorge Posada hit the ball into the cove during an exhibition game, the ball was scooped up by boater Mike Quinby who promptly threw it back onto the field on a fly.

SBC was built in the mold of Camden Yards. Rather than the B&O warehouse in right field, it is the Bay, with stunning vistas of the East Bay hills and the Bay Bridge from the upper deck. Architects resisted even more sweeping views in order to reduce the wind, and to give Bonds a better shot at reaching the Bay. Temperatures are not nearly as cold as at windy Candlestick, where former Giants pitcher Stu Miller was famously blown off the mound during the 1961 All-Star Game. Still, you won't catch many locals wearing short sleeves at night.

The inside is bustling with activity, from an 80-foot long Coca Cola bottle in left field, which houses slides for kids, and a 27-foot baseball glove at its spout, to a miniature SBC park, where kids can smack Wiffle balls over the fence. Outside, a statue of Willie Mays is a central meeting spot near the park's main entrance, and another of McCovey overlooks his cove on the Bay side.

Known as Pac Bell Park when it opened, the name changed in 2004 after Texas-based communications company SBC (Southwest Bell Corp.) bought the local phone company, putting some San Franciscans in the awkward position of clamoring for the park's original corporate name. SBC is the first privately financed park in Major League Baseball since Dodger Stadium in 1962.

The Giants' stadium changed name for the third time since it opened when it was officially renamed AT&T Park on March 1, 2006, because SBC Communications had rebranded itself as AT&T Inc. when it merged with AT&T Corp. in late 2005.

Right: General view of Pac Bell Park during the National Anthem before game three of the National League Championship series between the St. Louis Cardinals and the San Francisco Giants on October 12, 2002 in San Francisco, California. *Matthew Stockman /Getty Images*

Left: Stand-in Pitcher Kirk Rueter—#46 of the San Francisco Giants— throws a pitch during game five of the National League Championship series against the St. Louis Cardinals on October 14, 2002. The Giants won the game 2–1 and the series 4–1.
Getty Images

Far left: Fans stand in a moment of silence in a pre-game ceremony in honor of the victims of September 11 before the game between the Dodgers and the Giants at Pacific Bell Park on September 11, 2002. The Dodgers defeated the Giants 7–3.
Getty Images

Right: In recognition of the Hall of Fame player who wore the Giants' number 24 for 22 seasons, this nine-foot bronze statue of the great Willie Mays, welcomes fans to the entrance to the newly renamed SBC Park at 24 Willie Mays Plaza. The 24 palm trees that line the plaza are another part of the tribute to one of baseball's most honored and beloved players. *Scott Sommerdorf/San Francisco Chronicle*

Left: September 30, 1999: A general view of the last game at 3 Com Park, commonly known as Candlestick Park, between the Dodgers and the Giants. The Dodgers defeated the Giants 9–4.
Jed Jacobsohn/Allsport via Getty Images

Left: Exterior view of Candlestick Park as boats bring fans in for opening day game against St. Louis Casrdinals, April 12, 1960. *Jon Brenneis/Time Life Pictures/Getty Images*

Far left: General view of Candlestick Park, home of the San Francisco Giants in c. 1989. *Otto Greule Jr/Getty Images*

379

Left and Far left: Two views of Candlestick Park, home of the San Francisco Giants in c. 1989. *Both National Baseball Hall of Fame*

SEATTLE, WASHINGTON

Sicks' Stadium

Other names: Sicks' Seattle Stadium

Status: Demolished in 1979

Location: South Rainier Avenue, South McClellan Street, and Bayview Street; sight of Lowe's Home Improvement Warehouse

Capacity: 12,000 (original), 21,000 (final)

Opening day: June 15, 1938

First MLB game: April 11, 1969

Last MLB game: October 2, 1969

Cost to construct: $350,000

Architect: N/A

Dimensions (ft):	Initial	Final
Left Field:	325	305
Left Center:	345	345
Center:	400	402
Right Center:	345	345
Right Field:	325	320

Defining feature: Poor water pressure stopped the toilets from flushing when attendance exceeded 10,000.

World Series: none

All-Star Game: none

Kingdome

Status: Demolished in 2000

Location: Site of current Qwest Field

Capacity: 59,166

Opening day: April 6, 1977

Last MLB game: June 27, 199

Cost to construct: $67 million

Architect: Naramore, Skilling & Praeger

Dimensions (ft):	Initial	Final
Left Field:	315	331
Left Center:	375	376
Center:	405	405
Right Center:	375	352
Right Field:	315	312

Defining features: Dangling speakers, considered in play, were struck by hit balls several times. Fence in right (23 feet high) nicknamed "Walla Walla."

World Series: none

All-Star Game: 1979

Safeco Field

Address: First Ave. S and S. Atlantic St., Seattle, WA 98104

Capacity: 47,116

Opening day: July 15, 1999—San Diego Padres 3, Seattle Mariners 2

Cost to construct: $517 million

Architect: NBBJ

Dimensions (ft):		
Left Field: 331	Left Center: 390	
Center Field: 405	Right Center: 387	Right Field: 327

Defining feature: Open-sided retractable roof

Little-known ground rule: If the roof is open and climatic conditions warrant it, the roof can be closed in the middle of an inning. Once the roof is closed during a game, it will not be re-opened. If a game begins with the roof closed, it may be opened only between innings and the visiting team may challenge the decision to open it

Most expensive seat: $45

Cheapest seat: $6

World Series: None

All-Star Game: 2001

Memorable moments:

2000 August 1—Mike Cameron hits a 19th-inning home run to beat Boston 5–4.

2000 September 30—Alex Rodriguez hits two home runs and bats in seven runs to beat the Angels and move Seattle into a first place tie.

2000 October 6—Carlos Guillen scores Rickey Henderson on a ninth-inning squeeze bunt to sweep White Sox in the division playoffs.

2001 July 11—Cal Ripken, in his final All-Star game, hits a third-inning home run and is named the game's MVP.

2001 October 6—Mariners win their 116th game, tying the Chicago Cubs major-league record.

Right: Postcard showing Sicks' Stadium.

Baseball in Seattle has had a very checkered history. For many years, the city was home to the Pacific Coast League's Seattle Rainiers, whose owner, Emil Sick, gave his name to the city's first major baseball park—Sicks' Stadium. The concrete-and-steel ballpark was perfect for minor league baseball and a hit with the fans for many years. When Seattle was awarded a major league franchise—the Seattle Pilots—it was with the agreement that Sicks' Stadium would be expanded to 25,000 seats, and that it would be a temporary venue. Terrible winter weather delayed construction and on the Pilots opening day, April 11, 1969, only about 6,000 seats had been installed; some fans waited for benches to be set in place while the game started. Low water pressure (which shut down toilets when large crowds flushed too many times) and other problems plagued the ballpark, but the owners' financial difficulties were a bigger issue. The Pilots played their last game in Seattle on October 2 of the same year. In April 1970 the franchise was sold and moved to Milwaukee to become the Brewers.

Modern major league baseball returned

to Seattle in 1977 in the form of the expansion Seattle Mariners, who have spent their entire existence playing in the American League's West Division. To house the new team, Seattle built the Kingdome, where they made their debut in April 1977 in front of more than 57,000 fans. The multipurpose concrete-domed facility received mixed reviews from baseball fans. It had plenty of seating, with two decks around the entire stadium, and three for most of its circumference. On the other hand, the building was gray and quiet, especially when crowds were small, prompting its nickname—"The Tomb." It also had its quirks. Several large, suspended speakers were in play and frequently struck by hit balls. They were raised by about 30 feet before the 1981 season to minimize their impact. Forty-two large air-conditioning units kept fans comfortable, but they tended to blow air in from the outfield, cutting down on home runs.

The Mariners spent a little more than two decades in the dome and never achieved much success for their fans. They took the West Division title and Division Series titles in 1995, but never appeared in a World Series.

The Mariners left the Kingdome for the brand-new Safeco Field in July 1999. The 47,772-seat stadium features a retractable roof that is left open when the weather cooperates. Fans have given the new ballpark high marks for its quality game-

Left: Eerie lights Around the Kingdome, 1976. *Tim Thompson/Corbis*

Above: The Kingdome and industrial area south of downtown Seattle as seen from the Columbia Tower at night, 1986. *Stuart Westmorland/Corbis*

Left: When it opened in 1977, the Kingdome was the American League's first indoor stadium. In 1994 four ceiling tiles fell before the start of a game causing the team to play its final 15 games on the road. Repairs cost $70 million. The stadium, then home to the NFL Seahawks as well as the Mariners, was spectacularlydemolished in 2000. A new football only stadium now occupies the site.
National Baseball Hall of Fame

Below: The implosion of the Kingdome made way for Seattle's current two sports stadiumss—Safeco Field and Seahawk's Stadium that was renamed Qwest Field in June 2004, after Qwest bought the naming rights for $75 million. Mt. Rainier can be seen in the background. *Otto Greule Jr/Getty Images*

Left: The Seattle Mariners play the Texas Rangers.
Paul A. Souders/Corbis

watching experience, stunning views, and overall entertainment package. The field did not seem to hurt the Mariners, either. The team returned to the playoffs in both 2000 and 2001, advancing to the AL Championship Series both years—but also losing to the New York Yankees both times.

Over their history, the Mariners have fielded a number of fine ballplayers, though Gaylord Perry is the only Hall of Fame inductee who ever played in Seattle, and then only during the 1982 and 1983 seasons. A number of big-name recent stars have spent significant time with the Mariners, including Edgar Martinez, Ken Griffey Jr., Alex Rodriguez, and Randy Johnson, though other than Martinez all were lured to other teams by richer salary offers. At the time of this writing, Japanese sensation Ichiro Suzuki, one of baseball's top hitters, is the team's biggest star.

It took $517 million to move Seattle fans from baseball's worst stadium to one of its best, about the same dollar amount it took to construct every major-league park built in the United States through 1990—combined.

Real grass. Cedar-lined dugouts. Elevated bullpens. An old-fashioned, hand operated scoreboard and 11 video display

Left: Exterior view of Safeco Field on June 25, 2003. *Getty Images*

This page: Safeco Field with roof retracted. Built to the south of the Mariners' old home, the Kingdome, the new stadium was named after Safeco, a financial services company whose roots in Seattle date back to 1923. Safeco will pay $1.8 million per year for the next 20 years. *Otto Greule Jr/Getty Images*

boards. A concourse where fans waiting for salmon sandwiches, clam chowder, sushi rolls, or garlic fries won't miss the action.

There are 600,000 bricks in the facade, 40 miles of piping, 150 miles of electrical wiring, 200 miles of concrete, 535 metal halide lights, 600 tons of infield clay, and 20 to 30 miles of heating coils for the turf, which is a blend of Kentucky Bluegrass and perennial rye. And it wouldn't be Bill Gates' Seattle without Internet kiosks and luxury suites with high speed Internet access.

But what really cost money was the roof, which opens and closes like a well-vented convertible, covering the stands and the field, but leaving the side open to allow fresh air to blow in. When the roof is open, the right side of the upper deck offers views of downtown and the Puget Sound, though the city's landscape is not visible from most of the stadium.

The confines, though not the major leagues' coziest, are a vast improvement over the dark and cavernous Kingdome, the Mariners' previous home. The design offers a more mobile way to watch baseball. Wide concourses with lots of concessions and site lines allow people to move around during the game. The park also features one more women's bathroom than men's, which may be a first at a sports venue. Its restaurants, and even the field, are available for weddings, Bar Mitzvahs, and other events (for a substantial sum) when games are not being played.

The state-of-the-art park was built, owners said, to lure fans who in turn would bring in enough revenue to pay top-notch players to build a great team. Ironically, the stadium's astronomical cost put a serious dent in the owner's wallet, and now some of the Mariners' greatest, including Randy Johnson, Alex Rodriguez, and Ken Griffey Jr., have found homes elsewhere.

Far left and Left: Two views of Safeco Field at night—the annual fireworks show begins. July 4, 1999. *Natalie Fobes/Corbis; Philip James Corwin/Corbis*

Overleaf, left: An overhead view of Safeco Field taken during a 1999 season Seattle Mariner game. *MLB Photos via Getty Images*

Overleaf, right: Spectators watching a packed game at Safeco Field July 18, 1999. *Natalie Fobes/Corbis*

ST. LOUIS, MISSOURI

Robison Field

Status: Demolished

Location: Area bounded by Prairie, Natural Bridge, Vandeventer, and Lexington avenues

Capacity: 14,500 (opening day); 21,000 (final)

Opening day: April 27, 1893

Last MLB game: June 6, 1920

Cost to construct: N/A

Architect: N/A

Dimensions (ft):	Initial	Final
Left Field:	470	380
Left Center:	520	400
Center Field:	500	435
Right Center:	330	320
Right Field:	290	290

Defining feature: An amusement park once stood on the edge of left field.

World Series: none

All-Star Game: none

Sportsman's Park (second version)

Other names: Busch Stadium (first version)

Status: Demolished in 1966

Location: In an area bounded by Sullivan Avenue, North Spring Avenue, Dodier Street, and North Grand Avenue (Boulevard)

Capacity: 8,000 (opening day); 30,611 (1966)

Opening day: April 23, 1902

Last MLB game: May 8, 1966

Cost to construct: $300,000; $500,000 (renovation)

Architect: Osborn Engineering

Dimensions (ft):	Initial	Final
Left Field:	368	351
Left Center:	379	379
Center Field:	430	422
Right Center:	354	354
Right Field:	335	310

Defining features: Covered double-deck grandstand running the length of both foul lines. Lleft field scoreboard after 1953 topped by a giant Budweiser eagle.

World Series: 1926, 1928, 1930, 1931, 1934, 1942, 1943, 1944, 1964

All-Star Game: 1940, 1948, 1957

Busch Stadium (second version)

Status: Demolished in 2005

Location: 250 Stadium Plaza; site partially occupied by new Busch Stadium

Capacity: 49,676

Opening day: May 12, 1966

Last MLB game: October 19, 2005

Cost to construct: $20 million

Architect: Sverdrup & Parcel and Associates; Edward Durell Stone; Schwartz & Van Hoefen Associated

Dimensions (ft):	Initial	Final
Left Field:	330	330
Left Center:	386	372
Center Field:	414	402
Right Center:	386	372
Right Field:	330	330

Defining feature: Circular, multipurpose stadium, but one of the most attractive MLB ballparks. Ninety-six open arches surround the field just below roof level.

World Series: 1967, 1968, 1982, 1985, 1987, 2004

All-Star Game: 1996

The St. Louis Cardinals have a history stretching back to the founding of National Association's St. Louis Brown Stockings in 1892 but that name lasted just one year. They were the St. Louis Browns between 1883 and 1898, and then had a brief spell as the St. Louis Perfectos the following year before settling on the Cardinals in 1900. The team moved to Robison Field after their original home, Sportsman's Park, burned in 1898; they remained at Robison Field until the mid-1919 season.

Meanwhile, the Cardinals were no longer the only major league baseball team in St. Louis. In 1902, the Milwaukee Brewers—charter members of the new American League—moved to St. Louis after only one year of play and became the Browns. The team built a new ballpark on the site of the burned-down Sportsman's Park—maybe not a good choice considering it was filled with 8,000 wooden seats. Eventually the park was

Right: Left field view of Sportsman's Park Stadium.
MLB Photos via Getty Images

rebuilt with a concrete-and-steel, double-decked grandstand. In 1920 the Cardinals abandoned Robison Field and became co-tenants with the Browns at Sportsman's Park. A renovation in 1925 extended the double-deck grandstand down both foul lines, expanding the capacity to more than 30,000.

After the move to Sportsman's Park, the Cardinals became one of baseball's glory teams. Between the mid-1920s and mid-1940s they captured nine NL pennants—1926, 1928, 1930, 1931, 1934, 1942, 1943, 1944, and 1946)—and six World Series titles. They beat the New York Yankees twice, in 1926 and 1942, the Philadelphia As in 1931, the Detroit Tigers in 1934, the St. Louis Browns in 1944, and the Boston Red Sox in 1946.

The Browns, meanwhile, always played second fiddle to the Cardinals and finished either last or next to last exactly half of their 52 seasons in St. Louis. Their overall lackluster play coined the expression "First in shoes, first in booze, and last in the American League." The team hit bottom in 1936 when a paltry 80,922 fans turned up to watch them at home. The team rebounded to reach the World Series in 1944 but, in an eerie twist of fate, lost out to the Cardinals. Continuing financial problems plagued the Browns, and in 1953 they departed St. Louis for Baltimore, where they became the Orioles and enjoyed much more success.

That same year hometown brewing magnate August Busch bought the Cardinals and renamed their home Busch Stadium. Reportedly, Busch wanted to call the park Budweiser Stadium after his famous beer, but the league protested. Busch made some upgrades to the stadium and also installed the famous Budweiser eagle on top of the scoreboard that flapped its wings when the Cards hit a home run. The Cardinals stayed at Busch until 1966 when they moved to a new downtown ballpark—also known as Busch Stadium. The new version of Busch was a circular multipurpose stadium, but it was more attractive than other stadiums of the era. The arches below the roofline that ringed the stadium were a unique touch, and

Above: Left field view of Sportsman's Park Stadium. *MLB Photos via Getty Images*

Right: Postcard of Sportsman's Park.

the 46,000-plus red seats on two decks left no doubt about the team's primary color. They played their last game (a playoff contest against the Astros) there on October 19, 2005, and were scheduled to move into a new $400 million stadium—of course named Busch Stadium—for the 2006 season.

The Cardinals have never repeated their success from the first half of the century, but they have had some tremendous teams over the last 50 years. During the 1960s, they had three World Series teams—1964, 1967, and 1968, beating the Yankees, beating the Red Sox, and losing to the Twins in the three series. They returned to the World Series three times in the 1980s, beating the Brewers in 1982, losing to the Royals in 1985, and losing to the Twins again 1987. The Cardinals advanced to the playoffs only once in the 1990s, losing the championship series to the Braves in 1996. Then, starting in 2000 they began a five-year stretch with only one team not making the playoffs, in 2003. During this run they reached the World Series only once, in 2004, where they were swept by the Red Sox.

With such a long and successful history, it is hardly surprising that many Cardinals have made it to the Hall of Fame—nineteen in total. Perhaps the franchise's greatest player of all time (or at least the one most connected with the team) was Stan "The Man" Musial, a Cardinal from 1941 to 1963. He won the Most Valuable Player award in 1943, 1946, and 1949, led the league in hitting seven times, and played in 21 All-Star games. So popular and influential a figure was Musial that a statue in his honor was unveiled outside the Busch Stadium in 1968, three years before he entered the Hall of Fame.

Right: A view of a St. Louis Browns game on September 1, 1944. *Time & Life Pictures/Getty Images*

Far right: Aerial of Busch Stadium evening of June 13, 1983. *Nathan Benn/Corbis*

Below: Postcard showing the interior of Sportsman's Park.

SPORTSMEN'S PARK, ST. LOUIS, MO.—98

Right: A panoramic view of Busch Stadium and nearby skyscrapers in St. Louis, Missouri. *Joseph Sohm; ChromoSohm Inc./Corbis*

Page 404: General view of Busch Stadium during Game Three of the 2006 World Series. The Cardinals defeated the Tigers 5–0. *Paul Cunningham/MLB Photos via Getty Images*

Page 405: Busch Stadium before Game Four of the 2006 World Series. *Brad Mangin/MLB Photos via Getty Images*

Page 406: Busch Stadium during the game between the St. Louis Cardinals and the Colorado Rockies on May 10, 2006. The Cardinals defeated the Colorado Rockies 7–4. *Elsa/Getty Images*

Page 407: Another external view of Busch Stadiumbefore Game Four of the 2006 World Series. *Dilip Vishwanat/Getty Images*

Left and Right: Two views of the interior of Busch Stadium during the game between the Milwaukee Brewers and the St. Louis Cardinals on April 13, 2006. The Brewers won in 11 innnings 4–3. *Elsa/Getty Images*

ST. PETERSBURG, FLORIDA

Right: Tropicana Field during thegame against the Boston Red Sox on April 28, 2006. The Devil Rays defeated the Red Sox 5–2. *Photo by Eliot J. Schechter/Getty Images*

Tropicana Field was built to attract a Major League Baseball team to the Tampa Bay area. Originally called the Florida Suncoast Dome, it was renamed the Thunderdome while being used (1993–95) by hocket team Tampa Bay Lightning who made the stadium its home for three seasons.

Baseball came to the Tampa Bay area in 1995 when the MLB expanded. The Thunderdome changed its name on selling the naming rights to Tropicana Products in 1996. The first regular season baseball game took place on March 31, 1998, when the Devil Rays faced the Detroit Tigers, losing 11–6.

There has been much rebuilding and renovation in recent years—$70 million was spent when the Devil Rays came to town; there was a further $25-million facelift prior to the 2006 season; $10 million was spent on improvements during the same season; and further improvements were made in the offseason before the 2007 season.

Left: Pitcher Matt Clement of the Boston Red Sox delivers a pitch against the Devil Rays on April 28, 2006. *Eliot J. Schechter/Getty Images*

Right and Far right: Two exterior views of Tropicana Field dated 2006 (right) and 1998 (far right). *Victor Baldizon/Getty Images and Scott Halleran /Allsport*

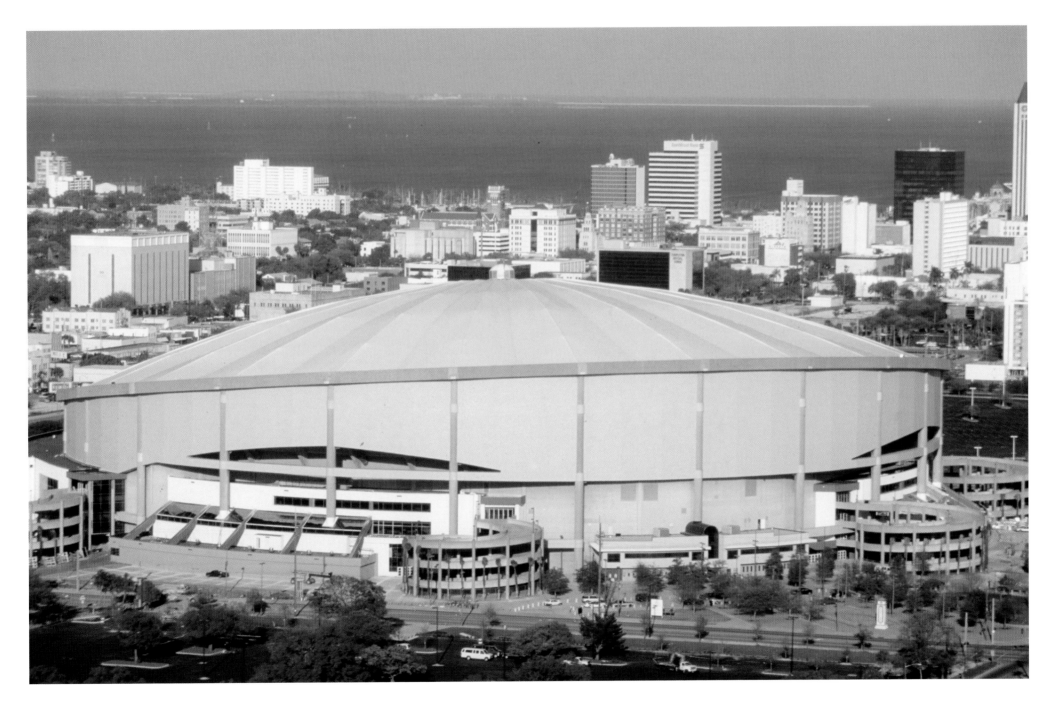

TACOMA, WASHINGTON

Cheney Stadium

Status: In use for minor league baseball

Address: 2502 S. Tyler Street Tacoma, WA 98405

Capacity: 9,600

Opening day: April 16, 1960

Cost to construct: $940,000

Architect: N/A

Dimensions (ft):

Left Field: 325

Left Center: 385

Center Field: 425

Right Center: 385

Right Field: 325

Defining feature: The life-size bronze statue of Ben Cheney, complete with opening day program and empty peanut shells, installed in his favorite seat in 1996.

Most expensive seat: $12

Cheapest seat: $4

The history of minor league baseball in Tacoma stretches all the way back to the Tacoma Tigers, a team that played in the Pacific National League and, with the exception of one year when they were known as the Cubs (1910), the club remained associated with Tacoma from the early 1900s to the beginning of the 1950s. They played in several different leagues— the Pacific Coast, which they won in 1904, Northwestern, Washington State, Northwestern International, Pacific Coast International, and Western International— before eventually bowing out in 1951.

Two men, lumber magnate Benjamin Bradford "Ben" Cheney and Clay Huntingdon, set out to remedy Tacoma's lack of AAA baseball. They began discussions in 1957 and, after two years of hard work, city officials met with representatives of the San Francisco Giants (Cheney had an 11 percent stake in the club) to discuss moving their AAA Phoenix club to Tacoma. An agreement was reached on the understanding that Tacoma would provide the team with a new stadium by April 1960. The building work on what became known as Cheney Stadium took just

three months and 14 days. The stadium was originally outfitted with seats and light standards that had been salvaged from San Francisco's Seals Stadium. Cheney Stadium is regarded as a nice place to watch baseball, with spectators feeling close to the action. The spacious single-level grandstand is angled behind the infield and is partially covered. Cloud-free days offer stunning views of Mount Rainier from selected seats on the third base side.

The Tacoma Giants' first game, against the Portland Beavers, was supposed to be played on April 14, 1960 but was postponed by heavy rain. Instead, the teams played a doubleheader, which they split, on April 16. The Giants went on to win the Pacific Coast League in 1961. They were renamed the Cubs five years later and in this incarnation won the Pacific Coast League in 1969. The Cubs turned into the Twins in 1971 and in 1978 became the Yankees, taking the league for the third time. They were briefly the Tugs in 1979, but returned to being the Tigers in 1980. In 1981 they started a fourteen-year affiliation with the Oakland As.

This Tigers disappeared in 1995 when the team became the Tacoma Rainiers and started an affiliation with the nearby Seattle Mariners; both the name and parent club remain in place. The Rainiers took the Pacific Coast League title in 2001. Several fine players have played for Tacoma in Cheney Stadium over the years, including Gaylord Perry, Juan Marichal, Mark McGwire, and Alex Rodriguez.

Left: Tropicana Field before the Devil Rays' home opener against the Baltimore Orioles on April 10, 2006. The Orioles defeated the Devil Rays 6–3. *Victor Baldizon/Getty Images*

TORONTO, ONTARIO, CANADA

Exhibition Stadium

Previous name: Canadian National
Exhibition Stadium

Status: Demolished in 1999

Location: West of downtown between
Gardiner Expressway and Lake Shore
Boulevard West

Capacity: 25,303 (original, football);
43,737 (baseball)

Opening day: April 7, 1997 (MLB)

Last MLB game: May 28, 1989

Cost to construct: $2 million (Canadian,
original); $17.8 million (Canadian,
renovations)

Architect: N/A

Dimensions (ft):

Left Field: 330

Left Center: 375

Center: 410

Right Center: 375

Left Field: 330

Defining feature: Odd shape caused by
original design for football, leaving a large
gap and no seating in right field.

World Series: none

All-Star Game: none

Rogers Centre

Previous name: SkyDome

Status: Home of Toronto Blue Jays

Address: 1 Blue Jays Way, Toronto,
Ontario M5V 1J1

Capacity: 50,516

Opening day: June 5,1989

Cost to construct: $600 million (Canadian)

Architects: Rod Robbie and Michael Allen

Dimensions (ft):

Left Field: 328

Left Center: 375

Center Field: 400

Right Center: 375

Right Field: 328

Defining feature: The dome of the
retractable roof is at 310 feet the tallest in
major league baseball. The 33-by-115-foot
Jumbotron scoreboard is the largest in the
world.

Most expensive seat: $205

Cheapest seat: $2

World Series: 1992, 1997

All-Star Game: 1991

Following the demise of the Montreal Expos in 2004 and their reemergence as the Washington Nationals, the Toronto Blue Jays became Canada's only major league baseball team. They have been around since 1977, have always played in the American League's Eastern Division, and have called two ballparks home. The somewhat unlovely, strangely shaped Exhibition Stadium was their original place of work and they played their first game there on April 7, 1977, beating the Chicago White Sox 9-4 in front of a crowd of 44,649. The game has the dubious distinction of being the only MLB played with snow covering the field. The stadium's left field "bleachers" had originally been built for football in 1948; the grandstand down the foul lines was built to convert the venue to a ballpark, but Exhibition Stadium was never very accommodating to baseball, but the Blue Jays stayed for more than a decade, advancing to the playoffs once during that time, in 1985. They played their last game at Exhibition Stadium on May 28, 1989.

The Blue Jays moved to what was the then state-of-the-art Skydome, featuring a retractable roof and artificial turf the same year. They played their first game there on June 5, losing 5-3 to the Milwaukee Brewers. The SkyDome is now called Rogers Centre, honoring Rogers Communications, which now owns both the stadium and the Blue Jays. It is the highest of all the domed arenas at 310 feet. Spectators have flocked to the new stadium, in part to enjoy amenities beyond baseball. For example, fans can enjoy games from one of 160 or so private boxes if they wish—as long as they have between $150,000 and $225,000 to spare each year. Those without bottomless pockets might prefer to watch a game from the facility's Hard Rock Café. The dome also has its own hotel, which offers 70 rooms with a field view.

The Blue Jays play in what has long been the American League's toughest division. Nonetheless, after the Jays moved to the SkyDome, they started winning consistently, taking division titles in 1989 and then consecutively from 1991 to 1993. The 1992 and 1993 Blue Jays took back-to-back World Series titles, knocking off the Braves and Phillies, respectively. Since those glory years success has eluded the team, and there have been no return trips to the playoffs.

No player has entered Cooperstown as a Blue Jay, but the team has had several quality players. George Bell holds the season home run with 47 in 1987, while Carlos Delgado is the team's career homer leader with 262. John Olerud recorded the highest season batting average (.363 in 1993), while Roberto Alomar, has the best career average (.307). Pitchers Jack Morris (1992) and Roger Clemens (1997) share the team record for most games won in a season with 21. Clemens also holds the season strikeout record with 292, while the career title goes to Dave Stieb with 1,658.

Below: Postcard showing the exterior of Toronto's Hanlan's Point stadium. Built on the Toronto Islands, Babe Ruth once played here and hit his first professional home run into the water of Toronto Harbour. The stadium on the site was demolished in 1937.

Left: Exhibition Stadium with the Blue Jays on field circa 1985. *John Reid/MLB Photos via Getty Images*

Below left: Aerial View of Exhibition Stadium, 1979. *MLB Photos via Getty Images*

Below: Postcard of Hanlan's Point exterior.

Right: The Skydome and CN Tower with the buildings of Toronto's downtown, seen from the water. Ontario, Canada. *Wolfgang Kaehler/Corbis*

Above left and Left: Game 2 of the 1993 World Series between the Blue Jays and the Philadelphia Phillies. *Rick Stewart/Allsport via Getty Images*

Above: Inside SkyDome with the roof open; photo taken in 1989 from above home plate. *Rick Stewart/Allsport via Getty Images*

Right: External view of Toronto's SkyDome and the looming height of the CN Tower taken during the 1989 season. *Rick Stewart/Allsport via Getty Images*

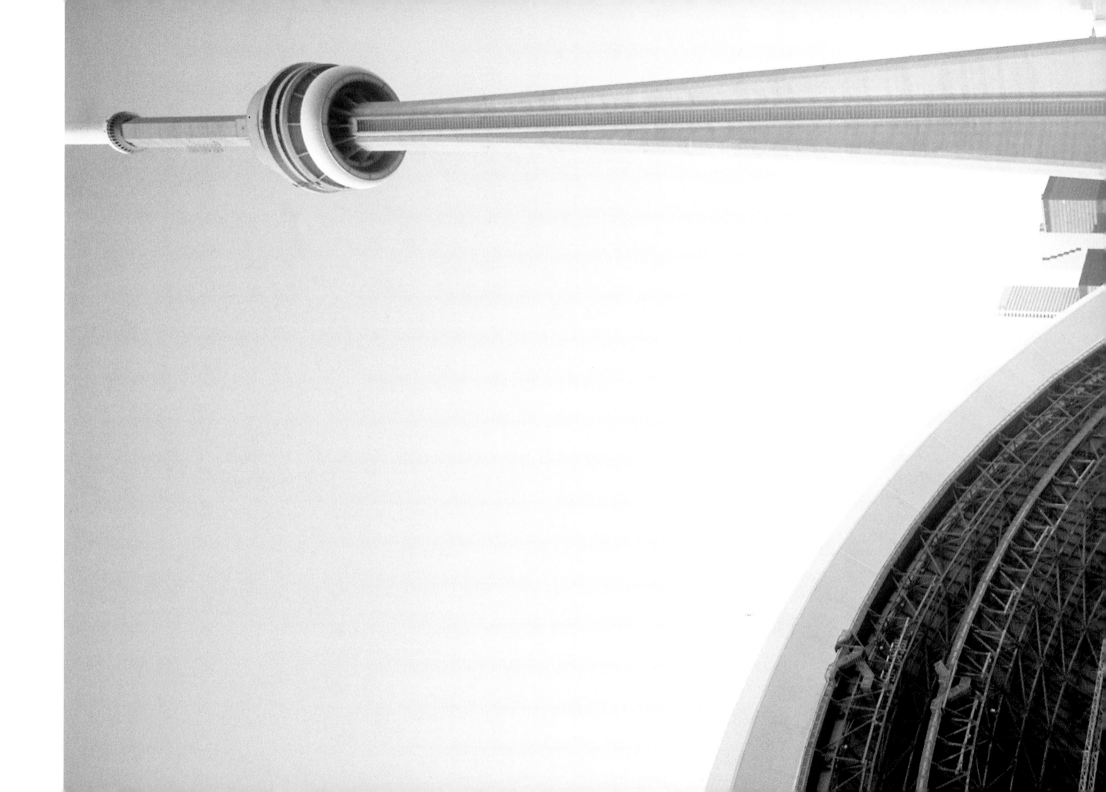

Left: Toronto's CN Tower rises over the SkyDome—creating real problems for sluggers.
Nik Wheeler/Corbis

WASHINGTON, D.C.

Griffith Stadium

Previous name: National Park

Status: Demolished in 1965

Location: Along Fifth and Seventh streets on the campus of Howard University

Capacity: 32,000 (1921), 27,550 (1961)

Opening day: July 24, 1911 (rebuilt stadium)

Cost to construct: N/A

Architect: Osborn Engineering

Dimensions (ft):

Left Field: 407 (1911)

Left Center: 391 (1911)

Center Field: 421 (1911)

Right Center: 378 (1954)

Right Field: 328 (1909)

Defining features: Center field wall detoured around five houses and a tree that encroached into field of play. Giant National Bohemian Beer bottle towered over scoreboard in right-center.

World Series: 1924,1925, 1933

All-Star Game: 1937, 1957

RFK Stadium

Previous name: D.C. Stadium

Status: Home of the Washington Nationals

Address: 2400 East Capitol Street, SE, Washington, D.C.

Capacity: 45,250 (opening day); 56,000 (current)

Opening day: April 9, 1962

Cost to construct: $24 million; $18.5 million (renovations)

Architect: Osborn Engineering

Dimensions (ft):

Left Field: 335

Left Center: 380

Center Field: 408

Right Center: 380

Right Field: 335

Defining feature: Round, multipurpose stadium with five tiers of seats, most of which are covered.

Most expensive seat: $45

Cheapest seat: $7

World Series: none

All-Star Game: 1962,1969

Several professional baseball teams, none particularly long lived, called Washington their home in the latter decades of the nineteenth century: the Washington Nationals (1873-1875 and 1884), the Washington Statesmen (1886-1889 and 1891-1894), and the National League's Washington Senators (1892-1899). When the American League transformed itself into a major league in 1901, the powers-that-be decided that the fledgling league needed a major presence on the East Coast, so in 1900 the Kansas City team moved to the capital and became the Washington Nationals or "Nats," more commonly known as the Senators (1901-1960). The new arrivals briefly played at the now long-gone American League Park from April 1901 to September 1902 and for the next season moved to a location that housed stadium's variously known as Beyer's Seventh Street Park, League Park, National Park, and Clark Griffith Park. The original structure burned down in March 1911 and—remarkably—was rebuilt by mid-season that year, this time of steel and concrete.

The new park seemed to be the right medicine for a franchise that had finished last in four out of their first nine seasons. Under the leadership of manager Clark Griffith, who took over in 1912, the team was more competitive. In 1919, Griffith purchased the team and continued revamping the franchise. The ball park was renamed Griffith Stadium in 1920 and that year saw the only addition to the stadium, new double-decking down the foul lines. Interestingly, the new stands did not connect to or line up with the original double-deck grandstands behind home plate. The stadium had other oddities, including a strange-shaped outfield—the center field wall was built around a tree and five houses whose owners would not sell their property. The stadium also had a presidential box on the first base side; the U.S. commander-in-chief traditionally tossed out the first pitch each year.

With an injection of new blood, the Nats took the American League Championship in 1924 and 1925. One more title came in 1933, but over the next twenty-six years the Nats were destined to have just four more winning seasons. A combination of the Depression and steadily falling attendance took a toll on the team's finances. Griffith died in October

1955 and his son, Calvin, took over. He became convinced that a move was in the team's best interest, and after 1960 they moved to Minnesota and became the Twins.

The capital was not left without a major league baseball team because a new expansion Washington Senators debuted for the 1961 season. They, too, played at Griffith Stadium, but stayed for just one season, playing their last match there on September 21. The Senators then moved to the new D.C. Stadium, one of the first multipurpose "cookie cutter" stadiums, playing their first game there on April 9, 1962. In 1968 the facility was renamed RFK Stadium in honor of the assassinated Attorney General Robert F. Kennedy. The Senators shared the stadium, with the NFL's Washington Redskins, which used RFK until they moved into their own new FedEx Field in 1996.

The Senators were not a good baseball team. In their first four seasons they hit the century mark in losses and they used up five managers in just a decade. Financial problems and a dwindling fan base soon brought an end to the second Senators and 71 years of continuous major league baseball in the capital. They played their last game—one marred by crowd trouble that led to it being forfeited to the New York Yankees—at RFK Stadium on September

30, 1971. The franchise moved to the Dallas-Fort Worth area and became the Texas Rangers.

It took more than three decades to bring baseball back to the nation's capital, but diehard fans were rewarded in 2005, when the former Montreal Expos made their home debut on April 15 as the reincarnated Washington Nationals. The Expos/Nationals had taken a bizarre route to the Capital—including an aborted MLB plan to kill the franchise, and a stint playing part-time in Puerto Rico—but Washington fans enthusiastically welcomed the team. The city invested more the $18.5 million upgrading RFK for baseball, and also agreed to build a new $535 million baseball-only stadium. After considerable political wrangling at site was selected at South Capitol and N streets SE, and the stadium was scheduled to be open for the 2008 season.

Below left: A 1924 World Series game between the New York Giants and the Washington Senators at Griffith Stadium The Senators won the series 4-3. *National Baseball Hall of Fame Library/MLB Photos via Getty Images*

Below: The RFK stadium on April 9, 1962. *National Baseball Hall of Fame Library/MLB Photos via Getty Images*

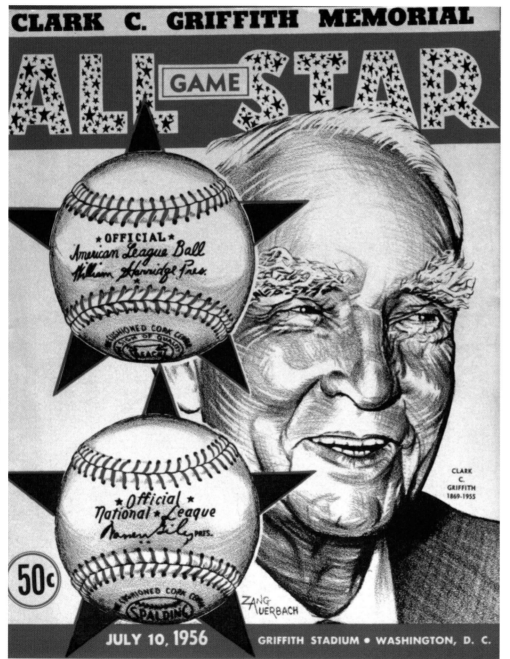

Above: Model of Griffith Field.

Left: Cover of the 1956 Major League Baseball All-Star Game Official Program portraying Clark C. Griffith, former pitcher, Washington Senators manager and team owner on the front. The game was held at Griffith Stadium on July 10, 1956. *Diamond Images/Getty Images*

Right: Joe DiMaggio batting on June 29, 1941. *Bettmann/Corbis*

Above: Mickey Mantle of the Yankees clouted the longest homer in the history of Griffith Stadium on April 17, 1953. The ball travelled 562 feet before it landed in a backyard (3) beyond the left field wall. Jimmy Foxx and Joe DiMaggio had hit them in the same direction but they wound up in the bleachers. Other titanic smashes were by Larry Doby (1) and Babe Ruth (2). Each measured about 450 feet. Bettmann/Corbis

Right: Composite of photos showing opening game ceremonies: Calvin Coolidge throwing out first ball; Kellogg raising flag; managers Harris & Huggins shaking hands; batting practice. *Library of Congress*

Above: James "Cool Papa" Bell of the Homestead Grays slides to avoid the tag during a Negro League game in Washington D.C. Cool Papa played for the Grays in 1932 and returned in 1943–46. *MLB Photos via Getty Images*

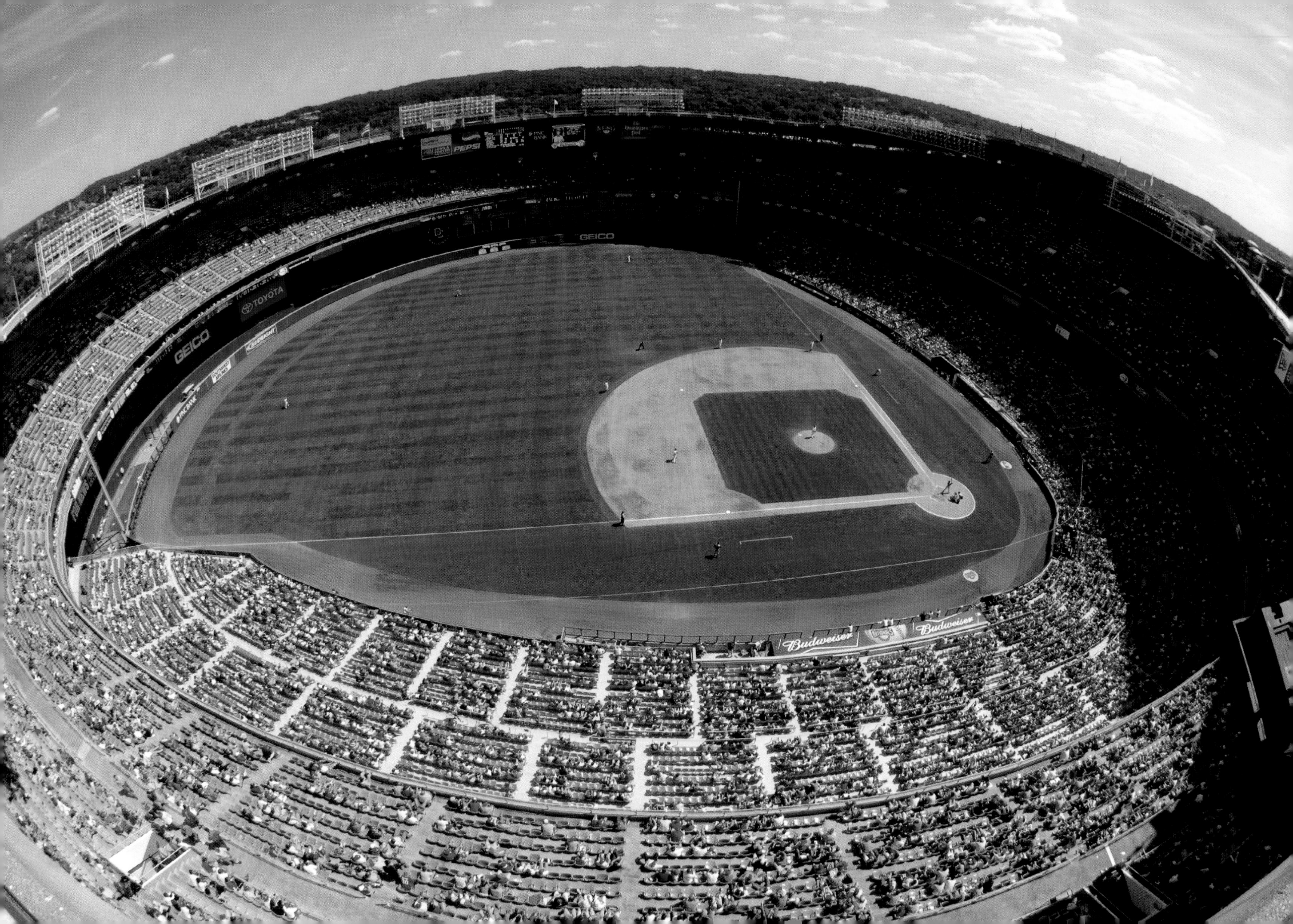
PEPSI
GEICO
TOYOTA
GEICO
Budweiser
Budweiser

Far left: RFK Stadium exterior during the game between the Los Angeles Dodgers and the Washington Nationals on May 27, 2006. The Dodgers won 3–1. *Jamie Squire/Getty Images*

Left: A general view of RFK Stadium prior to the game between the Arizona Diamondbacks and the Washington Nationals on April 17, 2005. *Jamie Squire/Getty Images*

Pages 434 and 435: RFK Stadium during the Washington Nationals 2005 home opener on April 14, in Washington, D.C. The Nationals defeated the Diamondbacks 5–3. *Rich Pilling/MLB Photos via Getty Images*

Page 436: April 17, 2005 at RFK Stadium in Washington, D.C. The Nationals defeated the Diamondbacks 7–3. *Jamie Squire/Getty Images*

Page 437: General view of RFK Stadium during the Washington Nationals first season in Washington, D.C. *Jamie Squire/Getty Images*

434

THE AMERICAN LEAGUE

The roster of American League cities sounds like a refrain from a Chuck Berry song: Detroit, Chicago, Baltimore, Boston, and K.C. When it was founded in 1901, the American League was the junior circuit, coming to life a quarter of a century after the National League, and bringing professional baseball to America's thriving metropolises. Of the eight original American League cities, only Washington, the nation's capital, is now without a professional team.

Some American League teams have come and gone, such as the Boston Pilgrims, the Cleveland Naps, the Seattle Pilots, and the Washington Senators. Roughly 50 stadiums have been home to American League teams. Several of the old classics—Detroit's Tiger Stadium, Cleveland's Municipal Stadium, and Chicago's Comiskey Park—closed in the 1990s.

The American League's oldest stadium is Fenway Park, which opened the same week the *Titanic* sank in 1912. Exactly 80 years later, Baltimore's Camden Yards sparked a new wave of classic-style parks, structures which sought to imitate the intimacy of Fenway and other older parks. There is now talk of a new ballpark in Minnesota, hope in Oakland, and—to the horror of some Bostonians—even a discussion of how to rebuild Fenway.

Fenway Park seen from inside the Boston Red Sox dugout during the game against the Yankees on July 25, 2003. The Yankees won 4–3. *Jerry Driendl/Getty Images*

AMERICAN LEAGUE EAST

AMERICAN LEAGUE CENTRAL

The American League's Eastern Division boasts some of baseball's most storied parks.

Fenway Park is where Babe Ruth began his career, and Yankee Stadium is where he reached power-hitting immortality. Ty Cobb, Walter Johnson, Hank Greenberg, Jimmy Foxx, Tris Speaker, each played on the very fields where Red Sox and Yankees still play. Fans still stream into the South Bronx park where Lou Gehrig bid baseball adieu and sit in the same Boston bleachers where Ted Williams hit his longest shot.

To the north, SkyDome with its convertible roof, showed the sporting world how to handle the elements. Orioles Park at Camden Yard reminded fans of the game's intrinsic beauty, while Tropicana Field in Florida jammed about as much entertainment as can fit inside a structure built for baseball.

There is talk of remodeling Fenway to meet 21st century standards. However the parks of the American League Eastern Division largely look like they are here to stay.

They are the best of parks. They are the worst of parks. The ball fields of the American League Central Division include Cleveland's Jacobs Field, so lovely it sold out 455 consecutive games, and Minnesota's Hubert H. Humphrey Metrodome, a baseball design so hideous that even Twins fans have demanded its demolition.

The American League central division includes one park from the 70s, one from the 80s, two from the 90s, and one from 2000. Though each offers its unique charms, Jacobs Field, Detroit's Comerica Park, and Kansas City's Kauffman Stadium, are all regarded as

wonderful places to watch a baseball game. Chicago's U.S. Cellular Field—opened just a year before Baltimore's Camden Yards would incite a demand for old-fashioned retro-parks—is functional. And Minnesota's Hubert H. Humphrey Metrodome, with its dim lighting, its hefty bag outfield, and its bright, ball-losing, Teflon ceiling is barely that. The Twins have already drawn up plans for a new retractable dome stadium, though they are lacking the means to pay for it. The rest of the parks of the American League Central Division should be around for a while.

AMERICAN LEAGUE WEST

Below: Wrigley Field from a right field skybox across the street from the ballpark during the game between the Phillies and the Cubs on July 23, 2003.
Jerry Driendl/Getty Images

The teams of the American League West are relatively young and so are their stadiums. The Athletics, who originally played in Philadelphia in the early 1900s, before moving to Kansas City in the 50s, and eventually to Oakland, are the only exception. The Anaheim Angels (originally the Los Angeles Angels, then the California Angels) came to life in the 60s, as did the Texas Rangers (from Washington), and the Seattle Mariners were born in 1977.

The Texas Rangers and the Seattle Mariners moved into new stadiums in the 1990s to rave reviews from their fans, who in the team's original homes had been subjected to Arlington's blistering heat and Seattle's impersonal dome. Anaheim has been quite comfortable in its home down the road from Disneyland since 1966. And Oakland A's fans enjoyed their oversized coliseum until the NFL Raiders returned in 1998, turning a baseball friendly stadium into a football arena uncomfortably forced to hold 82 baseball games a year.

The A's would like to build a park of their own, but after Seattle spent more than $500 million on its new park, it may be many years before Oakland follows suit.

THE NATIONAL LEAGUE

Left: A general view of Coors Field prior to the National League game between the Arizona Diamondbacks and the Colorado Rockies on June 30, 2003. The Diamondbacks defeated the Rockies 8–7 in 12 innings.
Brian Bahr/Getty Images

The National League of Professional Baseball Clubs, now known simply as the National League, was formed in 1876, the year of Custer's last stand, and exactly 100 years after the United States declared its independence. Some of its eight charter cities are familiar baseball towns: Chicago, Cincinnati, Philadelphia, St. Louis, and Boston. Others were unable to hold their teams: Hartford, Brooklyn, and Louisville.

The National League now consists of 16 teams, which have been divided into three divisions since 1994. Its newest franchises are located in places like Arizona and Colorado, which weren't even part of the union when the league was founded.

More than 80 National League parks have already opened and shut their doors. The old South End Grounds in Boston is now a T-station. The Hartford Ball Club Grounds now holds a church. Jefferson Grounds in Philadelphia, where on April 22, 1876, the first National League game was played, is now the site of an elementary school.

Today, the National League is experiencing a stadium explosion. Only five National League teams play in stadiums built prior to 1993. Seven new National League parks have been opened since 2000, including Citizen's Bank Park in Philadelphia and PETCO Park in San Diego, which opened their doors in 2004.

NATIONAL LEAGUE EAST

NATIONAL LEAGUE CENTRAL

The National League East is a division of haves and have-nots. The pre-turn-of-the-century teams, the Braves and the Phillies, play in brand-new, highly regarded ball parks. The expansion clubs, the Mets, the Expos, and the Marlins, play in parks that most of their fans would just as soon abandon.

Two stadiums in the National League East Division were built for Olympics. Another was built for football. Montreal's Le Stade Olympique was constructed for the 1976 Summer Olympics, and converted for the Expos the following year. The result was an oversized, clumsy park that never felt quite right for baseball. Twenty years later, the Braves learned from the Expos' mistakes. Atlanta's stadium for the 1996 Summer Games was specially designed to transform into a baseballfriendly park.

Miami's Pro Player Stadium, the home of the NFL Dolphins and perfect for Sunday afternoons in the fall, was worked over to accommodate the Marlins' often overheated fans in the summer.

New York's Shea Stadium was built for baseball, though it was also enlisted for football, concerts, boxing matches, and religious events. Philadelphia's Citizens, along with San Diego's PETCO Park, are baseball's newest stadiums.

The teams of the National League Central are among baseball's oldest. Baseball has been played in Chicago, Cincinnati, Pittsburgh, and St. Louis since the 19th century. However, the division's ballparks are among the game's newest.

Chicago's Wrigley Field, opened in 1916, is the National League's oldest park, and in the eyes of many purists, baseball's best. The manual scoreboard, outfield wall ivy, and close confines have come to define the game. Seventy-five years after Wrigley was built, four National League Central division teams opened 21st century parks.

The Houston Astros replaced their fully enclosed Astrodome with a downtown, retractable-dome stadium in 2000. Pittsburgh moved into a new ball yard on the banks of the Allegheny River that some claim is every bit as pleasant as Wrigley. Milwaukee also

NATIONAL LEAGUE WEST

Below: Shea Stadium at dusk during the National League game between the Philadelphia Phillies and the New York Mets on July 13, 2003. *Jerry Driendl/Getty Images*

opened a new park in 2001, replacing County Stadium, while Cincinnati moved from sterile Riverfront Stadium, later named Cinergy Field, to a new home in 2003. Not to be outdone, the St. Louis Cardinals are building a new stadium in time for the 2006 season, leaving Wrigley Field as the division's only 20th century park.

The National League West includes two of baseball's most storied franchises, the Giants (1880s) and the Dodgers (1890s), who, like so many Americans, left their New York homes in the late 1950s for California. The remaining three teams are relative babes—the Padres born in the 1960s, the Rockies in the 1980s, and the Diamondbacks in the 1990s.

The ballparks of the National League West have distinction. In AT&T Park, sluggers hit the ball into the San Francisco Bay. In Phoenix's Bank One Ballpark, they can hit the ball into a right field swimming pool. In San Diego's PETCO Park, batters smash balls off a left field warehouse, while in Denver's Coors Field, they take advantage of the thin, mile-high air.

Los Angeles' Dodger Stadium, opened in 1962, is the division's only park built before 1995, and is still regarded as one of the best places in the division to watch a baseball game. The National League West is the only division in baseball where there is no talk of any team building a new park for many years to come.

INDEX